Ancient Civilizations & the Bible

A BIBLICAL WORLD HISTORY CURRICULUM
FROM CREATION TO JESUS CHRIST

1:1
answersingenesis
Petersburg, Kentucky, USA

Answers in Genesis HISTORY written by Diana Waring

Ancient Civilizations & The Bible: From Creation to Jesus Christ

Fifth printing November 2014

For more information, contact
Answers in Genesis
2800 Bullittsburg Church Rd
Petersburg, KY, 41080

Photo credits by page: **17** ©2008 Jupiterimages Corporation **23** ©2008 Answers in Genesis **24** ©2008 Jupiterimages Corporation **51** ©2008 Answers in Genesis **83** ©2008 Jupiterimages Corporation **91** ©2008 Jupiterimages Corporation **101** ©2008 Jupiterimages Corporation **117** ©istockphoto.com/Lior Filshteiner **120** ©2008 Jupiterimages Corporation **147** Public Domain **154** Public Domain **183** ©istockphoto.com/Stefan Baum **190** ©2008 Jupiterimages Corporation **215** ©2008 Jupiterimages Corporation **222** ©2008 Jupiterimages Corporation **251** ©2008 Jupiterimages Corporation **258** ©2008 Jupiterimages Corporation **283** Public Domain **288** Public Domain

Cover Design: Brandie Lucas
Text Design: Diane King
Editors: Gary Vaterlaus and Lori Jaworski

ISBN: 1-60092-170-1

Printed in the United States of America.

www.AnswersInGenesis.org

"And He has made from one blood every nation of
men to dwell on all the face of the earth, and has
determined their preappointed times and the
boundaries of their habitation, so that they should
seek the Lord." Acts 17:26–27

Special Thanks to:

- Kathy Follette, Grace Balloch Memorial Library, who never said, "Impossible;"
- Josh & Cindy Wiggers of Geography Matters, for the blessing of their friendship and their fabulous maps;
- Paul Hawkins, international educator with Youth With A Mission, for his wise advice and counsel in issues of Biblical education;
- Janet Blomberg, interim international director of Asia Education Resource Consortium, for her kind encouragement and helpful suggestions;
- Rosalie Pedder, late friend, mentor, and international teacher in the areas of learning issues, for her invaluable ministry and encouragement;
- Ruth Beechick, author of numerous books, for her encouraging comments about the original version of this curriculum, and for her ongoing work;
- Rod White Eagle Wilson, Doctor of Divinity and international educator with Youth With A Mission, for his thoughtful Scriptural insights;
- my children, Isaac, Michael, and Melody, for all of their insight, input, and support;
- my beloved husband, Bill, without whom this would be literally impossible.

TABLE OF CONTENTS

Introduction

Welcome

You are about to embark on a journey. Though you can take this journey while relaxed in the comfort of your chair, you will, nonetheless, explore and discover the most panoramic events, interview some of the most fascinating people, and soar to the highest heights with God's perspective. As you are introduced to ancient civilizations from a biblical view, you will be given the opportunity to probe the aspects of those ancient times that you find interesting; to discover, through a variety of hands-on activities, the connections in history both between these ancient cultures and between their times and your own; and to present your understanding, not only through a test, but through the creative expression you find most appropriate.

This book was constructed with two objectives in mind:

- to discover history from a Christian worldview;
- to explore history through a curriculum that honors your God-given design.

What does it mean, "to discover history from a Christian worldview"?

- Noah Webster's 1828 dictionary defines history: "An account of facts respecting nations or states; a narrative of events in the order in which they happened with their causes and effects."
- James W. Sire, author of *The Universe Next Door*, defines worldview: "A set of presuppositions which we hold about the basic makeup of our world." This includes such questions as:
  - What is the nature of God and the universe?
  - Where did I come from?
  - What value do I possess?
  - What is the meaning of human history?

We will attempt to discover the biblical framework undergirding the chronological flow of people and events, so that we can understand what happened and why. Once we have this insight, we can move from head knowledge to heart knowledge, from academics to application.

This might sound overwhelming, stuffy, or boring to you. And it would be, if not for the second objective, "to explore history through a curriculum that honors your God-given design."

What does it mean, "to explore history through a curriculum that honors your God-given design?"

- First, for explore: "to travel to a place that is not well known to find out more about it."
- For honor, The Oxford American Dictionary says: "great respect, high public regard."

» And for your God-given design, we are referring to the way you were intricately formed by your Creator, and includes the ways you most enjoy and retain learning.

The way this curriculum has been formatted will open the doors for you to pursue your own explorations into regions of history that look interesting, so you can see why things are the way they are. And then, because we have great respect for the fact that you are created in the image and likeness of God, and are uniquely designed by Him, we offer you the choice of how to express what you are learning. Our options include a chance to sing, dance, cook, sketch, write, act, map, read, discuss, move, design . . . to interact with what you are learning and to express it in the way that best fits who you are and how God made you.

Putting an emphasis on "you" and focusing on learning activities tuned to the way you are designed is not to employ the recent "you/my" trend in marketing. In fact, we are very aware that self-centeredness is not a reflection of our Creator nor honoring to Him, and we have no desire to impart that to you through this curriculum. It is, instead, our concern that you excel; that you be enabled to learn thoroughly and deeply; and most of all, that your faith be increased as God reveals to you His faithfulness throughout history. This causes us to design opportunities for you to learn in the way you are most responsive, rather than in a one-size-fits-all approach.

Ravi Zacharias, an internationally renowned Christian apologist, said in an interview in the *Washington Times*, "The first thing Christianity does is raise the level of every individual. There's an essential dignity. Every human being is of essential worth." We believe this. Therefore, we have labored to create a history curriculum, which allows you the dignity of learning the wonders of HisStory in your own way.

Diana Waring
March, 2004
The Black Hills of South Dakota

Structural Overview

The Scope

The Course of Study...

- » Unit One: Creation & The Flood
- » Unit Two: The Rise of Civilizations
- » Unit Three: Egypt & The Exodus
- » Unit Four: The Children of Israel
- » Unit Five: Assyria & Babylon
- » Unit Six: The Persians & Medes
- » Unit Seven: Greece & The Hellenists
- » Unit Eight: The Rise of Rome
- » Unit Nine: Jesus Christ, Immanuel

The Structure

The Structure of Each Unit . . .

WEEK ONE: INTRODUCTION

- » Discuss Key Concepts
- » Read the unit lesson
- » Listen to the appropriate recordings
- » Read appropriate online articles
- » Consider and discuss opinions
- » Choose interesting books or Internet search

WEEK TWO: EXPLORATION & DISCOVERY

- » Research a topic of your choice
- » Learn the Words to Watch
- » Construct the timeline
- » Report findings on your research

WEEK THREE: HANDS-ON

- » Label maps
- » View art & architecture
- » Design art projects
- » Conduct science experiments
- » Listen to music
- » Cook the recipe

WEEK FOUR: EXPRESSION

- » Linguistics: Journalism, Prose, Poetry, Playing with Words
- » Art: Painting/Drawing, Graphic Design, Sculpting, Cartooning
- » Music: Compose, Practice Performance
- » Drama: Comedy, Tragedy, Reality, Reader's Theater, Puppetry
- » Movement: Pantomime, Dance, Action
- » Conceptual Design

The Foundation Beneath the Structure

These three foundational building blocks are integrally woven into this curriculum—they are already written into the lessons for you. This means that you do not have to figure out what learning style, modality, or intelligences you have, you can simply learn in the way that is most interesting and enjoyable to you.

There are three foundational building blocks undergirding this curriculum, three approaches to learning which help explain some of the differences in the ways people learn:

» Four Learning Styles

» Three Learning Modalities

» Eight Intelligences

Four Learning Styles

Learning Styles refers to the categorization of how a particular personality style best learns. The method we refer to was developed by Myers-Briggs. Here is a brief description of each of the four learning styles:

THE FEELER This is the "people person" learning style. A Feeler wants to know the people perspective, i.e., how this subject affects people; how does this impact our lives now; who were the people of history, as opposed to the events or things. This learner needs to be in good relationship with the people around him—his teacher, siblings, friends, etc. They love to be with other people in one-on-one conversations and in group activities, especially when they are part of a "team effort."	**THE INTUITOR** "Wait! I have an idea!" The Intuitor is the one brimming over with ideas about how this might have happened, or about how you might put on a play for the whole city portraying an historic event, or about what it must have been like to live in ancient times, and on and on. This learner is very good at coming up with suggestions, but is not as strong at seeing things through to completion. The Intuitor needs a lot of flexibility in schedule, and a "safe haven" for suggesting and trying out ideas.
THE THINKER "Give me the facts, ma'am, just the facts." The Thinker has a black & white approach to knowledge, wanting authoritative input, not just someone's opinions. This learner truly enjoys using textbooks, encyclopedias, charts, diagrams. There is a need to know exactly what the rules are in the class, when assignments or projects are due, what is required for good grades. They are organized and expect organization.	**THE SENSOR** The "hands-on," get-it-done-now person. The Sensor is the one who can make projects happen—taking them beyond the blueprint stage and into production. This learner does NOT enjoy sitting for long periods of time, looking through books for information, or discussing things for hours on end. Instead, the Sensor prefers to be involved with things that can be efficiently accomplished with physical effort.

Three Learning Modalities

Learning Modalities refers to the approach learners use to take in new information, how they best concentrate, process, and retain. Here is a brief description of each of the three modalities:

VISUAL	AUDITORY	TACTILE/KINESTHETIC
learn best by seeing, whether through reading, looking at pictures, watching a documentary, observing.	learn best by hearing, whether through audio recordings, conversations, lectures, or reading out loud.	learn best by touching objects or moving, whether through hands-on projects or physical action, such as jumping, running, dancing, even wiggling.

Eight Intelligences

Eight Intelligences refers to natural potential and areas of talent. Howard Gardner of Harvard University theorized that intelligence is made up of more than verbal and mathematical skills, and that people can strengthen their natural giftings and improve their weaknesses. Here is a brief description of each of the eight intelligences:

INTRAPERSONAL This could be described as Self-Smart. It is the ability to enjoy being alone, working independently, and relying on self-motivation. This person needs solitary time in order to think.	**NATURALIST** This could be described as Nature Smart. It is the ability to observe, investigate, experiment, and discover the natural world, including weather, animals, plants, and geologic structures. This person needs to go outside!
BODILY-KINESTHETIC This could be described as Body Smart. It is the ability to use one's body through touch and movement to accomplish what is desired. It includes being able to process knowledge through bodily movement or through sensation, enjoying physical activity, and being constantly in motion even while sitting down. This person needs to move!	**SPATIAL** This could be described as Picture Smart. It is the ability to see in pictures rather than words, and includes drawing and design, three-dimensional constructing (such as LEGO® bricks), and other visual arts, such as photography, sculpting, and painting. This person needs pictures, maps, diagrams, charts, photos, and other visual/spatial material.
MUSICAL This could be described as Music Smart. It is the ability to learn through rhythm and melody, sing or play musical instruments, enjoy listening to music, remember songs, and study more effectively when music is played. This person needs music, whether it is music lessons or musical recordings.	**INTERPERSONAL** This could be described as People Smart. It is the ability to understand and enjoy people. A person who is interpersonal learns best when other people are involved, whether through games, team work, or cooperative learning sessions. This person needs people.

MATH/LOGICAL	LINGUISTIC
This could be described as Number Smart. It is the ability to reason mathematically, discover abstract patterns, classify and organize, enjoy mathematical computations, and think logically. This person needs to see the logic and organization in what is being learned.	This could be described as Word Smart. It is the ability to enjoy and use language through word games, books, recordings, trivia, poetry, papers, discussion, and other forms of using words. This person needs words in order to communicate.

New Research on How People Learn

Traditionally, academic subjects have been taught in this manner:

1. Lecture (delivered by the expert)
2. Study (student studies textbook and memorizes material for test)
3. Test (True/False,Multiple Choice, Essay)
4. Grade (largely based on how well student regurgitated memorized facts)

Research on the brain and how people best learn has provided a new scenario:

1. Listen (read something new, hear something new, discuss something new)
2. Explore (ask your own questions and then search for answers)
3. Discover (find the answers to your questions, the "Aha!" moment)
4. Practice (interact with what you are learning through various, interesting activities)
5. Use (able to teach others, use it on a regular basis, mastery)

The emphasis has changed, from the teacher being the provider of the necessary information which the student memorizes, to the student being exposed to new information, and then actively engaging it. This shift, which we have incorporated into the curriculum, has profound implications for you: You are now an active participant in the sport of learning. Instead of passively taking in what a teacher or textbook tells you, you will have the opportunity to question, discuss, do teamwork projects, etc. What you actively put into this will be what you get out of it. There are few assignments to simply memorize, but there are many opportunities to actively participate in learning. This means, getting a good grade (for students in settings which give grades) is no longer a matter of memorizing material for a test.

You will be evaluated on how actively you participate:

- in class discussions,
- in exploration activities,
- in reporting your discoveries,
- in hands-on activities,
- in creative expressions.

The Difference Between Passive & Active Learning

You can choose to go passive:	or	You can choose to go active:
• do as little as possible • avoid participating in discussions • halfheartedly work on projects		• find what interests you and do it • share with others in discussion times and in other appropriate moments • give your best effort at the projects you choose
Result: • hate history • resist learning • not comprehend history or your place in it		**Result:** • meaningful learning • greater comprehension & retention • vastly more interesting!

Enjoy

"The works of the Lord are great, studied by all who have pleasure in them." Psalm 111:2

Did you know that it is biblical to enjoy learning? In fact, we were meant to actually find pleasure in studying the amazing things God has done!

The good news is that learning improves when it is enjoyable. Your brain actually imprints and retrieves new information better when you enjoy what you are learning. This means that not only is it permissible to enjoy what you are doing, enjoyment is a critical part of learning.

In this curriculum we have brought together several disciplines, including science, fine arts, writing, speaking, even cooking, to help you enjoy the process of learning history. You have the option of creating your own project (even beyond the ones suggested in the curriculum) so that you can find what will give you joy as you do the work.

Interaction and discussion, with other students, teachers, family members, etc., are vital parts of this curriculum, because they will help you better sharpen your own ideas and expand your horizons as you hear others' ideas. Interaction is often the most enjoyable part of learning, as well.

Choose

History courses are most often sets of names, dates, and places to be memorized. Success in the course, then, is directly related to how proficiently you are able to recall these names, dates, and places.

However, history is far richer, far deeper, far more extensive than that. You can learn about a moment in time by studying a specific person, or the type of weaponry used in battle, or the form of government, or the kind of artwork, or the scientific developments, or the method of recording information, or the architectural style, or the means of transportation. And, beyond these few studies, there are thousands more.

We believe that what you personally find interesting will be what you will enjoy studying. Since history incorporates all subject areas and all time periods, you ought to be able to find something interesting! So, we give you a choice. If you can choose something that you find fascinating, you will work harder, learn more, and retain it longer than if you are compelled to simply memorize names, dates, and places. Therefore, your success in this course will be directly related to your actively choosing and pursuing what interests you.

At Your Own Level

The object is to learn, to enjoy learning, and to understand what you are learning. Therefore, use the materials that you find interesting and accessible. It will not greatly contribute to your success if you try to read materials that are beyond your grasp, or are boring in the extreme.

I suggest looking for as many books as possible on the people or events you find interesting, and as many appropriate web sites as possible, then choose which ones will work the best for you. I have often found that children's books on history are more concise, more story-filled, and more memorable than ponderous tomes written for adults (though I have read my share of these, as well). So, if you find a fantastic book on King Cyrus of Persia, for instance, but you recognize it was obviously written for a much younger (OR much older) reader than yourself, don't worry about what other people will think! Read the book.

Academics to Application

Though it is impressive to know a lot of facts about history, it might change your life to learn from history. What we are learning will reflect in our actions:

"Knowledge puffs up, but love edifies." 1 Corinthians 8:1

As you learn more about God and His ways in history; as you discover time and time again that He seeks the restoration of relationship; and as you see that our relationship with Him changes our relationship with others, I pray that you will grow in love that edifies.

Personal Evaluation

Just as you are making choices about what you study, what projects you do, and what creative expressions you use to convey what you have learned—in other words, becoming an active learner— you need to evaluate yourself. Are you learning anything about history? Are you exerting yourself in your projects? Are you seeking to do your best on the creative expressions?

These personal evaluative questions will help you stay on track as an active learner. If you ask yourself, "Am I learning anything in this unit?" and the answer is, "No," then you need to figure out why not. One suggestion is to ask your parents and teachers for ideas, since they are as concerned about your success as you are (if not more so.)

If you ask yourself, "Am I exerting myself?" and the answer is "No," then discover what is wrong. Did you choose a project that you are not really interested in, or one that is too hard? Then perhaps you should change to a different project that is more promising. Are you tired? Then consider doing a project with a friend, as it helps to share the load.

If you ask yourself, "Am I doing my best?" and the answer is, "No," then it is time to consider what your goals are for this course. If it is to just put in the time required to get a grade and move on, then you are cheating yourself of a rich opportunity to discover what you love doing best. You may find that you love sculpting, or pantomime, or writing, or journalism, or designing . . . but if you never really try, you will probably never know. Be honest with yourself. After all, this is your education and your life. If you don't like what you see, seek to change something. If you do like what you are doing and what you are learning, be sure to tell someone, especially your teacher. Enthusiasm begets enthusiasm, and you might end up finding out things you didn't know about things you never knew.

Creation & the Flood

UNIT 1

Key Concepts

- A biblical view of the beginning
- The wonder of creation
- The impact of the Fall of man
- Early man as an intelligent, capable creature
- The Flood—its causes and effects

God's handiwork

"In the beginning God . . ."

Our study of human history begins at the very beginning of all things—Page One, if you will—with the focus and emphasis on the Creator. Many people who study history in our day do not start on that page. They begin with prehistoric man, just after he "evolved" from the ape—the ape being, as some suppose, our evolutionary predecessor! In textbooks, history books, and even children's picture books, we are presented with the accomplished fact of man's evolution from apes to ape-men to man, though actual evidence is noticeably lacking.

However, to those who recognize the reliability of Scripture for true knowledge and understanding—to those who accept the historic, scientific, and revelational truth of God's Word—the Bible becomes an insiders' look at the actual events of the beginning of history. You might consider it an absolutely accurate journalistic report of the "Lifestyles of the Perfect and Fallen." It is crucial to our understanding of history to start with the book of Genesis, which is an eyewitness account (with God being, obviously, the first and most reliable eyewitness) of the earliest history of man. Armed with this insight and understanding, we will be well-equipped to take our journey together through the history of ancient times.

In the first chapter of Genesis, we discover the amazing account of how God created the planets, the sun and moon, the stars, the plants and animals—in six actual days—and how He declared that they were good. Then, as the crowning act of the creation drama, God made man in His own image and likeness—male and female He created them. What does that mean? What does it mean to be created in the image and likeness of God Himself? The innumerable facets of this truth have occupied scholars and theologians for centuries. Interestingly enough, however, this is not merely an academic exercise for philosophers and ministers. It answers one of the deeply-felt needs common to all people in all time periods—"Who am I, and what value does my life possess?" This question is vitally important to each one of us, and when we discover in God's Word the answer (that I am a handmade creation of God, made in His very image), it provides what we need for living life with a purpose. I encourage you to spend some time considering this foundational question—"Who am I, and what value does my life possess?"—perhaps by journaling or sharing with your family or another student.

When we read in Genesis 1 and 2 about the way God created everything to be good, even VERY good, and as we see Adam and Eve living in a perfect place (can you imagine?), questions may begin to arise concerning what it would be like today in the world if things had continued in this state of perfection. Take a minute to suspend the everyday reality around you and consider our world without the effect of sin: What would nations look like? How would marriages and families function? What would technology and the economy be like if they were being run by people without sin? How would the artists and musicians and writers and dancers in a perfect world perform, and what kind of masterpieces in art would we be seeing? What would be the impact on the animal kingdom—would the lion lie down with the lamb? It is important for us to remember that God created a perfect world, and that His plan for mankind was to live in that perfect world. So, what happened? What went wrong? Why is there evil and suffering in the world today? That question is another one of the most significant to all people throughout history, and the Bible holds for us a true and reliable answer.

As the crowning act of the Creation drama, God made man in His own image and likeness—male and female He created them.

Have you recognized that sometimes we hear a story so often that it becomes almost meaningless? It is kind of like repeating a nursery rhyme over and over and over again:

Pease porridge hot, pease porridge cold,
Pease porridge in the pot nine days old...

What on earth does that mean? Our answer would probably be, "Nothing," because it makes no sense to us today. In the very same way, we often relegate Scripture—especially the early chapters of Genesis—to a mindless storybook nonsense.

We often relegate Scripture—especially the early chapters of Genesis—to a mindless storybook nonsense.

With that in mind, I'd like you to do something fresh and new. Please read these verses from Genesis 3 (on the next page) as if they were in vibrant Technicolor with camera lighting and surround sound.

All of the drama and tragedy in history has occurred because of the actual, historic event we term the Fall! Wars, enslavement, genocide, sickness and suffering of every kind can be directly traced back to mankind's Fall from relationship with God that took place in the Garden of Eden.

Remember my statement about our being made in the image and likeness of God? Consider that one vital aspect of our being made in the image and likeness of God is found in our capacity for relationship. God, the holy Trinity—God the Father, God the Son, God the Holy Spirit—was in divine relationship, each with the other, from eternity. How do we know?

> Then God said, "Let US make man in OUR image, according to OUR likeness... Genesis 1:26

The Impact of the Fall of Man

From the very beginning of time, human beings created in the image and likeness of God were made to be in relationship: relationship with God, relationship with one another, and relationship with the created world. It was to be a deep, intimate relationship, a day by day walking with God in the Garden, sharing all of the delights and discoveries of what He had created. The man's and woman's relationship was to be a human expression of this same kind of fellowship. He made us for relationship, deeper and more satisfying than anything we have ever imagined.

But, as we have discovered in Genesis 3, relationships were broken at the Fall of Man: the open and deep relationship between God and man, the fellowship and relationship between all people, and the relationship between people and the created world. As we'll see over the course of our study, the continuing effects of the Fall—evil and suffering of all kinds—are clearly visible throughout the pages of history.

However, along with this devastating thread of sorrows and suffering is woven the scarlet thread of Redemption. God, the Creator who made us in His image, did not leave us alone in our sufferings, but set in motion an

Genesis 3:1–23

Now the serpent was more cunning than any beast of the field which the Lord God had made. And he said to the woman, "Has God indeed said, 'You shall not eat of every tree of the garden?" And the woman said to the serpent, "We may eat the fruit of the trees of the garden; but of the fruit of the tree which is in the midst of the garden, God has said, 'You shall not eat it, nor shall you touch it, lest you die.'" And the serpent said to the woman, "You will not surely die. For God knows that in the day you eat of it your eyes will be opened, and you will be like God, knowing good and evil."

So when the woman saw that the tree was good for food, that it was pleasant to the eyes, and a tree desirable to make one wise, she took of its fruit and ate. She also gave to her husband with her, and he ate. Then the eyes of both of them were opened, and they knew that they were naked; and they sewed fig leaves together and made themselves coverings. And they heard the sound of the Lord God walking in the garden in the cool of the day, and Adam and his wife hid themselves from the presence of the Lord God among the trees of the garden.

Then the Lord God called to Adam and said to him, "Where are you?" So he said, "I heard Your voice in the garden, and I was afraid because I was naked; and I hid myself." And He said, "Who told you that you were naked? Have you eaten from the tree of which I commanded you that you should not eat?" Then the man said, "The woman whom You gave to be with me, she gave me of the tree, and I ate." And the Lord God said to the woman, "What is this you have done?" And the woman said, "The serpent deceived me, and I ate."

So the Lord God said to the serpent: "Because you have done this, you are cursed more than all cattle, and more than every beast of the field; on your belly you shall go, and you shall eat dust all the days of your life. And I will put enmity between you and the woman, and between your seed and her Seed; He shall bruise your head—and you shall bruise His heel." To the woman He said: "I will greatly multiply your sorrow and your conception; in pain you shall bring forth children, your desire shall be for your husband, and he shall rule over you." Then to Adam He said, "Because you have heeded the voice of your wife, and have eaten from the tree of which I commanded you, saying, 'You shall not eat of it': Cursed is the ground for your sake; in toil you shall eat of it all the days of your life. Both thorns and thistles it shall bring forth for you, and you shall eat the herb of the field, in the sweat of your face you shall eat bread till you return to the ground, for out of it you were taken; for dust you are, and to dust you shall return."

And Adam called his wife's name Eve, because she was the mother of all living. Also for Adam and his wife the Lord God made tunics of skin, and clothed them. Then the Lord God said, "Behold, the man has become like one of Us, to know good and evil. And now, lest he put out his hand and take also of the tree of life, and eat, and live forever"—therefore the Lord God sent him out of the garden of Eden to till the ground from which he was taken.

unfolding drama beyond the wildest imaginations of Hollywood. He made a promise to the serpent which gave Adam and Eve hope of His infinite mercy and grace, which would impact all peoples throughout time.

> And I will put enmity between you and the woman, and between your seed and her Seed; He shall bruise your head and you shall bruise His heel. [This is generally considered the first prophecy concerning Jesus.] Genesis 3:15

As we look at history, we will examine and consider these two threads woven into the pages of mankind: the sinful effects of the Fall and the powerful, redeeming grace of God. Another one of those significant questions people ask is, "What does history mean?" Keep your eyes open, looking for these threads of sin and redemption, and you will have the answer to that question.

One of the first human tragedies after the Fall was the brokenness of relationship between Cain and Abel. Genesis 4 tells us Cain killed his brother because he was angry that the Lord had accepted Abel's sacrifice and not his own. Jealousy, anger, murder, and lying are all visible at this very early moment in history. We also see the impact on the very ground that Cain had tilled—God told him that the ground would no longer yield its strength to him. What happens to a farmer when the ground produces nothing? It is devastating physically, emotionally, mentally, and financially. The devastation surrounding Cain goes much further even than that. His relationship with his parents and other siblings is so broken that he is terrified one of them will kill him for his sin against Abel. Finally, as he cries out his anguish before God, we see the greatest devastation of all. He says, "Surely You have driven me out this day from the face of the ground; I shall be hidden from Your face..." His relationship with God is severed, at least from his perspective. This is an amazingly accurate picture of what happens to individuals, families, and nations when sin reigns unrestrained.

After this destruction, God made provision for His promise in Genesis 3:15 by giving another son, a godly son, to Adam and Eve. This son they named Seth, which means, "appointed," because Eve knew, "God has appointed another seed for me instead of Abel, whom Cain killed." It was from this line that Noah would eventually come.

God, the Creator who made us in His image, did not leave us alone in our sufferings, but set in motion an unfolding drama beyond the wildest imaginations of Hollywood.

Early man as intelligent and capable

As we wait for the days to unfold before the Flood, let us discover some of the amazing historical information contained in Scripture. Genesis 4:20–22 describes the offspring of the great, great, great grandson of Cain. We find the "father" of those who live in tents and have domesticated livestock (nomadic ranchers), the "father" of all those who play the harp and flute (concert musicians), and the "instructor" of every craftsman in bronze and iron (the local Tech School professor). These three areas of knowledge and skill are all considered to be aspects of high civilization. When you read a secular history book, you will be told that the domestication of animals was a huge step for evolutionary man, as it allowed a more dependable source of food. Music is one of the most advanced technologies of an advanced civilization, according to musicologists. And iron and bronze both require high levels of technology to obtain, which is not supposed to appear for several thousand years more.

Since the Bible describes this technology and advancement as present in the very early days of mankind, who do secularists today teach an opposite view? Is it because most history books today begin with evolution rather than creation? If man has just recently evolved from pond scum, it will take him a while to evolve enough to be able to have "higher level" thinking skills. (For your consideration, the paleontological and archaeological data do not clearly support this theory). On the other hand, if Adam and Eve were handmade by the Creator God, in His very image, it would be perfectly reasonable to believe that they and their offspring were quite capable of thinking and creating. It is probable that they were actually more intelligent and able to create than people today, since they were so close to creation and the Garden of Eden, and we, in all of our doings and all of our technology are but a poor representation of what early man was able to accomplish. Isn't that a wild thought!

The Flood and its cause

More than fifteen hundred years after God created the world, the Bible records this horrific truth:

> Then the Lord saw that the wickedness of man was great in the earth, and that every intent of the thoughts of his heart was only evil continually. Genesis 6:5

Can you imagine a time when all but the family of Noah thought only evil thoughts every second of every day? With the long lives of men in the days before the Flood, evil men and women would have time to really develop their strategies of evil, and to train their offspring in all kinds of wickedness. If you have ever read the book, *Oliver Twist*, you can imagine Fagin as a nine-hundred year old trainer of pickpockets. On how many generations would one man such as that have influence? It boggles the imagination! And the evil being committed was far more deadly than mere pick pocketing. There was no reverence or honoring of God left in the earth, apart from Noah and his family.

Most history books today begin with evolution rather than creation.

The Scripture tells us that God was sorry that He had made man on the earth, and He was grieved in His heart (Genesis 6:6). God had intended such incredible blessings for mankind. He had created a world where people could walk in deep fellowship with God Himself, and in deep fellowship with the people and the creation around them. He had established a place of beauty and creativity, filled with every joy and delight imaginable, all at their disposal. But each of these amazingly good things was thrown away by mankind at this point, like so much rotting garbage. Evil was what they wanted, evil was what they craved, evil was the only thing that brought satisfaction—in the same way that heroin satisfies the addict only for a moment, and then the craving returns.

God made His plans for destroying the earth, but He did not carry them out immediately. He told Noah, a man who walked in relationship with Him (Genesis 6:9), about these plans for destruction, and instructed him to build an Ark. It is fascinating to consider that the God who had spoken the worlds into existence, and who could certainly have miraculously provided an Ark at the moment He decided to destroy the earth, instead gave the long and difficult task to a "preacher of righteousness" (2 Peter 2:5). Why the delay? Why give evil men many more years to commit heinous acts? What does Scripture say?

God was sorry that He had made man on the earth, and He was grieved in His heart.

> The Lord is not slack concerning His promise, as some count slackness, but is longsuffering toward us, not willing that any should perish but that all should come to repentance.
> 2 Peter 3:9

We see at this moment the twin threads of man's sin and God's mercy. Through the very visible building of the Ark, and through the preaching of Noah, God was giving men a chance to repent and escape the deluge. Tragically, only Noah's wife, his three sons and their three wives listened to Noah's warnings. They, along with a God-ordained selection of each kind of land animal and bird, escaped the worldwide flood, which not only destroyed the rest of mankind but dramatically changed the world itself. No longer would men live seven, eight, or nine hundred years. Instead, lives would be shortened considerably, to the point where seventy years was considered

Only Noah's family and the animals ordained by God were saved on the Ark.

normal. The original atmosphere, designed by God to water and nourish the earth, was changed to what we know today—capable of floods, droughts, storms, cyclones, hurricanes, tornados, and other weather-induced tragedies. The floodwaters laid down massive quantities of fossils in rock layers throughout the world. The Bible also records a dramatic change between mankind and the animal kingdom:

The earth from space

> And the fear of you and the dread of you shall be on every beast of the earth, on every bird of the air, on all that move on the earth, and on all the fish of the sea. Genesis 9:2

Many scholars and scientists believe that the Ice Age began soon after the Flood and lasted about 700 years. (See www.answersingenesis.org/go/ice-age for more information.)

From this point on, the world will look much like we see it today. Civilizations will rise and fall, discoveries will be made and forgotten, people will live and die, and throughout time we will encounter the two threads woven in and out of our story, HisStory.

Phase 1

Listen to This

What in the World? VOL. 1

DISC ONE:

- Welcome to World History (track 1)
- Creation (track 2)
- Early Man (track 3)
- The Flood (track 4)

True Tales VOL. 1

DISC ONE:

- Introduction (track 1)
- Dates for Creation (track 2)
- Early Man (track 3)
- Where Did Cain Get His Wife? *Interview with Ken Ham* (track 4)

Digging Deeper VOL. 1

DISC ONE:

- Noah's Ark

Look at This

- Creation: Where's the Proof? (www.answersingenesis.org/go/proof)
- Could God Really Have Created Everything in Six Days? (www.answersingenesis.org/go/six-days)
- Was There Really a Noah's Ark & Flood? (www.answersingenesis.org/go/ark-flood)

Key People

Adam & Eve
First people

Cain
First murderer

Seth
The godly line

Tubal-Cain
Instructor of metal craftsmen

Jubal
Father of musicians

Noah
Ark builder

Read for Your Life

The Holy Bible

> **CONSIDER:**
>
> Look in the Bible for these terms:
>
> - creation
> - rest
> - first Adam / last Adam
> - redemption
> - grace

CREATION:

- The Main Story: Genesis 1–4
- Other helpful verses: Exodus 20:11, Job 38:4–41:34, Psalm 8:3–9, Psalm 19:1–6, Psalm 65:5–13, Psalm 89:11–14, Psalm 95:1–7, Psalm 100, Psalm 104, Psalm 136:1–9, Psalm 148, Isaiah 40:12–31, Jeremiah 32:17, Matthew 19:4–6, John 1:1–5, Romans 1:20, Colossians 1:15–17, Hebrews 1:10, 11:3

THE FLOOD:

- The Main Story: Genesis 5–10
- Other helpful verses: Matthew 24:37–39, Hebrews 11:4–7, 1 Peter 3:20, 2 Peter 2:5

Talk Together

Opinion Column

- What did you find to be the most interesting aspect or the most fascinating person you encountered in your introduction to creation & the Flood?
- Adam was given the amazing work of naming the animals. If it were your task, what would the challenges be? What would the pleasures be?
- Noah labored for many years on the Ark, which must have seemed highly unusual to the people around him. Imagine yourself in his setting and consider what issues and difficulties he might have faced as he obeyed God.

Critical Puzzling

- Read Genesis 3. Ponder the choice Adam and Eve made to disobey God and eat the forbidden fruit, and then write your thoughts on these issues:
  - Name some of the results of their choice.
  - What is the ongoing impact of their choice on every person born after them?
  - Considering the whole of Scripture, which events did God set in motion to restore us to relationship with Him?
  - How has your own experience with God been affected by Adam and Eve's choice?
- One of Cain's descendants was Tubal-Cain, who was "an instructor of every craftsman in bronze and iron" (Genesis 4:22). This man demonstrates that early man had obtained a much higher level of technology than we have been led to believe by evolutionists. What are the implications of early technology and intelligence? (Use some of the resources listed below as a source for your answer.)

CODE:

AA (all ages)
RA (Read aloud)
E+ (elem & up)
UE+ (upper elem & up)
MS+ (Middle School & up)
HS (high school)

Resources for Digging Deeper

Choose a few books that look interesting, or find your own.

CREATION

Creation: Facts of Life

Gary Parker • This updated classic is filled with many of the latest findings in science. An excellent and concise introductory text for students and families. In his easy-to-read style, Dr. Parker looks at evidence for creation in DNA, embryonic development, homology, and more! Darwin's assumptions and fossil evidence are also addressed. **MS+**

Adam & His Kin

Ruth Beechick • A speculative, but fascinating look at what life might have been like during the first several chapters of Genesis. **RA UE+**

The Great Dinosaur Mystery and the Bible

Paul S. Taylor • Children often want to know, "What about the dinosaurs?" when we talk about creation. This is a great picture book to introduce the answers on a child's level (though I learned a lot, too!). **E+**

Understanding The Times
(ABRIDGED EDITION)

David Noebel • This book (especially Ch. 15 through 18) will greatly help to clarify the worldview positions of evolutionists and creationists. We think it is absolutely critical to understand the issue of worldview, and of its impact on every branch of learning. Dr. Noebel has written an excellent resource. **HS**

Darwin on Trial

Phillip E. Johnson • The controversial book that rocked the scientific establishment because it shows that the theory of evolution is based not on fact but on faith in philosophical naturalism. This fascinating book was written by a professor of law, and is laid out so simply that the nonscientist can follow the arguments. It is very helpful for understanding the fallacies in the evolutionist argument. **HS**

Evolution Exposed

Roger Patterson • This book helps teens to discern the chronic bias towards belief in evolution that permeates today's most popular high school biology textbooks. Evolution Exposed cross-references the evolutionary content with online articles and publications that provide both scientific and biblical answers. **HS**

Darwin's Black Box THE BIOCHEMICAL CHALLENGE TO EVOLUTION

Michael J. Behe • Don't let the subtitle scare you. This is a very readable book about a very complex subject. The result is that the reader will have an entirely new arsenal of defenses against evolution. Fascinating! **HS**

The Lie: Evolution

Ken Ham • Ken Ham is best known for his message on the relevance of creation and the importance of Genesis. Humorous and easy to read, this book equips Christians to defend the book of Genesis and opens eyes to the evil effects of evolution on today's society. **MS+**

Reasonable Faith THE SCIENTIFIC CASE FOR CHRISTIANITY

Dr. Jay Wile • Dr. Wile's book is a well-written, well-researched apologetic (defense) of Christianity. It describes the scientific evidences for God's intelligent design in creation, along with amazing descriptions of God's scientific reasons for some of the commands He gave (e.g., circumcision on the 8th day). **MS+**

Fearfully & Wonderfully Made

Dr. Paul Brand & Philip Yancey • Discover the amazing ways God has designed people in this story-filled book. It would make a great book for short read-alouds and discussions. **MS+**

In Six Days WHY 50 SCIENTISTS CHOOSE TO BELIEVE IN CREATION

Edited by John F. Ashton, Ph.D. • There is a general view in the media and Hollywood that only ignorant buffoons believe in creation. This book debunks that myth quite handily with essays by 50 scientists who hold doctorates from state-recognized universities. **HS**

THE FLOOD

Dry Bones and Other Fossils

Gary E. & Mary M. Parker • Written in an engaging style for children, this is a captivating, information-filled book that will give a basic understanding of the Flood and its impact on the earth. **E+**

Noah's Ark

Rien Poortvliet • This is an oversize, beautiful book of paintings and sketches about Noah's Ark. It is quite expensive, so check to see if your library can get it. **AA**

The True Story of Noah's Ark

Tom Dooley • With beautiful illustrations, this book will appeal to adults as well as children. **AA**

Noah's Ark: Thinking Outside the Box BOOK & DVD

Tim Lovett • Join this naval expert and mechanical engineer in his gound-breaking research regarding the design and shape of the Ark. **HS**

The Genesis Flood

John Whitcomb & Henry Morris • This is an excellent resource for understanding the scientific evidences for the biblical Flood, as well as the inadequacies of evolution to explain what is seen in the geologic, archaeological, and fossil record. **HS**

GENERAL

The Annals of the World

James Ussher, translated and revised by Larry & Marion Pierce • A classic survey of world history from creation to AD 70, written by a saintly scholar in the 1650s. An indispensable reference work for any study of ancient history. **HS**

Ancient History from Primary Sources

Harvey & Laurie Bluedorn • Including the literature of Egypt, Mesopotamia, Greece, and Rome, this compilation is an excellent resource. **MS+**

The Discovery of Genesis

C. H. Kang and Ethel R. Nelson • This incredible book shows the book of Genesis, in tremendous detail, as depicted in ancient Chinese pictographs (or ideograms). The authors' contention is that the founding of China in about 2500 BC was close enough to the time of the Tower of Babel that the memory of what had occurred prior was still fresh in the minds of the Chinese people. Highly recommended! **MS+**

History of the World

Josephus, edited by Paul Maier • Josephus was a Jewish historian who survived the destruction of Jerusalem in AD 70. He was taken to Rome and befriended by Emperor Titus, who asked Josephus to write an account of the history of the Jews. An original source document and one of the few histories written in antiquity, this book is a veritable gold mine of information. **MS+**

Genesis: Finding Our Roots

Ruth Beechick • Believing that Genesis forms the foundation of our understanding of all of life's major questions, Dr. Beechick has created this fascinating, insightful book, which provides students the opportunity to study in depth the first eleven chapters of Genesis. **UE+**

The Puzzle of Ancient Man

Donald E. Chittick, PhD • Dr. Chittick has compiled an astonishing selection of OOP Arts (Out Of Place Artifacts) with a thoroughly biblical explanation. Worth searching for! **MS+**

The New Answers Book

Ken Ham et al • This book is worth purchasing, as it will be referred to over and over again. The questions are pertinent questions students ask and the answers are well-researched and very understandable. **UE+**

The New Answers Book II

Ken Ham et al • A companion to *The New Answers Book*, answering even more questions on creation/evolution and the Bible. **UE+**

For more books, use these Dewey Decimal numbers in your library:

Bible: #220

Genealogy: #929

Creation: #213

Evolution: #575

Fossils & Prehistoric Life: #560

Ancient History: #930

Ancient Middle & Near Eastern: #930

Ancient Mesopotamia & Iranian Plateau: #935

What books did you like best?

The Internet also contains a wealth of information about creation and the Flood.

What sites were the most helpful?

Student Self-Evaluation UNIT 1, PHASE 1

Dates and hours:____________________________

Key Concepts

Rephrase the five Key Concepts of this Unit and confirm your understanding of each:

- A biblical view of the beginning

____

- The wonder of creation

____

- The impact of the Fall of man

____

- Early man as an intelligent, capable creature

____

- The Flood—its causes and effects

____

Tools for Self-Evaulation

Evaluate your personal participation in the discussions of this Phase. Bearing in mind that a good participant in a discussion is not always the most vocal participant, ask yourself these questions: Were you an active participant? Did you ask perceptive questions? Were you willing to listen to other participants of the discussion and draw out their opinions? Record your observations and how you would like to improve your participation in the future:

____

____

Every time period is too complex to be understood in one Phase of study. Evaluate your current knowledge of Creation & the Flood. What have you focused on so far? What are your weakest areas of knowledge?

____

____

Based on the evaluation of this introduction, project ahead what you would like to study more of in the following Phases:

____

Phase 2

Research & Reporting

Explore one or more of these areas to discover something significant!

Creation/Flood

Investigate various creation and flood stories in ancient or tribal cultures, including the Epic of Gilgamesh. Compare and contrast at least two of these versions with the biblical account. See www.answersingenesis.org/go/flood-legends for some ideas.

Creation in Scripture

Read Genesis and the New Testament Scriptures about creation, as well as any of the creation books available to you. Do the writers of the New Testament, as well as the words of Jesus, indicate they believed the Bible's account of creation was literal history? Do evolutionists? Using what you discover, write a defense of your position.

Intelligent Design

Find one of the books listed, or a book of your choice, for basic information on this branch of creation versus evolution. Report your findings. For more information, see www.answersingenesis.org/go/intelligent-design.

The Amazing Body

Do a research paper, with pictures, on the amazing intricacies of the ear, the eye, the brain, the heart, or any other part of the human body. Include the function of the organ, and its interrelation with other organs. Relate this to your study of creation. As a resource, see www.answersingenesis.org/go/design and look under human biology.

Metallurgy

Research the science of metallurgy. What is required to manufacture bronze? Iron? Explain how this demonstrates technological advancement. Consider how this contrasts with the evolutionary assumption of the technological and intellectual limitations of early man.

Music

Investigate what is necessary to create and play musical instruments. If possible, interview someone who makes or repairs instruments. Ask about the technology involved and the difficulties involved in this art. Interview someone who teaches a musical instrument. Find out what is involved in learning to play the instrument well. Ask at your music store for a video about instrument manufacturing. Explain how this demonstrates a sophistication of cultural development. Again, how does this contrast with the evolutionary assumptions about the abilities of the earliest humans.

Genealogy

Read the genealogies in Genesis 10, Matthew 1, and Luke 3. Research the term "genealogy." Collect the names and statistics of your family's ancestry, either through interviewing members of your family or researching through the library, Internet, or other organizations. (Save this information for the Family Tree Project in Phase Three.)

Order of Events

Make a chart listing the order of events during the Creation Week.

Floods

Research the powerful and devastating impact of floodwaters. If a community nearby has recently been flooded, interview someone who experienced it first hand.

Cavitation

Research cavitation and its danger at hydroelectric dams. Locate a video showing the catastrophic damage caused by cavitation.

Catastophic Plate Tectonics

The latest creation research points to Catastrophic Plate Tectonics (CPT) as one of the main sources for the waters of the Flood, and an explanation for why the landmasses look the way they do today. Research CPT and prepare a report on what it is and how it may have affected the earth in the past. See www.answersingenesis.org/go/cpt for more information.

How Deep is Deep?

Read and report on current ideas concerning how deep the water was at the Flood. Was it above Mt. Everest? Was Mt. Everest even there yet? Chart the various theories of the water levels.

Animal husbandry

A necessary science on the Ark! Find out some of the requirements for caring for reptiles, birds, and mammals. Comment on the difficulties of caring for a vast combination of animals.

Mt. Ararat

In the library or on the Internet, research any information about the mountains of Ararat and the search for Noah's Ark. Also, compare the varying opinions of the creationists concerning where they believe Noah's Ark is located.

Brain Stretchers

The Amazing Body, Part 2

Find out how scientists explain the complexity of the ear, eye, heart, etc., in light of their belief in a mindless evolutionary process. Compare/contrast this with the biblical account of creation.

Metallurgy, Part 2

Research what it would take for your family to make bronze. Give an inventory of the necessary equipment and facilities, the cost involved, and the value of the product. Is it feasible? Visit your town's blacksmith shop, machine shop, or foundry. Report what you discover and relate what it suggests about pre-Flood times.

Cavitation, Part 2

Research and report some of the potential effects that cavitation would have had on the earth's surface during the Flood.

Ark Design

Research the requirements for ship stability in the water. Seakeeping, structural integrity, and broach avoidance are important principles that need to be considered for any large vessel. Write a description (include drawings) of the engineering and construction techniques required to build the Ark. See www.worldwideflood.com for information on how the Ark might have looked and why.

Create Your Own Research Topic

____

____

Timeline

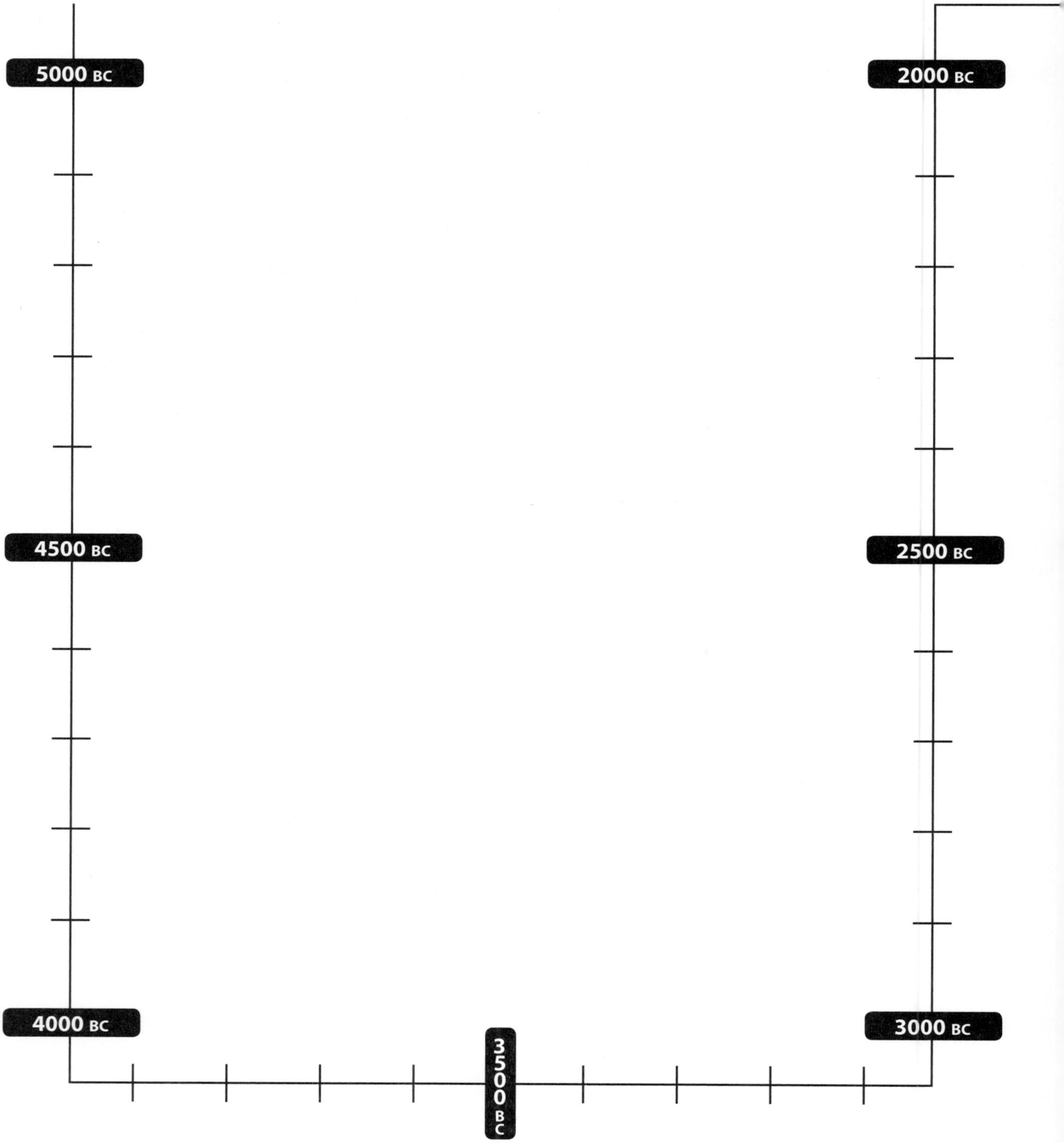

Consider this for your timeline

The Bible tells us that God created Adam and Eve on the sixth day of creation. Those who believe the Scriptures to express accurately and literally the events of history, such as the famous seventeenth century chronologist James Ussher, have set the date of creation around the year 4004 BC. There are other Bible scholars who disagree with this date, believing that the Bible does not necessarily include all the generations in the genealogies, and they set the date of creation at an earlier point, perhaps up to 10,000 BC. Those who do not hold to the Bible as literally true look to other sources for the date of early man, such as carbon dating of the archaeological record, which is riddled with difficulties; they set the date for the first true humans anywhere from 35,000 to 100,000 BC.

Ussher, utilizing the Genesis record as well as many other ancient, historical sources available to him, believed the date for the worldwide Flood to be 2348 BC. Though there are those who disagree, most history books document the explosion of ancient civilizations along the Fertile Crescent just after this date.

Key Events

- Creation
- The Flood
- The Ice Age

Be sure to include the people listed in Key People in Phase 1.

Words to Watch

prehistoric	technology	banish	antediluvian
metallurgy	repentance	evolution	genealogy
ancestor	creation	redemption	deceive
origins	Sabbath	altar	worldview
rebellion	naturalism	religion	Ark
pitch	cavitation	cubit	catastrophic
agriculture	buoyancy	uniformitarianism	animal
husbandry	hostility	rebellion	covenant
descendant			

Remember—The easiest way to learn a subject is to master its terms.

Other words you need to look up:

Student Self-Evaluation UNIT 1, PHASE 2

Dates and hours:______________________

Research Project

- Summarize your research question:

____

____

- List your most useful sources by author, title, and page number or URL where applicable (continue list in margin if necessary):

____

____

____

Now take a moment to evaluate the sources you just listed. Do they provide a balanced view of your research question? Should you have sought an additional opinion? Are your sources credible (if you found them on your own)? Record your observations:

____

____

Evaluate your research project in its final presentation. What are its strengths? If you had time to revisit this project, what would you change? Consider giving yourself a letter grade based on your project's merits and weaknesses.

____

____

Letter grade: ____

You have just completed an area of specific research in the time of Creation & the Flood. Now what would you like to explore in the upcoming Phases? Set some objectives for yourself:

____

Phase 3

Maps and Mapping

(These are all post-Flood mapping exercises, since no one knows what the geography of the pre-Flood world looked like.)

Physical Terrain

» Label and color the Tigris and Euphrates rivers on the outline map.

» Color the Fertile Crescent.

» Locate and indicate the mountain ranges, deserts, and green areas.

» Shade and label the Black Sea, the Caspian Sea, and the Persian Gulf.

Geopolitical

» Mark the possible locations of Mt. Ararat and the appropriate countries (Turkey, Iran).

» Locate the land of Shinar.

Explore

» ***Out from the Ark:*** Read Genesis 11:2. Look at a relief map of the region and try to trace the route taken by the post-Flood people from Mt. Ararat to the land of Shinar.

» ***Cradle of Civilization:*** Because the Garden of Eden was sealed off from man's presence after Adam and Eve sinned, and since the Flood thoroughly altered the geography of the earth, it is impossible to pinpoint where the events of Genesis 1–7 occurred. However, archaeologists believe the "cradle of civilization," which would be post-Flood, is located in the Fertile Crescent between the Tigris and Euphrates. Consult a relief map of the region where the Ark came to rest and a relief map of the Fertile Crescent. What reasons might there be that the Fertile Crescent, rather than the mountains of Ararat, was the cradle of civilization? (Consider this in terms of terrain and climate, though some of this will have been affected by the Ice Age.)

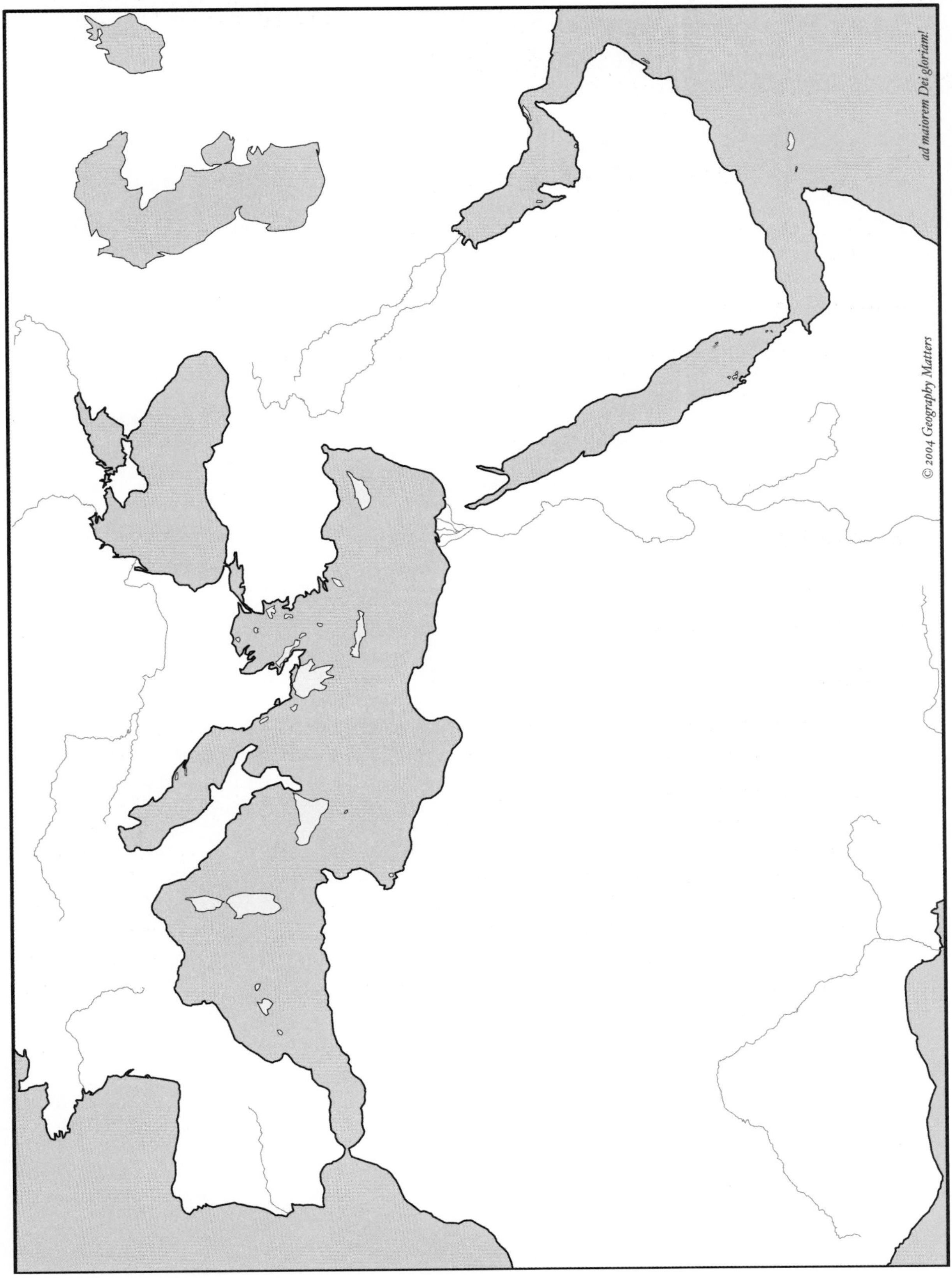
ad maiorem Dei gloriam!
© 2004 Geography Matters

CONSIDER:

Michelangelo painted the Sistine Chapel while lying on his back on scaffolding for several years!

CONSIDER:

Did you know that God is the Original and Greatest Architect? Hebrews 11:10: "For he waited for the city which has foundations, whose builder and maker is God." Look up architecture in a study Bible, and discuss the Scriptures listed, considering some of the implications of the concept: God is an Architect.

Art Appreciation

Creation by Michelangelo, the Sistine Chapel

» Do you think his painting reflects what the Bible describes?

» How does the painting differ from your own impression of this historic event?

- For a captivating look at his experience, watch the video, *The Agony and the Ecstasy*.

Noah's Ark by Edward Hicks

» What does this painting communicate to you about Noah's Ark?

» Edward Hicks (1780-1849) is one of the best known American folk painters. Is there any identifiable "American" aspect to his painting?

- Read more about Hicks's beliefs, and how that influenced his choice of subjects for painting.

Architecture

The earth is perfectly proportioned for its travel through space.

» Locate one of the photos taken of earth from space. Then consult a relief globe to discover the architectural design of the land masses and the corresponding bodies of water. Describe the design of the earth: Are the lines rigid and straight? Is there fluidity? There are significant "water features." How does that impact the design? Would you deduce that God is a fabulous architect?

Arts in Action

Select one or more, and let your artistic juices flow!

Family Tree

On poster board, draw a large tree with branches. At the roots, label the names of the children in your family. On the first two branches, write your mother's name and your father's name. From those branches, keep adding branches as far back as you can go. Since we all descend from Adam and Eve, through Noah, be sure to place their names at the very top of your family tree! Another option is to use fallen tree branches, or hanging cards with the names on them. Try making it three dimensional.

Copper Working

Learning to work with copper is an interesting means of understanding what early craftsmen dealt with. Locate a hobby shop and browse through their copper crafts. Be sure to ask questions about working with this substance, trying to learn all you can. Then, when you are ready, try your hand at creating a copper "work of art." (Suggestion: If you have Visual Manna's *Teaching History Through Art*, you will have a piece of copper foil and some suggestions of how to create art with it!)

Jewelry

Visit a jewelry store to learn about their use of metals and precious stones. Ask them how they make various pieces of jewelry. Then try making some metal jewelry.

Imitation

- Try your hand at creating the *Creation* by Michelangelo (trace, follow colors, etc.)
- Create a Noah's Ark in the style of Edward Hicks.

Creating at Home

Read Edith Schaeffer's book, *Hidden Art*. It is based upon the concept that we reflect our Creator when we create. There are many practical ideas for possible projects. Choose what appeals to you and make it! Possible areas to consider are gardening, floral arranging, cooking, clothes design, and making furniture. (Suggestion: Find a book or an expert who can help you get started in your creative endeavors.)

Construction

- Assemble the *Noah's Ark Paper Model* by Answers in Genesis
- Carve a soap boat
- Use LEGO bricks to construct a big boat
- Make a model wooden boat or a raft-size houseboat (a good backyard project!)

Carving

Start a year-long project carving wooden animals. Check in the library or with a local expert (perhaps your grandfather?) for how-to information.

Imagine

In whatever medium you prefer, create your version of the Garden of Eden. Explain some of your color, texture, and style choices.

Science

Do-It-Yourself Flood

» Create a "flood in a bottle" by putting sand, dirt, leaves, grass, and water in a tall plastic jar with a lid. Shake vigorously and observe the settling process. Do you see how different layers can be formed very quickly? Try varying the substances—how about rocks and oil?

Do-It-Yourself Cavitation

» Build a nice big sandbox dam and fill a big reservoir behind it. Watch the valleys it forms after you poke a hole in the dam.

Agriculture

» Plant a grape vine (if not possible, try potting a fruit vine or bushes like raspberries, strawberries, etc.). Go on a field trip to a vineyard. Learn about the cultivation of grapes. Learn about fermentation. Try making vinegar or drying grapes to make raisins.

Music

Many composers have created a tone poem or programmatic music where a scene is conveyed through the music. One of my favorites is *Pictures at an Exhibition* by Modeste Mussorgsky. If you can find this recording, listen especially to "The Ballet of the Baby Chicks in Their Shells." If you can find the artwork that inspired Mussorgsky, you may be surprised! Another wonderful example of a symphonic poem type of music is Beethoven's Sixth Symphony (*Pastoral* symphony). Listen for the sounds of nature recreated by the orchestral instruments.

Listen:

» Now listen to the oratorio "The Creation" by Franz Joseph Haydn. As you listen to this formal piece of music, try to hear the dynamics of creation. Why do you think Haydn called it "The Creation"? Does the music convey mental pictures to you?

Try This

» Listen to the music found in nature: the birds' song, the melodic tone of wind, the rhythm of falling rain. If you have a recording device, try to capture some of these sounds (and others)—a symphony of nature!

SING:

All Things Bright and Beautiful

How Great Thou Art

All Creatures of our God and King

Great is Thy Faithfulness

O Worship the King

I Sing the Mighty Power of God

Cooking

Apricots have an interesting history. One of the earliest homes of the apricot was in Armenia, in the region of Mt. Ararat. Might Noah and his family enjoyed the flavor of this fruit that is still grown in the Ararat Valley once they got off the Ark? We don't know, but it is interesting (and tasty) to consider. Enjoy!

Apricot Whip

1 pound dried apricots	½ cup sugar
2½ cups water	½ tsp almond extract
½ tsp salt	1½ cup heavy cream

Cook apricots in water & salt until tender (20 min.). Stir in sugar and flavoring. Puree in blender. Chill. Beat cream until stiff, fold into apricots, chill again. Serves 6

Student Self-Evaluation UNIT 1, PHASE 3

Dates and hours:____________________

Evaluate your projects

- List which of the activities listed in this Phase you did:

  ____

  ____

  ____

- Rate your enthusiasm: __________

  Explain: ____________________________________

  ____

- Rate the precision of your approach:__________

  Explain: ____________________________________

  ____

- Rate your effort towards the completion of the project: __________

  Explain: ____________________________________

  ____

Ask yourself what worked and what did not. What would you do differently in the future, and what would you repeat?

____

How specifically did these hands-on activities enhance your knowledge of Creation & the Flood? What made them worthwhile?

____

In the first three Phases of this Unit, what aspect of the time period has most captured your imagination? What would you like to creatively pursue to conclude your study?

____

Phase 4

In Your Own Way . . .

We have seen God's glory in the creation and His mercy in providing a way of redemption. And we have explored the causes and effects of Noah's Flood. Now, choose a selection of these activities, or create your own, which will best express what you have learned from this unit.

LINGUISTICS

Journalism

- Write an article for the *First World Times* called, "A Day in the Life of Seth." Be sure to find the human interest details.
- You are a newspaper reporter for the *Enoch Free News*. Your assignment is to interview Noah about this monstrosity he's building, and to write up his story for the newspaper feature, subtitled "Truth is Stranger Than Fiction."

Playing with Words

- Can you imagine thoughtfully naming hundreds of kinds of birds, cattle, and beasts of the field? Adam was AMAZING!
- Choose five from each category, and give them new names. Search for solid, interesting names which reflect the characteristics of the animal.
- Finish this limerick about Cain:
  There once was a man from Nod,
  Who offered his veggies to God . . .
- Try your hand at writing puns. Like this:
  "Hey Mom, you know what you call a fly that has no wings?"
  "No, son, what do you call a fly that has no wings?"
  "A walk!"

Prose

- Write a creative description of what the new world looked like after the Ark was opened and the people first came out.
- Write a first person account of life on the Ark, from the viewpoint of a seasick giraffe.
- Write a book for young children describing Noah, the Ark, and the Flood. You could use Scripture, write poems, or tell short stories.

ART

Painting/Drawing

- Illustrate the book for young children listed on the previous page. Create captions for the illustrations.

Graphic Design

- Design the T-shirt front and back, with logo and catchy saying, which Noah and his family would have worn to family reunions in the years after the Flood.

Cartooning

- The possibilities for cartoons on this subject are almost endless! Create a one-frame cartoon of one of the days of creation, or a multi-frame cartoon of Noah's neighbors, or design your own political cartoon about one of the topics of this unit.

Sculpting

- Sculpt Ark animals from your preferred material (Playdough, modeling clay, etc.)

MUSIC

Compose

Compose a song, either vocal or instrumental, about Adam and Eve entitled, "You and Me and the Forbidden Tree."

Use a familiar tune and write new words about life on the Ark.

Performance Practice

If you study an instrument, select an appropriate piece of music, with your teacher's help, which expresses some element from this unit. Prepare and perform the piece for an audience. Communicate with your audience the reason for your selection either in the *program notes* or in a short speech.

Create

Make your own instrument. It doesn't have to be fancy, it just needs to create pleasing sounds. Consider an instrument made of natural materials, such as a dried gourd filled with large beads. Or create your own rainstick, or perhaps a washtub bass. A homemade flute or drum from a hollow log would be perfect! If there are more than one instrument makers/players, form a musical group. Then either compose an original piece of music or learn to play a tune, so you can share your "music" with others!

DRAMA

Comedy

Act out a humorous introduction of Adam and Eve by God. Possible questions might include, "Excuse me, where did you say you were from?"

Create a skit about Noah's excitement when he realized the floodwaters were receding. Variation: Show the animals' excitement!

Tragedy

Reenact the Fall of Man. Include some of the tragic consequences. Finish your presentation with some of the prophecies of the coming Redeemer, because for those who would receive Him, the story need not end in tragedy.

Puppetry

Use puppets to tell young children the story of Noah and the Ark. Be sure to include realistic animal sounds!

Prop Needs

____

____

Costume Ideas

____

____

Role/Player

____

____

Set Suggestions

____

____

MOVEMENT

Pantomime

Using movement only (no words!), show the six days of creation.

Convince your audience that you are herding animals onto the Ark, two by two and seven by seven.

Dance

Choose a selection of music that expresses to you the creation or Flood, then choreograph a dance that depicts some aspect of this unit. You may use ballet, modern, jazz, or improvisational dance. Make sure your moves communicate the appropriate emotion to the audience.

Action

Stage a stylized conflict between God's goodness and man's rebellion. It is effective to have groups of two doing the same actions.

CONCEPTUAL DESIGN

Game-Making

Using the first two chapters of Genesis, create a game for children, which will give them practice in naming both the days of creation and what was created on each day. You will need to decide if this is a board game, an action game, a rhyming game, a musical-chairs game, etc.

CREATE YOUR OWN EXPRESSION

____

____

____

____

Student Self-Evaluation UNIT 1, PHASE 4

Dates and hours:____________________________

Evaluate Your Projects

- What creative project did you choose:

____

- What did you expect from your project, and how does the final project compare to your initial expectations?

____

____

- What do you like about your project? What would you change?

____

____

In Conclusion

Revisit the five Key Concepts from the beginning of this Unit. Explain how your understanding of and appreciation for each has grown over the course of your study.

____

____

____

____

____

____

Record your concluding thoughts on Creation & the Flood:

____

____

____

The Rise of Civilizations

UNIT 2

Key Concepts

- The descendants of Noah
- The Tower of Babel
- Sudden civilizations
- Archaeology—its uses and limits
- Abraham & Ur

Artist's representation of the Tower of Babel

The adventures of early mankind continue . . .

As Noah and his family came out of the Ark and began a new life in a vastly changed world, we see described in the Bible the foundations of nations, the emergence of many languages, and the first of the world empires. There is contained within those first post-Flood people the same virus that had infected the antediluvian (pre-Flood) population: active rebellion, willful disobedience, and separation from God. But with these problems also comes the second thread of God's provision and promise of redemption, as we shall soon discover in the life of Abraham.

> Now the sons of Noah who went out of the ark were Shem, Ham, and Japheth. And Ham was the father of Canaan. These three were the sons of Noah, and from these the whole earth was populated. Genesis 9:18–19

Isn't it amazing to consider that everyone who lives on the face of the earth today is a descendant of Ham, Shem, or Japheth, which, of course, means that we are all descendants of their father, Noah!

The Tower of Babel

Genesis 11 gives us a very descriptive account of the attitudes and plans of the people of earth at this post-Flood moment. As they came to the plains of Shinar (the very fertile area between the Euphrates and the Tigris rivers in the area of Babylon), they said,

> "Come, let us build ourselves a city, and a tower whose top is in the heavens; let us make a name for ourselves, lest we be scattered abroad over the face of the whole earth."
> Genesis 11:4

Notice whose name they were intent on glorifying! Do you see in their words an attitude of trust in God? How instead would you describe their attitude? These descendants of Noah were evidently not concerned with walking in obedience to the Lord who had told their ancestors to "be fruitful and multiply, and fill the earth." You can almost see mankind thumbing its nose at the God in whose image they were made. It is sobering to consider how quickly we, as the race of mankind, forget His goodness and mercy, even His miraculous provision to us, and turn our face toward rebellion.

The Scriptures describe the phenomenal power that was available when they had one mind and one language among all the people. The fact that they were of one mind and their hearts were set to do evil, combined with this ability to communicate freely without the misunderstandings common when two or more languages are present, unleashed an unstoppable ability to accomplish whatever post-Flood mankind wanted to do, as they worked together in their rebellion.

> "Indeed the people are one and they all have one language, and this is what they begin to do; now nothing that they propose to do will be withheld from them."
> Genesis 11:6

Everyone who lives on the face of the earth today is a descendant of Ham, Shem or Japheth.

In His mercy and long-suffering, God chose not to destroy mankind again, but to supernaturally and permanently confuse their language, so that they would no longer be able to plot and plan rebellion unimpeded. Can you imagine these people suddenly unable to understand what their neighbor was so emphatically trying to tell them? Picture for a moment the terror and fear that must have accompanied this dramatic change, as they struggled to find anyone with whom they could converse. Breathlessly they would run from place to place trying to find their husbands, wives, mothers, fathers, children. We could assume that nuclear families spoke the same tongue—be it an early form of Swahili, Hebrew, Latin, Malay, Chinese, German, or any of the dozens of original language families. Perhaps a few close relatives would have at least a related language and could join them as they began to make plans to flee from the center of such confusion. Whether or not we can accurately reconstruct the scenario, God used this moment to scatter our ancestors over the face of the earth. His plan for the boundaries of their habitation and their preappointed times would be fulfilled, whether they were willing or not.

Those who study languages and their distribution throughout the world have proposed that there are about ninety original language families, and possible as few as seventy, the same as the number of families named in Genesis 10. Secular theories of language evolution can't explain this discovery; only the biblical account of Babel makes sense of the facts.

The Table of Nations

In Genesis 10 we are given the detailed family names of Noah's sons and grandsons, and the general geographic regions to which they were scattered. This detailed list is often called the "Table of Nations." Simply put, the descendants of Japheth were the northern people (who inhabited the northern coastal regions of the Mediterranean), the descendants of Ham were the southern people (who migrated to the southern part of Mesopotamia, as well as Egypt), while the descendants of Shem were the people of the central area in the Middle East (as far north as Syria and as far south as Arabia). From these early days, and for various reasons including the Ice Age, drought, warfare, "greener pastures," and exploration, tribes of people began to colonize the entire earth—from the continents to the islands, from North to South, and from East to West.

The Bible tells us that God used this movement of people across the face of the earth for His redemptive purpose, to give each people group the hunger and opportunity to seek the Lord in each group's unique settings and circumstances:

> And He has made from one blood every nation of men to dwell on all the face of the earth, and has determined their preappointed times and the boundaries of their dwellings, so that they should seek the Lord. Acts 17:26–27a

God chose not to destroy mankind again, but to supernaturally and permanently confuse their language.

Genesis 10:8–10 describes one of the great grandsons of Noah as a builder of cities and as a mighty hunter before the Lord. This one man, Nimrod, received such prominence in Scripture because he was a "mover and shaker" in the earth, building such notable cities as Babel (or Babylon, capital city of the Babylonian civilization), Erek (ancient Uruk, a city close to Ur), Akkad (the Akkadian empire was an early power in Mesopotamia), Nineveh (one of the capital cities of the Assyrian civilization), and Calah (later called Nimrud, after its builder). Though we have limited information in Scripture concerning this man, it is obvious just from this list of foundational cities

2

Mankind continues to build with the technology and knowledge gained before the Flood and retained in their memory.

that he was a power to be reckoned with (notice that three of the cities that Nimrod built were centers of mighty pagan empires), and that as a "mighty hunter before the Lord," he was held in awe by the people who followed him. There have been scholars who, based on Scripture and the writings of antiquity, believe that Nimrod actually headed the rebellion at the Tower of Babel, and was the world's first dictator. *Unger's Bible Handbook* points out that there is a tremendous difference in the character of a godly leader—a "shepherd" of the people—and a godless leader—a "hunter." Consider that carefully. Would you prefer to be ruled over by one known as a "shepherd" (like David) or by one known as a "hunter" (like Nimrod)? That should give a comparative taste of what it may have been like to live in the time of Nimrod.

Sudden civilizations

From this moment of man's rebellion and God's scattering, we see the evidence of civilizations in the archaeological record. From the ancient Chinese to the Indus Valley, from Ur to Egypt, from the Minoans to the Olmecs, mankind continued to build with the technology and knowledge gained before the Flood and retained in their memory. Ancient Ziggurats and even more venerable pyramids dotted the landscape of antiquity with puzzling regularity. Discoveries in archaeology show that ancient music had many common characteristics in civilizations widely separated across the globe. Gigantic, carved stone heads were found in Central America showing the distinctive looks of two different people groups—European and African—neither of which were native to the region! These discoveries, along with ancient maps, such as the Piri Reis Map (a Turkish map dated to about AD 1513) containing the actual coastline of Antarctica (which was not known by modern geographers until the 1900s!), show that there was a tremendous amount of travel in antiquity with the accompanying technologies of boat building, surveying, navigating, and economics. (There is evidence of trade between widely divergent ancient cultures across the earth.)

Rather than the secular view of primitive man barely able to outrun the saber tooth tigers, slowly banding together into small communities, and eventually into larger cities, resulting, after many thousands of years, in what we call "civilization," we see rather a highly technical, fully developed group of civilizations that seem to pop up in the archaeological record without warning. It is disconcerting to secular historians and archaeologists, to say the least. They have even given an acronym to describe the advanced technology found in the archaeological record—OOP Arts (Out Of Place Artifacts)!

Archaeology—its uses and limitations

It might be helpful at this point to discuss the functions and limitations of archaeology. Archaeology comes from two root words, which mean "ancient" and "study." So it is the study of antiquity through the material remains (such as fossils, relics, artifacts, and monuments). This is a recent branch of science, dating from the 1800s. It is considered a historical science; it is different from the operational sciences, like physics or chemistry, since it does not provide an opportunity to test one's hypothesis in the lab over and over again. Instead, it is a matter of searching for the proverbial needle in a haystack of stone, dirt, and rubble. There have been some absolutely spectacular finds in archaeology that have illuminated the historic past in fascinating and incredible ways, which we will examine in later chapters. However, archaeology is also significantly limited in that the discoveries are partial, fragmentary, and perhaps even misleading at times. (See Appendix H, "Archaeology and the Bible," in Ussher's *Annals of the World* for a devastating critique of archaeology.)

To explain what I mean, imagine you and your family went through a holiday time where you ate box after box after box of chocolate-covered cherries. All the empty boxes filled a metal trash can, and before the garbage truck could remove the debris, the garbage can was swept away by a minor flood into a mud pit. Hundreds of years later, archaeologists suddenly discover your garbage can. If they don't find anyone else's garbage from your neighborhood, they may erroneously conclude that people of your region in your time period lived solely on chocolate-covered cherries! Though that seems silly to us, it is the kind of struggle archaeologists deal with since they simply don't know what they have not yet found. They are left to make assumptions with the collection of material they have found.

Archaeology is a wonderful tool for the historian, but it is not nearly as reliable as the Bible itself. So, as you read about discoveries in archaeology, always remember that it does not tell the whole story nor the eternal perspective. If archaeologists, or historians interpreting archaeological finds, say that their discovery disproves the Bible, recognize that their tools are falling apart and need to be replaced!

We see rather a highly technical, fully developed group of civilizations which seem to pop up in the archaeological record without warning.

Abraham & Ur

One of the earliest cities found in the archaeological record is the city of Ur, with its ziggurat, its worship of the moon goddess, and its royal tombs with ornate harps and perfectly coiffured dead servants. The Bible tells us a fascinating truth about Ur: it was a place for a friend of God to get out of!

> Now the Lord had said to Abram: "Get out of your country, from your kindred and from your father's house, to a land that I will show you. I will make you a great nation; I will bless you and make your name great; and you shall be a blessing. I will bless those who bless you, and I will curse him who curses you; and in you all the families of the earth shall be blessed." Genesis 12:1–3

As Abram obeyed, he journeyed from the very southern end of Mesopotamia (close to the Persian Gulf) all the way to Canaan (by the Mediterranean), and then on to Egypt. We see in the biblical account a description of pharaohs, kings, armies, cities, battles, and amazing deliverances out of dangerous situations! Even from this early time in human history, we have all the intrigue, all the greed, all the lust, all the evil that whirl through our cultures today. The names and dates have changed, but the basic ways we deal with one another have not changed at all. Mercifully, God has continued throughout the ages to work in and through us, and often in spite of ourselves. He didn't wind the earth up and walk away.

From the rebellion of the Tower of Babel to the blessing God intended through Abraham, we see the two threads continuing to weave through the pages of HisStory. From here, the Bible begins to follow the specific steps of Abraham and his descendants. Though there are many other stories of antiquity, even stories of God's amazing work in preserving the knowledge of Himself in ancient cultures (a fascinating study!), we will pursue the story of Abraham's seed and the various civilizations and cultures the Bible describes. Through this we will watch the unfolding of God's marvelous plan to bless "all the families of the earth."

The table below shows names of some of Noah's descendents reflected in history.

Name	Descendant of Noah	What is it?
Aramaic	Aram	Language that came out of Babel and still survives, likely with changes down the ages.
Cush	Cush	Ancient name of Ethiopia. In fact, people of Ethiopia still call themselves Cushites.
Medes	Madai	People group often associated with the Persians.
Galacia, Gaul, and Galicia	Gomer	These regions are the old names for an area in modern Turkey, France, and Northwestern Spain respectively, where Gomer was said to have lived. His family lines continued to spread across southern Europe.
Gomeraeg	Gomer	This is the old name for the Welsh language on the British Isles from their ancestor, Gomer, whose ancestors began to populate the Isle from the mainland.
Javan	Javan	This is still the Hebrew name for Greece. His sons, Elishah, Tarshish, Kittim (Chittim), and Dodanim still have reference to places in Greece. For example, the apostle Paul was from the region of Tarshish (Acts 21:39) and a city called Tarsus; Jeremiah 2:10 mentions Kittim, which is modern day Cyprus; the Greeks worshiped Jupiter Dodanaeus (from Japheth/Dodanim); the Elysians were ancient Greeks.
Meshech/ Moscow	Mechech	Mechech is the old name for Moscow, Russia. One region called the Mechech Lowland still holds the orignal name today.
Canaan	Canaan	Canaan is the region of Palestine that God removed from the Canaanites for their sin and gave as an inheritance to the Israelites. It is often termed the *Holy Land* and is where modern day Israel resides.
Elamites	Elam	This was the old name for the Persians prior to Cyrus.
Assyria	Asshur	Asshur is still the Hebrew name for Assyria.
Hebrew	Eber	This people group and language was named for Eber. Abraham was a Hebrew and most of the O.T. is written in Hebrew.
Mizraim	Mizraim	This is still the Hebrew name for Egypt.

Phase 1

Listen to This

What in the World? VOL. 1

DISC ONE:

- » Descendants of Noah (track 5)
- » Sources & Evidences (track 6)
- » Oldest Cities (track 7)

True Tales VOL. 1

DISC ONE:

- » The Table of Nations (track 5)

DISC TWO:

- » The Origin of "Races" *Interview with Ken Ham* (track 1)
- » The Dispersion after Babel *Interview with Bodie Hodge* (track 2)
- » The Discovery of Troy (track 3)
- » The Discovery of Ur (track 4)

Look at This

- » In the Days of Peleg (www.answersingenesis.org/go/peleg)
- » The Sixteen Grandsons of Noah (www.answersingenesis.org/go/grandsons)

Read for Your Life

The Holy Bible

- » The Main Story: Genesis 11–36
- » Helpful Verses: Psalm 105:1–15; Romans 4; Galatians 3:5–14; Hebrews 11:8–21

Key People

Ham
Father of the people who traveled South

Shem
Father of the people of the Middle East

Japheth
Father of the people who traveled North

Nimrod
Builder of the first post-Flood cities

Abraham
Father of the Hebrew and Arab nations, and of all those who have faith in God

Talk Together

Opinion Column

- What did you find to be the most interesting aspect, or the most fascinating person, you encountered in your introduction to the rise of civilizations?
- Why do you think God called Abraham out of Ur?
- One of the things that sets the Bible apart from other religious books is that it describes people accurately—with all of their failures and faults, as well as their successes. Why do you think the Scriptures tell us that Abraham, a man who deceived two kings, was a friend of God?
- Think about Abraham and his experiences with God. In your own life, when has it been easy to trust God and when has it been difficult?

Critical Puzzling

- Noah, his wife, and his three sons and their wives were the eight people who survived the devastation of the Flood, so from them descend all of the people of the earth. How should that impact our attitude about other nations, cultures, people groups?
- What are some of the possible reasons that the archaeological record shows that civilization seems to just "pop" onto the scene?
- Consider what might have been necessary for humanity to build cities, provide a dependable food supply, reestablish metal working, and any other industries vital for civilization.
- Read about Nimrod, the great-grandson of Noah, in Genesis 10:8–10. He was a prolific builder of cities. How much of Nimrod's character can be known from the character of the cities he built?

Resources for Digging Deeper

Choose a few books that look interesting, or find your own.

BIBLICAL PERSPECTIVE

The Puzzle of Ancient Man

Donald E. Chittick, PhD • Dr. Chittick has compiled an astonishing selection of OOP Arts (Out Of Place Artifacts) with a thoroughly biblical explanation. Worth searching for! **MS+**

The New Unger's Bible Handbook

Merrill F. Unger, revised by Gary N. Larson • This book is one of my most-used reference books in the study of ancient history and the Bible. Highly recommended! **MS+**

Life in the Great Ice Age

Michael & Beverly Oard • In this colorful novel, your whole family will learn what life was like during the Ice Age after the Flood. Packed full of scientific facts that can be used to defend creation and the Flood, and oppose evolution. Read through this book as a devotional with your children! **UE+**

Strongholds of the 10-40 Window

Edited by George Otis, Jr. • This is an intercessor's guide to the world's least evangelized nations. It includes basic facts, historical background, Christian outreach, and specific prayer requests from resident Christians. This book will help you turn head knowledge to heart compassion as you pray for the nations. **MS+**

Treasures from Bible Times

Alan Millard • If you can find this book, you will have found a treasure indeed. Beautiful pictures, archaeological data and helpful maps make this a tremendous resource. **MS+**

After the Flood

Bill Cooper • This is an amazing book concerning the truth of the Scriptures! Mr. Cooper spent more than twenty years examining the accuracy of the Table of Nations in Genesis 10, and found the descendants of Ham, Shem, and Japheth throughout the pagan king lists—which are the best chroniclers of families and chronologies in the ancient world. One of the watershed books of our time. Highly Recommended! **HS**

Asia: A Christian Perspective

Mary Ann Lind • Though our main focus in this study guide is the rise of civilization in the Fertile Crescent, Egypt, and Greece, what I found particularly helpful about this book was the historical background of some of the Asian civilizations such as India and China. This book tells about the rise of Confucianism, Hinduism, and Buddhism—a significant part of understanding Asian cultures and early Asian civilizations. **MS+**

ARCHAEOLOGY

Old Testament Archaeology

Dr. Alfred Hoerth • Not a book, this is actually a full-color chart from Rose Publishing, which lists archaeological finds, a description of them, and their importance to Bible students. A great tool! **UE+**

The Bible in the British Museum

T. C. Mitchell • Another incredible resource from the British Museum, this book lists all of the artifacts in the museum that reference Bible events, times or people. **HS+**

Then & Now

Stefania Perring & Dominic Perring • A fascinating look at the archaeological ruins of antiquity by two British archaeologists. This is the book that shows the ruins of Nimrud (in ancient Assyria), which was built originally by Nimrod! Includes several civilizations that we will be studying in this study guide. Each picture of an ancient site is accompanied by a full color overlay depicting how that place would have looked in its prime. **AA**

The Bible Comes Alive

Clifford & Barbara Wilson • Dr. Wilson, a renowned Australian archaeologist and educator, has gathered photographs from his own collection on Middle Eastern archaeology. Set up to follow the order of the books of the Bible, these photos and texts run from creation to Revelation! Includes many photographs of artifacts and sites from the Bible! **MS+**

The Usborne Young Sientist: Archaeology

Barbara Cork & Struan Reid • A brief, concise overview of what archaeologists do and some of what they have found. Excellent pictures help to tell the story. **UE+**

Dig This! How Archaeologists Uncover Our Past

Michael Avi-Yonah • This a great introduction to the ways and means of archaeologists. It has lots of pictures of archaeological digs, which is tremendously helpful in trying to understand what a dig is really like. **E+**

Gods, Graves and Scholars

C. W. Ceram • Often listed as required reading for college-level archaeology, this is a riveting book describing the real-life adventures of archaeologists from the 1800s to the early 1900s. The author's worldview is not a biblical worldview, but he unwittingly relates astonishing evidences that confirm the Bible's accuracy! Wondering if this book was really interesting, I asked my junior and senior high boys to read it. They couldn't put it down! **MS+**

Archaeology for Kids

Richard Panchyk • For students truly interested in understanding archaeology, this is a hands-on, activity-based approach. You may want to skip the sections on early man. **UE+**

Mesopotamia

Julian Reade • This book provides a fascinating look at early Mesopotamia, including Ur. This is the book where I learned that there was a mass-produced, bevelled-rim bowl which was probably used the way we use throw away wrappers on fast food! **HS+**

Digging to the Past: Excavations in Ancient Lands

W. John Hackwell • This children's book has wonderful descriptions of excavating archaeological sites. Even if you can't find this book or the one listed above, try to find an elementary book on archaeology to help your students comprehend the incredible "detective work" that is necessary to decipher ruins. **E+**

Treasures Under the Sand

WOOLLEY'S FINDS AT UR

Alan Honour • An incredible book! This is a children's biography of Leonard Woolley, the man who began excavating Ur in 1922. Unfortunately, the author's worldview doesn't see the Bible as literal history, and so the dates and explanations of Old Testament events are mistaken. Even with its problems, I still recommend it. This is the book that describes, among other things, Woolley's work with T. E. Lawrence (Lawrence of Arabia) prior to WWI. **UE+**

ANTIQUITY

Ancient Crete

Frances Wilkins • A fascinating look at an ancient civilization that was unknown until the early 1900s. The Minoans were a highly advanced people who flourished from soon after the Tower of Babel to around 1400 BC. **UE+**

The Sumerians

Elaine Landau • It is difficult to find books that are both appropriate and understandable for younger students about this time period. This book, however, is worth the search. **E+**

Dazzling! Jewelry of the Ancient World

Jewelry is an art form, it involves advanced technology, is a form of economics, and was seen to be valuable in the afterlife. For example, the ancient royal tombs in Ur, excavated by Leonard Woolley, were found to contain vast quantities of jewelry. **E+**

CITIES

City Planning in Ancient Times

Richard L. Currier & Arthur Segal • This book shows the high level of city planning found in even the earliest civilizations. It is a very good introduction to what goes into planning cities. **UE+**

Street Smart! Cities of the Ancient World

Lerner Geography Department • Another book showing how well planned many of the cities of antiquity were. Fascinating reading! **E+**

GENERAL

Kingfisher History Encyclopedia

This is the best resource book for world history that we've seen. Though offered by a secular publisher, it is an excellent tool for seeing the "big picture" in history. It replaced the old *Kingfisher Illustrated History of the World* **UE+**

Ancient Times A WATTS GUIDE FOR CHILDREN

Guy I. Austrian • This book is a series of short articles about people, ancient nations, early developments such as the alphabet, and concepts such as democracy. This would make a good resource. **UE+**

Usborne World History ANCIENT WORLD

Fiona Chandler • If you are familiar with Usborne books, you know that they are filled with short descriptions and great pictures. This is a wonderful, concise, fact-filled book about ancient nations and people. **E+**

For more books, use these Dewey Decimal numbers in your library:

Bible: #220

Ancient History: #930

Ancient Middle & Near Eastern: #930

Ancient Mesopotamia & Iranian Plateau: #935

Archaeology: #930.1

Also, look for biographies on the archaeologists listed.

What books did you like best?

____

____

____

____

The Internet also contains a wealth of information about the rise of civilizations.

What sites were the most helpful?

____

____

____

____

Student Self-Evaluation UNIT 2, PHASE 1

Dates and hours:______________________

Key Concepts

Rephrase the three Key Concepts of this Unit and confirm your understanding of each:

- The descandants of Noah

  ____

- The Tower of Babel

  ____

- Sudden civilizations

  ____

- Archaeology—its uses and limitations

  ____

- Abraham & Ur

  ____

Tools for Self-Evaulation

Evaluate your personal participation in the discussions of this Phase. Bearing in mind that a good participant in a discussion is not always the most vocal participant, ask yourself these questions: Were you an active participant? Did you ask perceptive questions? Were you willing to listen to other participants of the discussion and draw out their opinions? Record your observations and how you would like to improve your participation in the future:

____

____

Every time period is too complex to be understood in one Phase of study. Evaluate your current knowledge of the rise of civilizations. What have you focused on so far? What are your weakest areas of knowledge?

____

____

Based on the evaluation of this introduction, project ahead what you would like to study more of in the following Phases:

____

Phase 2

Research & Reporting

Explore one or more of these areas to discover something significant!

Early Civilizations

- Find one of the books listed, or a book of your choice, to compare information on early civilizations. Key concerns will be: location, appearance, religion, writings, dates.
- Research and report on the "Rise and Fall of the Sumerian Civilization."
- Research the rise of civilizations in the Indus Valley and China. Compare and contrast these civilizations with the civilizations in the Fertile Crescent.
- Investigate and report on the location of the descendants of Ham, Shem, and Japheth.
- Find out about the climate, terrain, and political situation of the Fertile Crescent during the time of Abraham. Describe (specifically) the changes in his life and situation after he left Ur for Canaan and Egypt.

Cities

- Research and report on what structural requirements are necessary in order to build a city. (Water, sewer, residences, roads, etc.) Then consider the technology required to accomplish building those structures.
- Try to discover what archaeologists know about the size of Nimrod's cities. Report your findings.

Architecture

- In the library, or on the Internet, research the Great Pyramid, the Ziggurat of Ur, and the Pyramid of the Sun in Mexico. Report on your findings, answering these questions: What are the similarities between these three structures? What are some possible explanations archaeologists present to explain these similarities? What is the biblical explanation for their similarity?

Archaeology

- Using the books listed on archaeology, or others you discover, research what archaeologists can determine about a civilization based on the ruins, and what they cannot. Can this tell you anything about the claims of non-Biblical archaeologists that attack the biblical record?
- List all of the tools, supplies, equipment, and special needs an archaeology team must assemble before attempting an excavation. To go deeper, you may want to follow the story of an actual archaeological dig, from preparation to discovery.
- The Chronology of Archaeology on page 65 gives dates and names. Research the events listed and report your findings.

Bible

- In Scripture, discover the position of Abraham in regard to God's plan of redemption. Make a chart showing the flow of redemption from Adam to Abraham and Abraham to Jesus.

Culture

- Investigate the history and culture of the Fertile Crescent from the time of Abraham to the present. Report your findings.

Brain Stretchers

Genetics

See www.answersingenesis.org/go/one-race for information about how we can explain the various people groups and their differences. Compare this to a secular evolutionary explanation. Report on your discoveries.

DID YOU KNOW?

During the excavation of Ur, a clay tablet was discovered with a mathematical theorem very similar to the Pythagorean theorem? Check it out!

Early Travel

Look in the library for the books by Thor Heyerdahl, especially *Ra*. Report your findings on his theories of the ability of ancient people to travel across the earth. Compare his theories with creationists, and note the similarities and differences.

Language

Research the major language "families." Make a chart showing these language groups and their location in the world. What can you learn from this about the possible source, relationship, spread, and development of languages? You may want to consider investigating how this affects Bible translation work.

Mathematics

Discover the level of mathematical proficiency in early civilizations. (Consider: What was used for money? for calculating? for astronomy? An interesting place to start would be to trace the concept of "zero.")

Create Your Own Research Topic

____

____

____

Chronology of Archaeology

Date	Name	Place
1760s	Karsten Niebuhr	Persepolis—Brought back bricks with cuneiform—His book was what Napoleon used on his trip to Egypt
1798	Napoleon/Denon	Egypt—First drawings of Upper & Lower Nile Dhautpoul—found Rosetta Stone, hieroglyphs
1802	Denon	Book published
1802	Grotefend	German school teacher, first to understand how to decipher cuneiform
1821	Champollion	French scholar, deciphered Rosetta Stone
1837	Henry Rawlinson	English soldier, copied Behistun inscriptions
1843	" "	Translated inscriptions (Old Persian, Babylonian, Elamite)
1843–46	Paul Emile Botta	French consul, first to discover Assyria—Khorsabad, palace of Sargon II
1845+	Austen Layard	British (French born) adventurer, excavated Nimrud (biblical Calah)
1849+	" "	Uncovered Nineveh (Father of Assyriology)
1868+	Heinrich Schliemann	Uncovered Troy (against all odds)
1876+	" "	Excavated Mycenae (Agamemnon?—Opposed Troy)
1899–1913	Robert Koldewey	Excavated Babylon, discovered Ishtar Gate, walls of Babylon, Hanging Gardens, and perhaps the Tower of Babel
1900–26	Sir Arthur Evans	British, uncovered Minoan civilization (predecessor to Mycenaean civ.) Palace of Knossos
1927+	Leonard Woolley	Excavated Ur of Abram
1964	Paolo Matthiae	Excavated Ebla (contemporary civilization of Sumer and Egypt)

Timeline

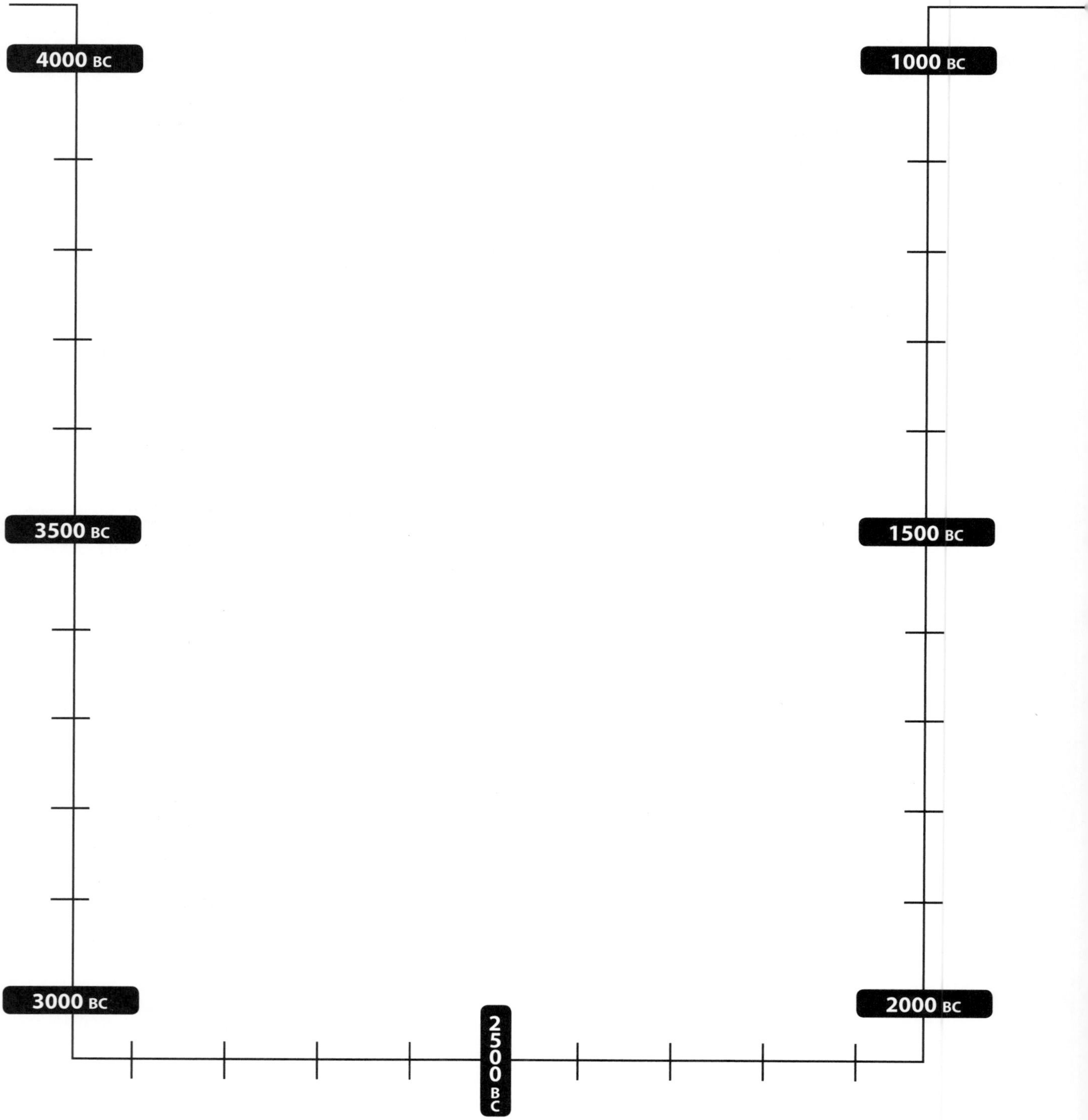

Consider this for your timeline

The dates for Nimrod should reflect the earliest dates of Babylon and Nineveh, since he was the original builder of these cities.

Most scholars believe that the scriptural reference to the earth being "divided" in Peleg's day refers to the division that occurred at Babel when God confused the languages. Others see it as a description of the irrigation systems that were set up in Mesopotamia, which harnessed the water for reliable food crops and increased wealth.

Archbishop James Ussher puts Abraham's birth in 1996 BC. He added up the years given in the geneaologies of Genesis 5 and Genesis 11, and used other biblical references as well as accepted dates for later biblical events. (See www.answersingenesis.org/go/ussher to see how Archbishop Ussher calculated his dates.) This is within the range of many other Bible scholars, who put the date for Abraham's birth anywhere between 1876 BC and 2136 BC, depending on which biblical manuscripts are used, and which dates are selected for other events.

Key Events

- Tower of Babel
- Sumerian civilization
- Egyptian civilization
- Chinese civilization
- Indus Valley civilization
- Assyrian civilization
- Minoan civilization
- Ebla civilization

Be sure to include the people listed in Key People in Phase 1.

Words to Watch

Remember—The easiest way to learn a subject is to master its terms:

Fertile Crescent	antiquity	engineering	Tower of Babel
Sumer	civilization	dispersion	clay tablet
Ur	architecture	ziggurat	cuneiform
archaeology	babble	excavation	nation
people group	antediluvian		

Other words you need to look up:

Student Self-Evaluation UNIT 2, PHASE 2

Dates and hours:______________________

Research Project

- Summarize your research question:

____

____

- List your most useful sources by author, title, and page number or URL where applicable (continue list in margin if necessary):

____

____

____

Now take a moment to evaluate the sources you just listed. Do they provide a balanced view of your research question? Should you have sought an additional opinion? Are your sources credible (if you found them on your own)? Record your observations:

____

____

Evaluate your research project in its final presentation. What are its strengths? If you had time to revisit this project, what would you change? Consider giving yourself a letter grade based on your project's merits and weaknesses.

____

____

Letter grade: _____

You have just completed an area of specific research in the time of the rise of civilizations. Now what would you like to explore in the upcoming Phases? Set some objectives for yourself:

____

Phase 3

Maps and Mapping

Physical Terrain

» Label and color the Tigris and Euphrates rivers on the outline map.

» Color the Fertile Crescent.

» Draw in and color the mountain ranges.

» Look in a resource book to discover the areas which are desert and the areas which are fertile, and color them appropriately on your map.

Geopolitical

» Place Nineveh, Nimrud, and Babylon on the map.

» What countries (both ancient and modern) are they located in?

» Draw the boundaries of Sumer (Mesopotamia), Egypt, and Canaan on your map.

» What is the name of the country or countries that today occupy the same area as Sumer and Canaan?

» Mark the city of Ur.

» Trace Abraham's route from Ur to Egypt to Palestine.

Explore

» ***Christian Outreach to Countries in the Fertile Crescent:*** What is the status of Christian outreach to these countries in the Middle East? Discuss the difficulties facing Christians seeking to serve God in these nations; brainstorm creative ways of overcoming these difficulties.

» ***Limited Archaeological Access in Bible Lands:*** Discover the challenges that face archaeologists, especially biblical archaeologists, in these countries, and then consider the impact this limited or restricted access has on our understanding of these ancient lands.

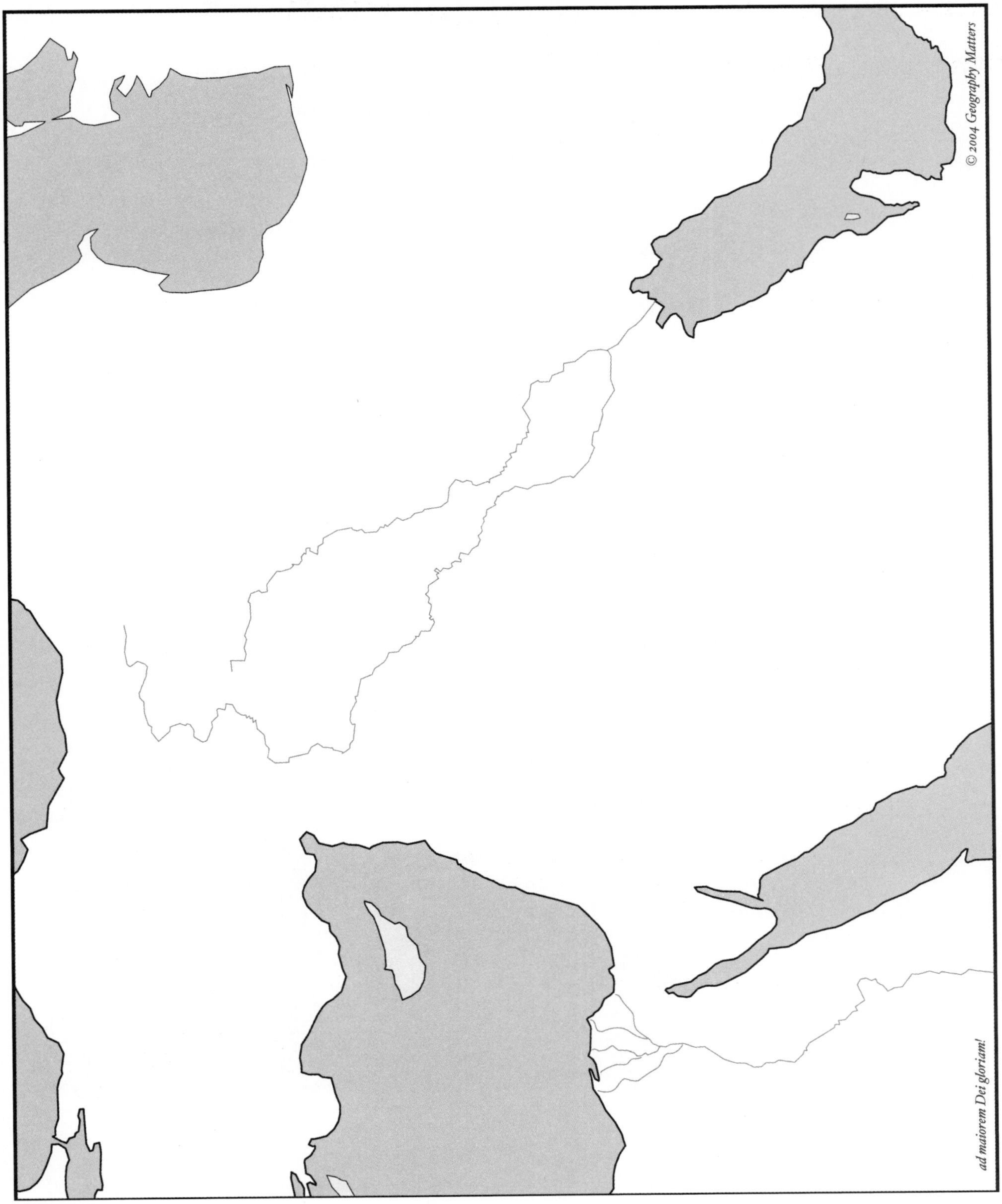
© 2004 Geography Matters
ad maiorem Dei gloriam!

CONSIDER:

Pieter Bruegel The Elder (circa AD 1530–1569) was a Flemish painter who lived during the time of the Spanish war against the Netherlands. He was among the first artists to paint with an appreciation of landscape.

Art Appreciation

Tower of Babel by Pieter Bruegel, the Elder

» Does the painting reflect what the Bible describes?

» How does the painting differ from your own impression of this event?

» How does Bruegel's painting reflect his own time period rather than antiquity?

The royal headdress of Queen Pu-Abi of Ur *(displayed in the British Museum)*

» What does this show you about the culture of Ur?

» How does it display the craftsmanship of the time?

- Leonard Woolley found this amazing piece of jewelry while excavating the royal burial grounds in Ur.

The Royal Standard of Ur *(displayed in the British Museum)*

» What activities are shown on the Standard of Ur?

» What facial expressions do you notice on the people?

- Archaeological digs have brought to light beautiful ancient mosaics made from colored tiles, such as this one discovered in Ur.

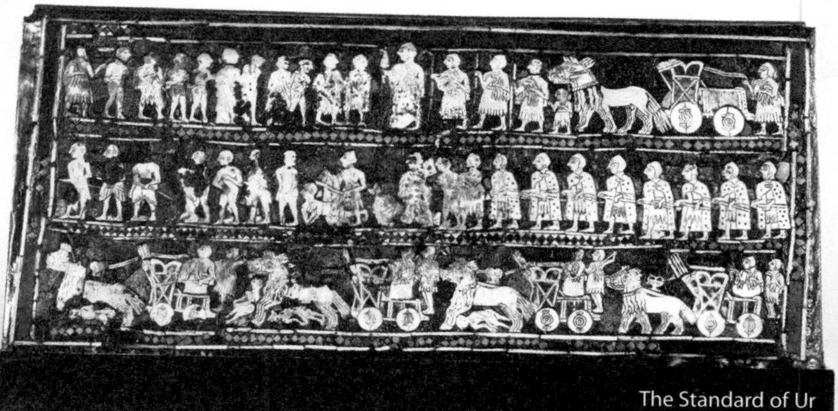

The Standard of Ur

Architecture

When the earliest cities in Mesopotamia, such us Uruk and Ur, were built, the buildings were constructed with the local materials available to the builders—mud, sometimes mixed with straw. From these mud bricks, temples, palaces, houses, and city walls were built. Unfortunately, mud bricks don't last as long as other building materials, so archaeologists have had to try to envision the design of ancient cities and their architecture. One of the most prominent features of these ancient Mesopotamian cities is the ziggurat, or temple tower. Ziggurats were pyramid-like, stepped structures, with the actual temple on a platform at the very top. Their architects used the technique of slightly curving the walls, so that the tall structures would not appear top heavy.

» Look for a photo of the reconstruction of the Ziggurat of Ur, as well as artists' renditions. How would you describe this building?

Arts in Action

Select one or more, and let your artistic juices flow!

Imitation

Try your hand at imitating Bruegel (trace, follow colors, etc.).

Create your own Standard, like the Standard of Ur.

Architecture

Construct a small city from LEGO bricks, cardboard, etc. Where are the utilities? Where are the parks, the transportation routes, the city/government center, the homes, the places of worship?

Mosaics

There are many different kinds of materials to choose from in making mosaics. For this project you can make a mosaic using bits of colored paper or tiles glued to wood. Start with an outline for your design, then glue the pieces of paper within the outline. Check out the library for more information on how to create this art form.

Clay Pots

Find a book or an expert who can get you started with the simplest method—the coil pot. You will need a fair amount of clay for this project, depending on the size of your pot. You could also consider using Playdough.

Jewelry

Try your hand at making ornate jewelry, in the style of the Sumerians. You might construct a headdress, arm bands, necklaces, or earrings. Check the library for a how-to book.

Science

Archaeologists who excavated the ancient cities of Mesopotamia found that many sites had been continuously occupied for many hundreds of years. They discovered this by examining the artifacts found in the different layers, or strata, of earth. This allows them to separate and date the various artifacts to the proper time period.

Try This

» Carefully dig a hole outside at least twelve inches deep by eight inches wide. The deeper you go, the more layers you may find. Examine the layers which are revealed in the hole. Do you see a difference in color and texture of the dirt? Measure the depth of each layer and record this in a notebook. How many layers did you find?

Music

Though evolutionists believe that the advanced technology and complexity needed for musical instruments would require music to develop long after earliest man, the archaeological record does not show this. In fact, exquisite harps were discovered in the royal tombs of Ur, and archaeologists now know that there were also drums and double reed instruments in this early civilization.

Listen

» There are many types of harp music available. Listen to a selection of different styles, such as Celtic, classical, and folk. As you listen, consider the level of difficulty in playing this ancient instrument. Does this show you anything about early man in post-Flood times?

Try This

» Find a book in the library (or an instrument maker) that can show you how to construct a simple instrument: a drum, a bamboo flute, a whistle, a harp.

Cooking

The Fertile Crescent was a remarkably productive area for crops. Located between the two great rivers, the Tigris and Euphrates, the Fertile Crescent was occasionally flooded, which brought rich, wonderful soil for the farmers. Here is a recipe that is typical of Middle East cooking.

Lentils with tomatoes

1 cup brown lentils	1 tsp ground cumin
2 tbsp. oil	½ cup beef broth
1 large onion, minced	4 tomatoes, peeled and chopped
2 cloves garlic, minced	Salt & pepper

Soak lentils in cold water for 3 hours. Drain, then place lentils in pot of boiling salted water and cook over medium heat 30 min. Drain, reserve. Heat oil in large saucepan. Add onions and garlic, sauté about 5 minutes. Stirring constantly, add cumin and cook over high heat for 2 minutes. Add broth and lentils. Mix, then simmer, uncovered, over low heat until lentils are almost tender (15 minutes.) Stir in tomatoes and season. Continue simmering until tomatoes are tender, about 15 minutes. Serve immediately. Serves 4.

Student Self-Evaluation UNIT 2, PHASE 3

Dates and hours:________________________

Evaluate Your Projects

- List which of the activities listed in this Phase you did:

____

____

____

- Rate your enthusiasm: ____________

  Explain: ____

  ____

- Rate the precision of your approach:____________

  Explain: ____

  ____

- Rate your effort toward the completion of the project: ____________

  Explain: ____

  ____

Ask yourself what worked and what did not. What would you do differently in the future, and what would you repeat?

____

How specifically did these hands-on activities enhance your knowledge of the rise of civilizations? What made them worthwhile?

____

In the first three Phases of this Unit, what aspect of the time period has most captured your imagination? What would you like to creatively pursue to conclude your study?

____

Phase 4

In Your Own Way . . .

In this unit we have seen another major rebellion of mankind against God, the divine judgment which scattered people across the globe, and the resulting rise of civilizations in the archaeological record. We have also considered the reality of Abraham's time and his life in God's plan of redemption. Now, choose a selection of these activities, or create your own, which will best express what was most significant to you.

LINGUISTICS

Playing with Words

Have each student learn a few words in a separate foreign language, or create your own language (such as "grunt-grunt," gibberish, a tonal language, or a clicking language)—then try to communicate using these words that no one else understands! (A very small taste of the confusion at the Tower of Babel.)

Journalism

At the Tower of Babel, what would have been the impact of the sudden emergence of many different languages? Be a newspaper reporter at the Tower just after God confused the languages. Write the fast-breaking story!

Prose

- Write a short story about the farewell party in Ur for Abraham's family.
- You are on the archaeological team working with Leonard Woolley in 1922. Write a letter home to your church family describing the discovery of Abraham's hometown.

Poetry

Write a rhyming *Ode to Archaeology*. You could imitate Joyce Kilmer's famous poem,

I think that I shall never see
A poem lovely as a tree . . .

Script Writing

Write a "then and now" skit: Abraham leaves Ur while Leonard Woolley discovers Ur.

ART

Painting/Drawing

Create a collage-style drawing of your impressions of the people and events of this unit.

Graphic Design

Design the poster for the "then and now" skit.

Cartooning

Make a political cartoon showing the unanticipated results at the building of the Tower of Babel.

Sculpting

Make a sculpture showing the separation of the three sons of Noah into their geographic locations.

MUSIC

Compose

- Compose an original song entitled, "To Ur is Human; To Leave, Divine."
- Write new lyrics to the tune of "Camptown Races" about Nimrod's rebellious cities. You could start like this:

  "Nimrod built a city wrong,
  doo dah, doo dah,
  Founded it on being strong,
  oh doo dah day..."

  Another option would be to use a different familiar tune.

Performance Practice

If you are familiar with harps, prepare a short demonstration of the technical requirements for this instrument, referencing the discovery of harps in the burial pits of Ur in order to show the high level of advancement this discovery indicates.

DRAMA

Comedy

- Do a humorous skit about archaeologists sifting through a garbage dump that is 4,000 years old.
- Act out the "then and now" skit listed above.

Tragedy

Portray the imaginary story of Abram's best friend, Elimech, who would not leave his beloved Ur to travel to an unknown land on the word of an unseen God.

Puppetry

Put on a puppet show describing Abraham and Sarah's adventures. Consider the age level of your audience as you decide which scenes to show.

Prop Needs

____

____

Costume Ideas

____

____

Role/Player

____

____

Set Suggestions

____

____

MOVEMENT

Pantomime

Act out the discovery of Ur in 1922 without benefit of words. Be sure to show Mr. Woolley's excitement when he discovers it!

Dance

Find a piece of music, which communicates the confusion of the Tower of Babel and create a dance showing the breakdown of languages and the division of people.

Miniature Action

Using chairs, tables, people, and other props, construct a city, complete with utilities and food supplies. A narrator can describe for the audience what early cities looked like.

CONCEPTUAL DESIGN

Design-A-Tool

With what you have learned about archaeology in this unit, design a tool (on the drawing board) which would make life a lot easier for the archaeologist in the field.

CREATE YOUR OWN EXPRESSION

Student Self-Evaluation UNIT 2, PHASE 4

Dates and hours:____________________________

Evaluate Your Projects

- What creative project did you choose:

  ____

- What did you expect from your project, and how does the final project compare to your initial expectations?

  ____

  ____

- What do you like about your project? What would you change?

  ____

  ____

In Conclusion

Revisit the five Key Concepts from the beginning of this Unit. Explain how your understanding of and appreciation for each has grown over the course of your study.

____

____

____

____

____

____

Record your concluding thoughts on the rise of civilizations:

____

____

____

Egypt & the Exodus

UNIT 3

Key Concepts

- Ancient Egypt & God's plan
- Joseph's life
- Moses & The Exodus
- Possible routes

The Egyptian Sphinx

Let my people go . . .

> Go and gather the elders of Israel together, and say to them, "The Lord God of your fathers, the God of Abraham, of Isaac, and of Jacob, appeared to me, saying, 'I have surely visited you and seen what is done to you in Egypt; and I have said I will bring you up out of the affliction of Egypt to the land of the Canaanites and the Hittites and the Amorites and the Perizzites and the Hivites and the Jebusites, to a land flowing with milk and honey.'" Exodus 3:16–17

Egypt. Land of mystery and antiquity, the scene of biblical refuge and tyrannical slavery, home of the pharaohs and the pyramids, a place where the complex process of mummification was extended even to crocodiles . . . one of the most fascinating places on earth. Geographically unusual, Egypt is a long, narrow strip of rich, dark earth in northeastern

3

Africa bordered by the unrelenting dryness of the desert, drawing its life from the annual flooding of the Nile River. Ham's son Mizraim founded Egypt (still called Mizraim in Hebrew) after the dispersion at the Tower of Babel.

Beauty, wealth, medicine, mathematics, technology, military might, vast trade networks—this was the culture of ancient Egypt. But, along with all of its wonders, Egypt at this time embraced a polytheistic (many gods) religion, in which even the lowly cat was seen as divine. This brought a terrible bondage and darkness to the Egyptian people, and eventually, as we shall see, it brought a catastrophic confrontation between the Creator of the Egyptians and the gods of the Egyptians.

But that's jumping ahead! Let's return to the journey of Abraham and bring the story up to speed. God had promised that He would make of Abraham a great nation and through him "all the families of the earth would be blessed" (Genesis 12:1–3). So Abraham and his wife, Sarah (called Abram and Sarai until God changed their names at the time of His covenant with them—Genesis 17), moved lock, stock, and barrel to the area of Canaan, located between the Jordan River and the Mediterranean Sea. During a local famine, Abram and Sarai traveled to the bountiful land of Egypt. Genesis 12 gives a fascinating description of Abram's unusual encounter with the reigning pharaoh. Ussher's chronology sets this encounter in the year 1921 BC. Using the new Egyptian chronology suggested by David Rohl (see the end of this article for more information), it is possible to theorize that Abram's brief sojourn in Egypt was toward the end of the time period known to historians as the "Old Kingdom."

Beauty, wealth, medicine, mathematics, technology, military might, vast trade networks—this was the culture of ancient Egypt.

The Old Kingdom is also known as the Pyramid Age, since it was the time that the most magnificent pyramids were built. When the Nile was in flood and the farmers could not work the land, the pharaohs had them work alongside craftsmen to build these gigantic tombs. It has been estimated that perhaps as many as 100,000 men labored for twenty years (four months at a time) to build each one of the pyramids. That's a LOT of manpower! The Old Kingdom was also known for its intellectual achievements in medicine, engineering, mathematics, and astronomy. Toward the end of this kingdom, the pharaohs lost increasing amounts of tax revenue and governmental power over the outlying "nomes," or districts. After several years of insufficient flooding of the Nile, many nomarchs (or governors of nomes), declared themselves kings, and Egypt slid into the chaos of the First Intermediate Period.

When Abram and Sarai returned to Canaan, they took matters into their own hands concerning what God had told Abram about becoming the father of descendants more numerous than the stars of heaven.

After a sticky relational mess between Abraham, Sarah, and Sarah's maid resulted in a son named Ishmael (the beginning of the Arab nation), God told Abraham that, despite his and Sarah's advanced age, they would, indeed, bear a son to fulfill the promise God had given. When Sarah heard this, she laughed. Thus her son, born the following year, was given the name "Isaac," which means laughter! From this son and his son, Jacob, the nation known as Israel was born. Isn't it amazing that from Abraham came two mighty nations, and the source of three world religions—Judaism, Christianity, and Islam! What do you think would be the impact on the world today if Abraham and Sarah had trusted God's timing for a son, rather than trying to help bring about the promise of an heir through Hagar, Sarah's maidservant?

Joseph's Life

Fast forwarding through the next several chapters of Genesis, we meet Joseph, Jacob's favored son. Joseph—the dreamer of dreams, the wearer of a many-colored coat, the hated of his brothers—was secretly sold as a slave to traders heading to Egypt (Genesis 37). Ussher dates this event in Joseph's life to 1728 BC, which corresponds to the end of the Eleventh Dynasty or the beginning of the Twelfth Dynasty using the new Egyptian chronology.

Egypt began to recover from the confusion of the First Intermediate Period when Mentuhotpe reunited the country in the Eleventh Dynasty. By far the most important dynasty of the Middle Kingdom, however, was the Twelfth. It began when the vizier Amenemhet took the reigns of power and made himself Pharaoh. He moved the capital from Memphis to Itjawy (whose site is not certain, but may be in the Nile Delta). There is not agreement between Bible scholars concerning which pharaoh was the pharaoh who elevated Joseph from a prisoner to the position of vizier (second in command of the kingdom). However, several candidates have been proposed by Bible scholars, among them Sesostris II (Associates for Biblical Research) and Amenemhet III (David Rohl).

Joseph was secretly sold as a slave to traders heading to Egypt.

In Genesis 41 we are told that one night this pharaoh had a disturbing dream about cows. No one in his retinue of magicians and wise men could interpret the dream, which made him very angry. Suddenly, his chief butler remembered his fellow prisoner who had correctly interpreted a dream.

> Then Pharaoh sent and called Joseph, and they brought him hastily out of the dungeon; and he shaved, changed his clothing, and came to Pharaoh. Genesis 41:14

Isn't the Bible great in its details? Not only are we told that Pharaoh called for him, but we get a glimpse of the great commotion this caused the jailers. You can almost see them falling all over themselves, trying to find Joseph a razor (the Egyptians liked to be clean-shaven!) and some decently fitting clothes appropriate for an audience with an angry pharaoh.

When Joseph appears, Pharaoh tells him that he has a reputation of being able to interpret dreams. Listen to Joseph's reply:

> "It is not in me; God will give Pharaoh an answer of peace."
> Genesis 41:16

Who receives the glory from that statement? How is that attitude different from the builders of the tower of Babel (Genesis 4:11)? How is it different from those today who want to get close to someone who is powerful or famous? Joseph was not into promoting Joseph, he was into glorifying God. And that was so amazingly refreshing to the pharaoh, that when he heard Joseph's interpretation of the dream and his recommendation to prepare for the famine during the time of plenty, he decided to make Joseph—a thirty-year old Hebrew foreigner and former slave/prisoner, his vizier—second-in-command throughout the land of Egypt!

> "You shall be over my house, and all my people shall be ruled according to your word; only in regard to the throne will I be greater than you. . . . See, I have set you over all the land of Egypt." Genesis 41:40–41

During the time of tremendous plenty, Joseph oversaw the gathering of grain, which was stored in the cities. There was such an overabundance that, according to the Bible, they finally stopped counting the grain since it was as the sand of the sea—without number! It is interesting to note that discoveries have been made of Egyptian art showing government officials overseeing the gathering of a huge grain harvest into storehouses.

Joseph was not into promoting Joseph, he was into glorifying God.

As the time of famine came, and the people began to cry out, Joseph opened the storehouses of grain and sold it to the Egyptians. As the famine worsened, people from the surrounding nations also came to Egypt to buy grain. That was the motivation for Joseph's brothers to come from Canaan to Egypt in 1707 BC, but it brought about a far greater result than a few loaves of bread! You can read one of the most amazing stories ever recorded, about the reunion of these brothers with one they thought lost forever, in Genesis 42–45. Only God Himself could have worked such good from such evil: the dramatic salvation of a family through the vicious enslaving of a hated brother.

The seven years of famine resulted in Pharaoh owning all of the money, livestock, land, and people of Egypt (except for the priests and their land). Normally, famines do not create great wealth, but, due to Joseph's administration, this was a significant exception. The famine also resulted in Joseph's entire family moving to Egypt, into an area known as Goshen, which the Bible describes as being the "best of the land." Most biblical archaeologists would agree that Goshen is located in the Wadi Tumilat, in the northeastern part of the Delta (in Lower or northern Egypt). They remained there until the Exodus out of Egypt.

A fascinating clue to Joseph's presence in Egypt can be seen in an ancient canal known as the "Bahr Yusef" (or The Joseph Canal), which was built during the time of the Twelfth Dynasty, connecting the Nile River to Lake Moeris through 200 miles of canal. It is still used today in irrigation, as it has been for centuries. Doesn't it amaze you to discover a still-existing proof of Joseph's presence and prestige in Egypt?

After Joseph's death, the Bible tells us a chilling truth:

> Now there arose a new king over Egypt, who did not know Joseph. And he said to his people, "Look, the people of the children of Israel are more and mightier than we; come, let us deal wisely with them, lest they multiply, and it happen, in the event of war, that they also join our enemies and fight against us, and so go up out of the land." Therefore they set taskmasters over them to afflict them with their burdens. And they built for Pharaoh supply cities, Pithom and Rameses. Exodus 1:8–11

Only God Himself could have worked such good from such evil.

Moses and the Exodus

The Hebrews, the descendants of Abraham, Isaac, and Jacob, were enslaved at this point by the ruling pharaoh. The Egyptians feared these descendants of Jacob (the "children of Israel"), and so not only increased their workload, but also commanded the Hebrew midwives to kill all of the baby boys born to the Hebrew women. In the midst of this oppression and suffering, Moses was born. Rather than obeying Pharaoh and throwing him to the crocodiles in the Nile, his mother fashioned an "ark of bulrushes" for him, and gently placed his basket in the reeds of the Nile. Pharaoh's daughter found the baby, recognized him as a Hebrew, and rather than obeying her father's command (Exodus 1:22), took him home to the palace to raise as her own son. Hebrews 11:24–26 tells us:

> By faith Moses, when he became of age, refused to be called the son of Pharaoh's daughter, choosing rather to suffer affliction with the people of God than to enjoy the passing pleasures of sin, esteeming the reproach of Christ greater riches than the treasures in Egypt; for he looked to the reward.

Amazing as it may seem, this man who "had it all"—who was raised in the very lap of pharaonic luxury, who, according to Josephus (a first-century Jewish historian), successfully led an Egyptian army to war with Cush (Ethiopia), who was adopted kin of the most powerful ruler of that

3

time—gave it all up to be identified with and suffer affliction with the children of Israel. At age 40, after murdering an Egyptian who was beating a Hebrew, Moses was forced to flee for his life from the wrath of the pharaoh and go to the land of Midian (in western Arabia). For forty years Moses tended sheep as God prepared him for his next role. Beginning in Exodus 3, we see how God takes this reluctant prince turned shepherd and turns him into a powerful leader, able to confront the might of Egypt with the power of the Lord.

Thus begins one of the most dramatic confrontations in human history. As Moses with his brother Aaron brought the word of the Lord to Pharaoh—"Let My people go"—Pharaoh hardened his heart, which brought, plague by plague, destruction and devastation to his nation. After the tenth and final plague, the death of the firstborn of both man and beast, the children of Israel were released from their enslavement, with their wages given in silver and gold by their Egyptian neighbors.

This man . . . gave it all up to be identified with and suffer alongside the children of Israel.

However, when Pharaoh realized that he had just lost a whole nation of slaves (estimates run up to three million people!), he changed his mind. Gathering his entire army, he chased after the fleeing Hebrews all the way to the Red Sea, which you might call his "Waterloo." It was there that the Hebrews crossed safely to freedom, and with Pharaoh's army drowned, God decisively ended the contest between the finite Egyptians gods and Himself, the infinite Creator of all. It was the final sign to the Egyptian people indicating who was really Lord. They had seen their pharaoh as divine, as a god, but now they understood who was truly reigning in heaven.

Again, there is not a consensus among scholars concerning which pharaoh drowned in the Red Sea with his army. The two most likely candidates, based on the new Egyptian chronology, are Amenemhet IV of the Twelfth Dynasty and Dudimose I of the Thirteenth Dynasty. It is interesting to note that, in favor of the first candidate, Amenemhet's tomb was never found, and his widow reigned only a short time after his demise. From that point, Egypt enters into the Second Intermediate Period (13th to 17th Dynasties) under weak pharaohs and conquering foreigners known as the Hyksos.

After the Hyksos were driven out of Egypt, a new period, known as the New Kingdom, began. This was the time that the greatest expansion of Egypt beyond its borders occurred, and it lasted for approximately five hundred years. One of the most interesting pharaohs of this period was Akhenaton, who declared that there was only one god, the god of the sun. He built a new capital city, whose ruins today lie near Tell el Amarna. When he died, his beliefs were declared heretical by the priests, and everything went back to the old ways. His successor was Tutankhamon, the boy pharaoh who is believed to have been mysteriously murdered at about age

Exodus 14:19–31

And the Angel of God, who went before the camp of Israel, moved and went behind them; and the pillar of cloud went from before them and stood behind them. So it came between the camp of the Egyptians and the camp of Israel. Thus it was a cloud and darkness *to the one,* and it gave light by night *to the other,* so that the one did not come near the other all that night.

Then Moses stretched out his hand over the sea; and the LORD caused the sea to go *back* by a strong east wind all that night, and made the sea into dry *land,* and the waters were divided. So the children of Israel went into the midst of the sea on the dry *ground,* and the waters *were* a wall to them on their right hand and on their left. And the Egyptians pursued and went after them into the midst of the sea, all Pharaoh's horses, his chariots, and his horsemen.

Now it came to pass, in the morning watch, that the LORD looked down upon the army of the Egyptians through the pillar of fire and cloud, and He troubled the army of the Egyptians. And He took off their chariot wheels, so that they drove them with difficulty; and the Egyptians said, "Let us flee from the face of Israel, for the LORD fights for them against the Egyptians."

Then the LORD said to Moses, "Stretch out your hand over the sea, that the waters may come back upon the Egyptians, on their chariots, and on their horsemen." And Moses stretched out his hand over the sea; and when the morning appeared, the sea returned to its full depth, while the Egyptians were fleeing into it. So the LORD overthrew the Egyptians in the midst of the sea. Then the waters returned and covered the chariots, the horsemen, *and* all the army of Pharaoh that came into the sea after them. Not so much as one of them remained. But the children of Israel had walked on dry *land* in the midst of the sea, and the waters *were* a wall to them on their right hand and on their left.

So the LORD saved Israel that day out of the hand of the Egyptians, and Israel saw the Egyptians dead on the seashore. Thus Israel saw the great work which the LORD had done in Egypt; so the people feared the LORD, and believed the LORD and His servant Moses.

eighteen. With the Twentieth Dynasty, the power of Egypt dramatically waned, and it was soon under the control of foreign rulers.

When we look at the contest of power between the gods of the Egyptians and the Creator of the Egyptians during the Exodus, we need to discover God's heart from the Scriptures, lest we think wrongly of Him:

> And the Lord will strike Egypt, He will strike and heal it; they will return to the Lord, and He will be entreated by them and heal them. In that day there will be a highway from Egypt to Assyria, and the Assyrian will come into Egypt and the Egyptian into Assyria, and the Egyptians will serve with the Assyrians. In that day Israel will be one of three with Egypt and Assyria, even a blessing in the midst of the land, whom the Lord of hosts shall bless, saying, "*Blessed* is Egypt My people, and Assyria the work of My hands, and Israel My inheritance." Isaiah 19:22–25

The Egyptians were not the bad guys in the Exodus scenario. That role belonged to Pharaoh.

3

The Egyptian people were not the bad guys in the Exodus scenario. That role belonged to the pharaoh. But God did use the plagues and the Exodus to demonstrate to the people of Egypt who was worthy of their worship. This nation, which many centuries later would be a haven to Joseph, Mary, and Jesus at the time of Herod's rampage, was intended by God to be a blessing and a safe place of refuge, not a place of enslaving others or being enslaved by false religions. As we know, however, pride goes before destruction and a haughty spirit comes before a fall (Proverbs 16:18), and the pharaohs of ancient Egypt had a tremendous amount of pride. In fact, the book of Ezekiel describes the pride of a later pharaoh:

> Behold I am against you, O Pharaoh king of Egypt, O great monster who lies in the midst of his rivers, who has said, "My River is my own; I have made it for myself." Ezekiel 29:9

He thought he had made the Nile River? By himself? What a foolish delusion. That is what happens when you think you are a god.

Dating the Exodus

With all of the specific biblical information about the Hebrews's time in Egypt (Goshen, Joseph's viziership, Hebrew enslavement, supply cities built of mud and straw bricks, the destruction of Pharaoh's army in the Red Sea, etc.), you would think the Egyptologists, archaeologists, and historians would be shouting to the world, "Here!" "Here!" "Over here!" as they found verification of the biblical events in Egyptian relics and digs. Perhaps you may have noticed the silence instead? Perhaps you may have wondered about the silence, or even, the vocal dissent which dismisses the biblical record, all the way from creation through the time of David and Solomon, as myth and legend. Let's consider the problems and the possible solutions.

Neither of these choices is a good one for those who believe the Bible describes accurately the events of its time.

In the third century BC, Manetho, an Egyptian priest, compiled a history of Egypt, including a list of the pharaohs, divided into thirty-one dynasties. (This list was reconstructed by the priests from memory because Cambyses had destroyed all the written records of Egypt in 526 BC. Manetho's list differs from the list the priests had given Herodotus about two hundred years earlier.) That seems fairly simple and straightforward, doesn't it? A list of kings, grouped into families—everything made nice and tidy. This was more or less accepted for many years as the standard by which to date the various pharaohs and their reigns. The problem for Bible believers is that, as the pharaohs march through time, one by one, the years and events of their reigns do not correspond with biblical events and people—not in recovered documents of the time nor in the dating of archaeological debris. In the *traditional* chronology, the Exodus (which Ussher lists as 1491 BC, and many scholars who follow the errors of Edwin Thiele, have set at 1446 BC) falls during the New Kingdom. However, since there are some *serious* difficulties with this time period, including the capital city of the 18th Dynasty being located 475 miles from Goshen (a long daily walk for Moses as he confronts Pharaoh), another suggestion was made to date the Exodus to the 19th Dynasty under Rameses II since his capital city was in Goshen. The problem with this choice is that, under the traditional chronology, Rameses II ruled Egypt from 1290–1224 BC, which does not agree with the biblical date for the Exodus. So, neither of these choices is a good one for those who believe the Bible describes accurately the events of its time.

> Decisions have been made in the last sixty years . . . to throw out the veracity and historicity of Scripture.

A new wave of archaeologists and Bible believers have begun to question the accepted chronology of Manetho. You see, it is not clear from the archaeological record whether the pharaohs lived one at a time, shared their reign, or reigned over only a portion of Egypt while another dynasty (or two, or three) ruled over other parts of Egypt. And, to make it more difficult, when archaeologists uncover a monument with a list of pharaohs, the years of their reign are often not included or obliterated through the aging, so, along with pottery fragments, isolated hieroglyphic inscriptions, and surviving documents, the information needed for creating an accurate timeline is scanty at best. Even though this forms—along with wrong assumptions made by early Egyptologists—the shaky foundation of Egyptian chronology,

Egyptian Papyrus Painting

decisions have been made in the last sixty years in academic circles, in museums, universities, and scholarly journals, to throw out the veracity and historicity of Scripture because the Egyptian artifacts have not lined up with the names, dates, and events of the Bible.

That is, until the mid-1990s. In 1995 David Rohl, working on his doctoral thesis at University College in London, released his book, *A Test of Time: The Bible From Myth to History*, which has brought about a flurry of new ideas. Basically, through the research Rohl has done with existing documentation, he has theorized that the Third Intermediate Period of Egyptian history is 200 years shorter than previously thought, due to parallel dynasties. That, along with other adjustments in the chronologies, results in a reduction of 345 years in the ancient Egyptian timeline. David Down, field archaeologist and author of *Unwrapping the Pharoahs*, agrees with a reduction in the Egyptian chronology, though he would differ slightly from Rohl's dates.

Rohl thinks that Rameses II, rather than being the pharaoh of the Exodus, is actually the pharaoh who ransacked the temple in Jerusalem in 971 BC (called "Shishak" in 1 Kings 14:25)—and, not surprisingly, there is good archaeological evidence for this event! Ussher calls this pharaoh Sefonchis, and Isaac Newton says it was Sesostris, also called Bacchus. This scenario puts Joseph and the Exodus in the Twelfth (and possibly the Thirteenth) Dynasty. Amazingly, in 1987 a statue was discovered in a palace in Goshen, which had a most un-Egyptian face, with red hair and a coat of many colors. Could it be a statue of Joseph? Rohl thinks the answer to that question would be "Yes!"

Tremendous research is taking place, since the Egyptian chronology has been adjusted, to discover whether there is now, in the right places, all the evidence for the Hebrews that was previously missed. We will consider some of the new evidence from old discoveries in the next chapter. With all that's happening, with all the discoveries opening up the evidence of the Bible's accuracy for all to see, it is an exciting moment to be a student!

Phase 1

Listen to This

What in the World? VOL. 1

DISC TWO:

- Historical Chronology (track 1)
- Problems with Chronology (track 2)
- Egyptian History (track 3)

True Tales VOL. 1

DISC TWO:

- The Rosetta Stone (track 5)

Digging Deeper VOL. 1

DISC TWO:

- The Seven Wonders of the Ancient World: Introduction & The Great Pyramid (tracks 1–2)

Look at This

- The Mystery of Ancient Man (www.answersingenesis.org/go/pyramids)
- The Mysterious Hyksos (www.answersingenesis.org/go/ten-plagues)

Read for Your Life

The Holy Bible

- The Main Story: Genesis 39–50, Exodus 1–15, Acts 7:1–38 (the short version of the story)
- Helpful Verses: Deuteronomy 32:1–12; Psalms 66, 78, 95, 136; Isaiah 19, Ezekiel 29–32; Hebrews 11:8–29

Key People

Menes
First pharaoh to unite Egypt

Khufu (Cheops)
The Great Pyramid was built for his tomb

Hatshepsut
The best known woman pharaoh

Tutankhamen
His tomb was found intact

Rameses II
Fought the Hittites at Battle of Kadesh

Joseph
Hebrew vizier of Egypt

Moses
Leader of the Hebrews

Talk Together

Opinion Column

- What did you find to be the most interesting aspect, or the most fascinating person, you encountered in your introduction to Egypt and the Exodus?
- *"You meant evil against me; but God meant it for good" (Genesis 50:20).* Knowing that God is always good—that His ways are always righteous and pure—explain why Joseph went through the difficult situations of being sold into slavery, being accused wrongly, and being thrown into prison. As you answer this question, consider the implications in your own life.
- Honestly, thinking about the reality of the situation, why do you think Moses chose to identify with the Jews who were now slaves in Egypt, rather than to enjoy the pleasures of Pharaoh's court?

Critical Puzzling

- From the Scripture readings and the audio recordings, what can you discover about the Egyptian culture in regard to their treatment of other peoples? What aspects of their culture would you consider to be warlike? Can you draw parallels to any modern cultures?
- How did God demonstrate His love to both the descendants of Jacob and the Egyptians?
- The article describes Egypt as intended by God to be a safe haven, a refuge. What examples of this do you find in Scripture?

Resources for Digging Deeper

Choose a few books that look interesting, or find your own.

THE EXODUS

Celebrate the Feasts

Martha Zimmerman • This book is filled with the why's and how-to's of celebrating the feasts of Israel. We learned so much about the meaning of the Last Supper, and the incredible picture of the Messiah depicted in the feast of Passover from this book—which also shows how to celebrate this and the other feasts. **AA**

The Story of Passover

Norma Simon • A beautiful children's picture book teaches about the historic passover and how it has been celebrated both in history and currently. **E+**

Exodus

Brian Wildsmith • Filled with wonderful illustrations, this hardbound children's book brings the story of the Exodus to life. **E+**

Video: The Ten Commandments **AA**

Video: Prince Of Egypt **AA**

EGYPT

Cultural Atlas for Young People ANCIENT EGYPT

Geraldine Harris • The Cultural Atlas books are among the most informative, best laid-out history books for young people. Highly recommended! **MS+**

Pyramid

David Macaulay • An incredible look at the construction of a pyramid—you actually get the sense that you are inside a pyramid with the workers! **AA**

Growing Up in Ancient Egypt

Rosalie David • This is an excellent introduction to the many facets of living in ancient Egypt. Though it is written for children, the information and layout makes it valuable to all ages. **E+**

The Pharaohs of Ancient Egypt

Elizabeth Payne • Landmark books are always a good value, and this is no exception. Excellent for younger students. **UE+**

Tut's Mummy Lost and Found

Judy Donnelly • For elementary students, this book shows the fascinating adventure of Howard Carter who found King Tut in 1922. **E+**

Look What Came From Egypt

Miles Harvey • What a wonderful picture book of Egypt! Filled with photos and simple descriptions, this will be a great introduction for elementary students. **E+**

Make it Work! Ancient Egypt

Andrew Haslam & Alexandra Parsons • This is one of a series of the most incredible hands-on books of projects I've ever seen! It shows how to construct clothing, make jewelry, create instruments, even make a chariot! **UE+**

The Riddle of the Rosetta Stone KEY TO ANCIENT EGYPT

James Cross Giblin • An absolutely fascinating book about the man who deciphered the Rosetta Stone. **AA**

Seeker of Knowledge THE MAN WHO DECIPHERED EGYPTIAN HIEROGLYPHS

James Rumford • If you collect excellent children's books, this is one for your shelves. It is the story of Jean-François Champollion, told with exquisite style and illustrations. **E+**

Hatshepsut—His Majesty, Herself

Catherine Andronik • Another excellent children's book, this one is concerned with one of the most interesting and unusual pharaohs of ancient Egypt. **E+**

Unwrapping the Pharaohs

John Ashton & David Down • Ashton and Down provide fascinating information about the architecture, timelines, and culture of Egypt during the times of Moses, Joseph, "King Tut," and others. Discusses the "problem" of dating the Exodus and provides real solutions.

Pharaohs and Kings

David Rohl • Discover for yourself the compelling reasons for revising the traditional Egyptian chronology, and see how this affects the archaeological evidences for Joseph and Moses in Egypt. Fascinating! **MS+**

Ancient Egypt—A Cambridge Junior History

Philip Cummins • Cambridge University Press has published some of my favorite history books. This is an excellent introduction to ancient Egypt for pre-high school students. **UE+**

HISTORICAL FICTION

The Golden Goblet

Eloise Jarvis McGraw • We really like this author! This book focuses on the intrigue and mystery of one orphaned boy's life. Another exciting means of making ancient Egypt come alive! **UE+**

Mara, daughter of the Nile

Eloise Jarvis McGraw • Riveting historical fiction! This is a wonderful way to make the ancient Egyptians, the political intrigues, and the places of power come to life. **UE+**

The Cat of the Bubastes

G. A. Henty • A fascinating look at the religious life of the Egyptians, with a Judeo-Christian insight. Historical fiction at its best: includes Moses! **MS+**

What books did you like best?

____

____

____

____

The Internet also contains a wealth of information about Egypt and the Exodus.

What sites were the most helpful?

____

____

____

For more books, use these Dewey Decimal numbers in your library:

Bible: #220

Ancient Egypt: #932

Ancient Palestine: #933

Anthropology: #300

Also, look for biographies on the key people listed.

Student Self-Evaluation UNIT 3, PHASE 1

Dates and hours:____________________

Key Concepts

Rephrase the four Key Concepts of this Unit and confirm your understanding of each:

- Ancient Egypt & God's plan

____

- Joseph's life

____

- Moses & the Exodus

____

- Possible routes

____

Tools for Self-Evaulation

Evaluate your personal participation in the discussions of this Phase. Bearing in mind that a good participant in a discussion is not always the most vocal participant, ask yourself these questions: Were you an active participant? Did you ask perceptive questions? Were you willing to listen to other participants of the discussion and draw out their opinions? Record your observations and how you would like to improve your participation in the future:

____

____

Every time period is too complex to be understood in one Phase of study. Evaluate your current knowledge of Egypt & the Exodus. What have you focused on so far? What are your weakest areas of knowledge?

____

____

Based on the evaluation of this introduction, project ahead what you would like to study more of in the following Phases:

____

Phase 2

Research & Reporting

Explore one or more of these areas to discover something significant!

Hieroglyphics

Research and explain what hieroglyphic writing is, and how it was deciphered in modern times. (Look up the Rosetta Stone and Jean Francois Champollion.)

Math

Research and report on the use of triangulation in surveying ancient Egypt. Why was regular surveying required? Is triangulation still used in surveying?

Chronology

Compile a list of the major names, dates and accomplishments of Egypt's dynasties. Using David Rohl's research or Ted Stewart's research, how does this list compare with the events listed in the Bible?

Egyptian History

- Summarize the factors that led to Egypt's far-reaching dominion and the factors leading to its decline. Be sure to include the impact of the Nile.
- Investigate the history of Egypt from the earliest times to the present. Report your finding.

Bible

- Research the life of Joseph in the Scriptures.
- Research the life of Moses.
- Investigate the book of Exodus in the Old Testament. To whom did God speak? What were the messages? How did the people (both Egyptian and Israelite) respond? How did God deal with each of them?

Wilderness Living

Research and report on the weather conditions and ecosystems in Egypt and in Midian. How would this have affected the children of Israel as they wandered for forty years?

Deserts

- Compare and contrast the desert in Egypt with other deserts, such as the Sahara or Mojave. How did the Nile River impact the desert of ancient Egypt? How is this different today?
- Using a recent cultural anthropology study or a missions resource, learn more about nomadic desert dwellers (like the Bedouins), their lifestyle, and how they care for their animals. Write a report showing the lifestyle of the desert dweller, then, extrapolate what we can learn from this in regard to the Israelites in the wilderness.

Passover

Read Exodus 12. Now, using either *Celebrate the Feasts* or another book describing the Jewish feast of Passover, chart the similarities between the feast and the original historic event of Passover.

Egyptian Afterlife

Why were the ancient Egyptians so concerned about the afterlife? What are some of the ways they demonstrated their concern? What scientific techniques used in mummification remain a mystery to us?

Building the Great Pyramid

Discover how big the Great Pyramid is, and as much as is known about how it was built. What is the average weight of each stone? How much, approximately, does the Great Pyramid weigh?

Brain Stretchers

Egypt & Israel

Compare and contrast the history of ancient Egypt and the history of ancient Israel. What cultural distinctives (i.e. religion, war, politics, class structure) continue in each nation throughout the centuries of antiquity?

The Sinai

Find one of the books listed at the beginning of this unit, along with the encyclopedia or other history resource book, for basic information on what would be needed in a hot, dry climate to sustain life for people, flocks, and herds. Is it available on the Sinai Peninsula? Would it be available in the land of Midian (Arabia)? Make a chart listing the necessary requirements to sustain life, and show which of these requirements are fulfilled in each of these two locations. Keep in mind that God made miraculous provisions for the Israelites and that the climate is different today.

Geography of the Exodus

Read Exodus and note the geographical descriptions of the flight from Egypt, the crossing of the Red Sea, and the route to and depiction of Mt. Sinai (reference Gal. 4:25 also.) Next, find a description of the traditional site of Mt. Sinai and the Sea of Reeds. In what way do these sites support or conflict with the biblical text? Write a report explaining what you discover.

Create Your Own Research Topic

____

____

____

____

Timeline

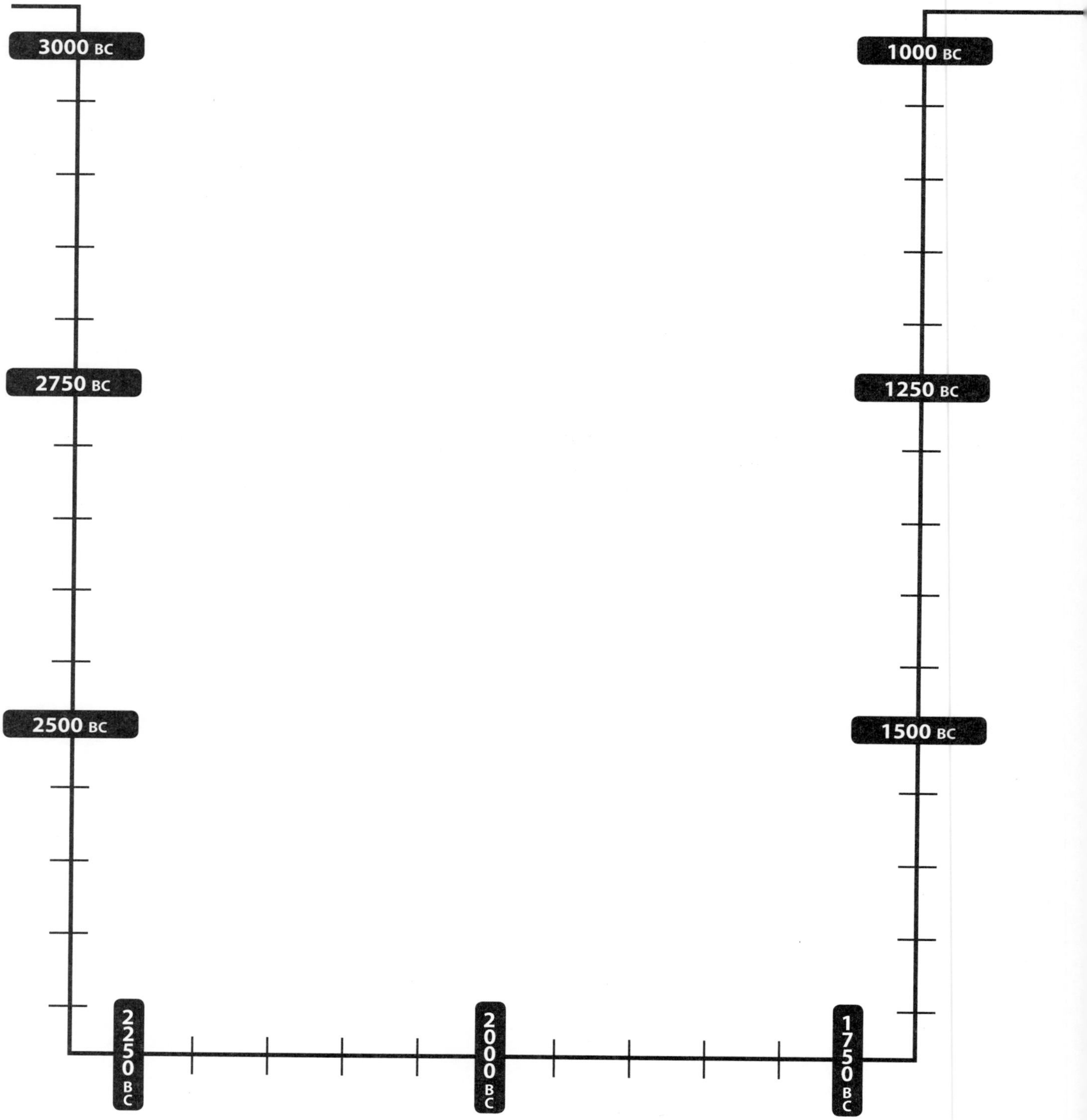
3000 BC
2750 BC
2500 BC
2250 BC
2000 BC
1750 BC
1500 BC
1250 BC
1000 BC

Key Events

- Joseph to Egypt
- The Exodus
- Early Dynasties
- Middle Dynasties (especially Rohl's dates for the Twelfth Dynasty)
- Late Dynasties

Be sure to include the people listed in Key People in Phase 1.

Consider this for your timeline

The Exodus is thought by many to have occurred approximately 1446 BC. Archbishop Ussher dates it to 1491 BC and David Rohl to 1447. Others believe that the Exodus took place much later, in the 1200s BC. Do your research and make your own decision.

The difficulty in pinpointing dates and pharaohs lies with the Egyptian chronologies. When we look back in history, we often expect to find a "digital clock" marking the exact moment when an event occurred. Unfortunately, especially in ancient civilizations, that is not the case. Instead, there are many educated guesses about the time frame in which certain key events and players happened.

Words to Watch

Remember—The easiest way to learn a subject is to master its terms:

Midian	plague	Goshen	famine
sorcerers	Nile River	slavery	magicians
Mt. Horeb	exodus	pharaoh	Mt. Sinai
quota	hieroglyphics	petroglyph	Passover
irrigation	triangulation	survey	pyramid
mummification	afterlife	sphinx	

Other words you need to look up:

Student Self-Evaluation UNIT 3, PHASE 2

Dates and hours:______________________________

Research Project

- Summarize your research question:

____

____

- List your most useful sources by author, title, and page number or URL where applicable (continue list in margin if necessary):

____

____

____

Now take a moment to evaluate the sources you just listed. Do they provide a balanced view of your research question? Should you have sought an additional opinion? Are your sources credible (if you found them on your own)? Record your observations:

____

____

Evaluate your research project in its final presentation. What are its strengths? If you had time to revisit this project, what would you change? Consider giving yourself a letter grade based on your project's merits and weaknesses.

____

____

Letter grade: ____

You have just completed an area of specific research in the time of Egypt & the Exodus. Now what would you like to explore in the upcoming Phases? Set some objectives for yourself:

____

Phase 3

Maps and Mapping

Physical Terrain

» Color and label the Nile River in Egypt.

» Color the flood plain of the Nile (which is the fertile area of Egypt).

» Color the desert area of Egypt.

» Color the Mediterranean and the Red Sea.

Geopolitical

» Draw the boundaries of Egypt (including the area of their copper and turquoise mines).

» Divide Egypt into Upper Egypt and Lower Egypt.

» Label the cities of Memphis, Thebes, and the Valley of the Kings.

» What modern day cities are close to these ancient cities?

» Label the area of Goshen in the Nile delta.

» Label and color the Sinai Peninsula.

» Label the land of Midian.

» What modern day country holds the land of Midian?

Explore

» ***Christian Outreach to Egypt and Saudi Arabia:*** What is the status of Christian outreach to these countries in the Middle East? Discuss the difficulties facing Christians seeking to serve God in these nations, and brainstorm creative ways of overcoming these difficulties.

» ***God's Purposes in Earth's Geography:*** How would the terrain and climate of Egypt, with the Nile River, the flood plain, the desert, and the Upper & Lower portions of Egypt all have affected the Egyptian culture and God's purpose for it?

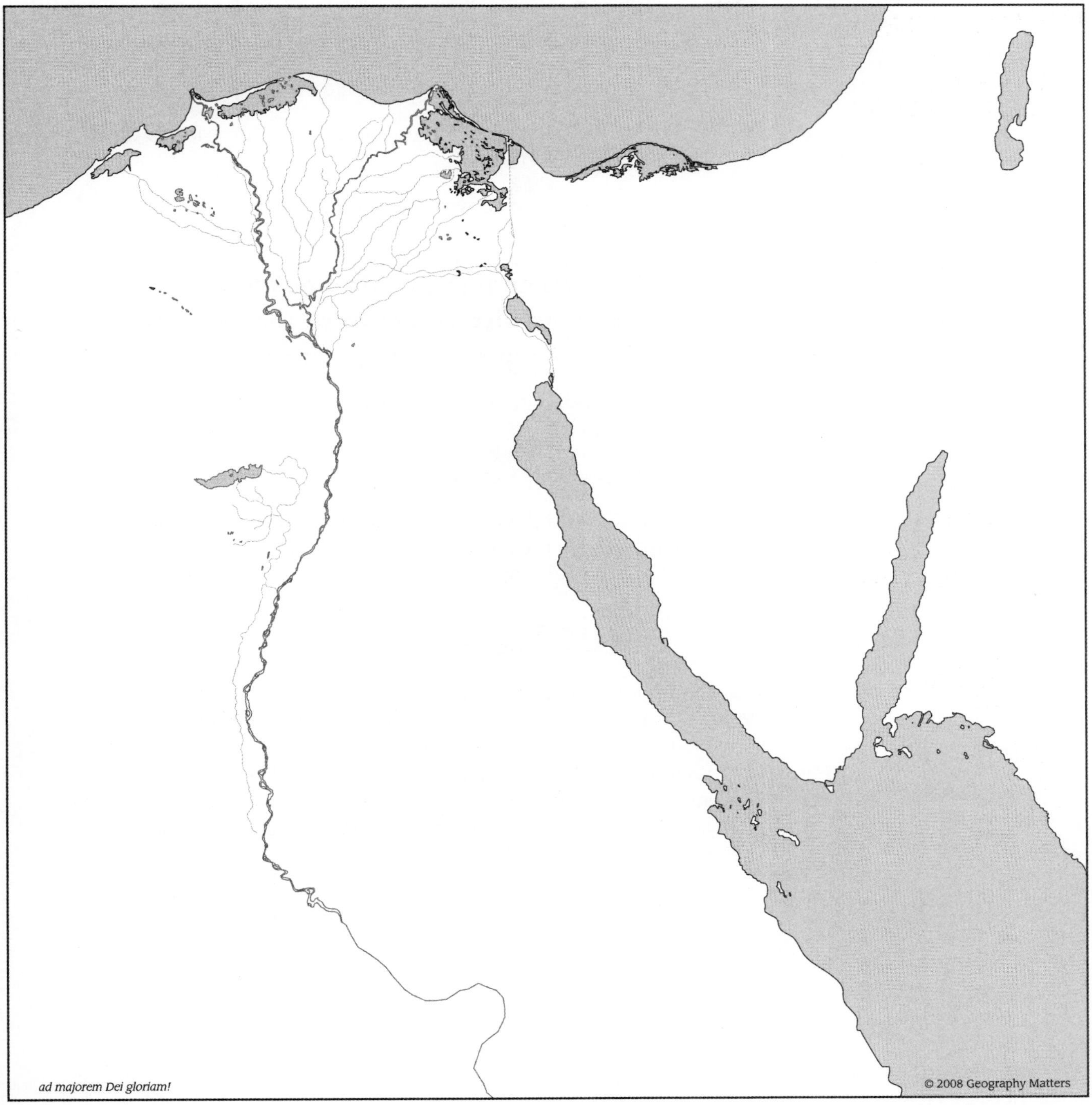
ad majorem Dei gloriam!
© 2008 Geography Matters

CONSIDER:

Bernardo Luini (c. AD1480–1532) studied under Leonardo da Vinci, and was himself, a master artist. His style of painting was also influenced by the Florentine artists of an earlier time.

CONSIDER:

When it was originally built, the outside of this pyramid was covered with brilliant white Tura limestone, which would have made it even more impressive. Though most of it has been removed over the centuries, there is still enough in place that one can imagine the splendor of this architectural wonder of the world.

Art Appreciation

The Deliverance of the Israelites **by Bernardo Luini**

» Does the painting reflect what the Bible describes?

» How does the painting differ from your own impression of God's deliverance?

» Does Luini's painting convey the epic nature of the destruction of Pharaoh and his army?

Egyptian Tomb Painting**: Look in a book about Egypt, a book with historic art, or on the Internet for examples of Egyptian tomb painting.**

» How would you describe the style of painting used by these Egyptian artists?

» What kinds of scenes are depicted?

» Does this style of painting make you think the Egyptian artists were sophisticated in their art? Do you consider them to be childish to the Western eye? Why do you think they painted in this style?

Architecture

The Great Pyramid at Giza is one of the Seven Wonders of the Ancient World. It was probably standing when Abraham ventured into Egypt—a long time ago. It still stands today! It is believed to weigh five million tons, and has more than two million blocks of stone. Napoleon thought there was enough stone in this pyramid, along with two other pyramids nearby, to build a wall ten feet high and one foot thick all the way around France!

» Look for a photo of the Great Pyramid of Khufu (or Cheops). What are some words that would describe this building?

Arts in Action

Select one or more, and let your artistic juices flow!

Imitation

Try imitating Luini, or the ancient Egyptian artists (trace, use colors, etc.)

Sphinx Carving

Try carving a Sphinx out of soap. Remember Michelangelo's advice: just carve away anything that doesn't look like the Sphinx!

Egyptian Portraiture

Sketch a simple portrait of yourself or someone else, in the style of the Egyptian tomb paintings. (Notice how they usually paint flat profiles.) Then make a dry plaster (a secco) painting: using very smooth plaster of Paris, brush a ⅛" layer of plaster over a piece of wood. When dry, lay your sketch over the wood and trace the outline with a nail. Use tempera to paint picture. Remember to keep it simple!

Egyptian Jewelry

Egyptians liked to use jewelry in adorning themselves. (This came in very handy when the Israelites took their back wages out of the country!) Find a book showing the look of Egyptian jewelry, and try your hand at creating some. There are many, many possibilities for materials, colors, size, and shape!

Science

Brick Making

» Using water, clay soil (or potter's clay), and straw, mix up a batch of "bricks." Make wooden rectangular forms to put the mixture into. Let it dry (it may take several days.) What's the difference between sun-dried brick and kiln-dried brick?

Levers & Pulleys

» Ancient Egyptians may have used levers and pulleys to build the pyramids. Construct a system of pulleys and ropes to try lifting a heavy object like a concrete block. Notice that the more pulleys used, the easier it is to lift something. Consult the library for more info (see also "block and tackle").

Music

In ancient Egypt, as we have seen in other early civilizations, people played various kinds of instruments, such as flutes, harps, and drums. But they were not the only ones in Egypt with instruments! Exodus 15 tells us that Moses' sister, Miriam, played the timbrels (tambourine) during the triumphant song of deliverance after Pharaoh and his army were drowned in the Red Sea. One of the five elements of music, rhythm is the distinctive pattern of long and short notes in each piece of music. Along with the pattern of notes is the underlying pulse, or beat, of the music. The beat can be slow or fast or medium. We use the term tempo to mean the speed of music. So, slow music, like a lullaby, has a slow tempo, and fast music, like a march, has a faster tempo.

CONSIDER:

Have you ever listened to a tambourine? Sometimes it's played consistently and regularly on the beat, but sometimes the tambourine player will make different patterns: a long, held-out "shimmering" sound, or a series of short, quick taps. The performer is creating a pattern of sounds, some longer and some shorter.

Listen

» Find a recording of a percussion ensemble, such as the Lawrence University Percussion Ensemble (LUPE), or a recording of tribal drumming, to see just how creatively rhythm can be used.

Try This

» Recite these children's verses:
"Pat-a-cake, pat-a-cake, Baker's man..."
"Twinkle, twinkle, little star..."
"Hot cross buns..."

» Now, try clapping (not saying) one of these verses. Can anyone guess which pattern you are clapping? That pattern is called the rhythm.

» For a greater challenge, try clapping familiar tunes, such as Christmas carols or church songs.

» Now, speed up the clapping, which changes the tempo. Next, slow down the clapping. Which speed allows the clearest presentation of the above verses?

» Play a rhythm game where one person claps a short rhythm and everyone tries to repeat it. Take turns!

Cooking

Since this unit looks at two different people groups, the Egyptians and the Israelites who fled Egypt, we will make two different recipes. Do you remember what the children of Israel complained about in the wilderness in regard to good ol' Egyptian food? (You may want to listen to Keith Green's "So You Wanna Go Back to Egypt".) Sample the following and see what they were talking about! (Be sure NOT to complain!!)

Stewed Beef with Okra (Egyptian)

2 tbsp oil
2 tbsp butter
1½ pound stew beef
(or lamb) cubed
2 onions, chopped
2 cloves garlic, minced
½ tsp ground coriander
1 pound tomatoes, peeled & sliced
1 tbsp tomato paste
2 10-oz. pkgs frozen okra
Salt & pepper

Heat oil and butter in casserole. Add meat cubes & saute until brown. Add onions, garlic, coriander, and fry for one minute. Add tomatoes, paste, seasoning. Cover stew with water, bring to boil, reduce heat, cover, simmer 1 hour. Add okra, cook 30 minutes more.

Unleavened Bread (The Exodus)

4 cups unbleached flour
1 tsp salt
1½ cup water, room temp

Combine flour and salt. Add enough water to make a dough that will clean sides of bowl and gather into a ball. Turn out onto lightly floured surface, knead 10 minutes. Shape into ball and cut in half. Cut each half into 8 pieces and form into 16 balls. Roll out each ball to form about a 7" circle. Place on ungreased baking sheet and bake in 500 degree oven for about 5 minutes. Makes 16.

Student Self-Evaluation UNIT 3, PHASE 3

Dates and hours:______________________

Evaluate Your Projects

- List which of the activities listed in this Phase you did:

  ____

  ____

  ____

- Rate your enthusiasm: ___________

  Explain: ____

  ____

- Rate the precision of your approach:___________

  Explain: ____

  ____

- Rate your effort toward the completion of the project: ___________

  Explain: ____

  ____

Ask yourself what worked and what did not. What would you do differently in the future, and what would you repeat?

____

How specifically did these hands-on activities enhance your knowledge of Egypt & the Exodus? What made them worthwhile?

____

In the first three Phases of this Unit, what aspect of the time period has most captured your imagination? What would you like to creatively pursue to conclude your study?

____

Phase 4

In Your Own Way . . .

In this unit we have seen how the descendants of Abraham entered Egypt, a biblical land of refuge. After God's powerful intervention through Joseph in what could have been utter devastation to both the Egyptians and the Hebrews, a generation arose who did not remember the past. Instead, they focused on the increasing might of the Hebrews, and out of fear for their own safety, they enslaved them. In one of the most powerful historic events of all time, God delivered the Hebrews, the descendants of Abraham, in the Exodus. In this, and through other Scriptures, we have discovered God's mercy and love to both the Egyptians and the Hebrews. Now, choose a selection of these activities, or create your own, which will best express what was most significant to you.

LINGUISTICS

Playing with Words

Make a pun about Egypt. Like this:
What do you call a pyramid that smells bad?
A stynx!

Journalism

- Be a newspaper reporter for the Palestine news daily, *The Patriarch*, and write the human interest story "Family Finds Long-Lost Son in Egypt."
- Imagine you were invited to a formal dinner at Nefertiti's palace. Write a detailed description of the guests, their outfits, and the food served for the magazine, *Lifestyles: Egyptian Royalty at Home*.

Prose

Write a fictional account of an Egyptian orphan who flees to a Hebrew family during the plagues, then comes with them on the Exodus.

Poetry

- Discover the connection these words have to the unit, and then write a rhyming poem using them: sea, flee, free; pharaoh, marrow, narrow; pulley, bully, fully; flood, blood, mud; slave, brave, save
- Write an acrostic poem from the Hebrew perspective describing the night of the first Passover.

ART

Painting/Drawing

- Create a mural of the Great Pyramid, the Sphinx, and the surrounding Egyptian desert. If you have a current photo from which to draw, you might want to add the ubiquitous camels!
- Paint the scene from the Exodus where God sends a wind to part the Red Sea. You might consider making it abstract to focus on the overall experience.

Graphic Design

Design an ad for a real estate developer who has land for sale—just outside the flood plain of the Nile. Remember that the Egyptians described the land as either black (from the rich deposits of flooding) or red (the unrelieved desert ground).

Cartooning

As a political cartoonist, draw a cartoon for the *Mt. Sinai Herald*, showing the confrontation between Pharaoh and Moses.

MUSIC

Compose

Exodus 15 contains the song that Moses and the children of Israel sang after their deliverance through the Red Sea. Select some portion of those verses and put them to music. If composing a melody is initially too overwhelming, start by creating a text-setting, which means setting a selection of text to rhythm. Try to get the most dramatic use of pauses and rhythmic emphasis.

Performance Practice

There is a tremendous amount of drama in this unit. With your teacher, select an appropriate dramatic piece, with great contrast, to play at the end of this unit. Explain to your audience the way that the music represents what you learned about Egypt and the Exodus.

DRAMA

Comedy

Do a humorous skit about Moses explaining to his wife that the reason he was late for dinner was because God was talking out of a burning bush!

Reality

Act out the Exodus. Use your imagination to create props, sets, and costumes. Be sure to include realistic fear, as well as rejoicing! Add appropriate songs and worship choruses.

Puppetry

Produce a puppet show on the life of Joseph. You could choose to begin with his time in prison. For inspiration, check out *Joseph and the Amazing Technicolor Dreamcoat*.

Prop Needs

____

____

Costume Ideas

____

____

Role/Player

____

____

Set Suggestions

____

____

MOVEMENT

Pantomime

- Pantomime Joseph's being called out of prison, cleaned up, and dressed, to appear before Pharoah. Show how he listens to Pharoah's dream, interprets it, and is then honored with responsibility for the entire land of Egypt. If two students wish to do this together, one could portray Joseph and the other Pharoah.
- Pantomime the plagues of Egypt. Be sure to show how the Hebrews were saved out of them.

Dance

Dance the enslavement and bondage of Israel in the land of Egypt, showing how they cried out to God. Remember, after the Red Sea parted, Miriam danced to show her thankfulness to God.

Action

Perform a stylized action/dance of Pharoah and his army chasing the Israelites to the Red Sea, with the tragic end for the Egyptians and the victorious deliverance for the Hebrews.

CONCEPTUAL DESIGN

There is a tremendous number of possible explanations as to how the pyramids were built, including poured concrete, the brute strength of slaves, and kite power. Design an imaginative (it doesn't have to work in real life) pyramid-building machine.

CREATE YOUR OWN EXPRESSION

Student Self-Evaluation UNIT 3, PHASE 4

Dates and hours:____________________

Evaluate Your Projects

- What creative project did you choose:

- What did you expect from your project, and how does the final project compare to your initial expectations?

- What do you like about your project? What would you change?

In Conclusion

Revisit the four Key Concepts from the beginning of this Unit. Explain how your understanding of and appreciation for each has grown over the course of your study.

Record your concluding thoughts on Egypt & the Exodus:

The Children of Israel

UNIT 4

The Jordan River

Key Concepts

- Strategic Location & God's Purpose
- The Chronology
- The Glory
- The Divided Kingdom
- Application

Into the Promised Land...

> So the Lord saved Israel that day out of the hand of the Egyptians, and Israel saw the Egyptians dead on the seashore. Thus Israel saw the great work which the Lord had done in Egypt; so the people feared the Lord, and believed the Lord and His servant Moses. Exodus 14:30–31

Out of Egypt! Deliverance and freedom! A new hope and a new future! Standing on the other side of the Red Sea, watching with incredulity as the towering waters collapsed on Pharaoh and his army, the escapees must have felt a torrent of thoughts and emotions. Consider: first, the thrill of being alive and free when they expected to be either dead or re-enslaved, and secondly the very present and human concern, "What do we do now?"

Moses, their God-appointed leader, faced a number of obstacles in leading this massive group of people (estimated between one and three million!) and their livestock, not least of which was finding food and water for them in a dry and thirsty land. As they journeyed into the wilderness, God both led them and provided for them—but not without testing. As someone once observed, "You can deliver the man out of Egypt, but you can't deliver Egypt out of the man!" There was an ongoing process of actively putting their trust in the God who had proved His trustworthiness. These things take time and experience, however. So, God very wisely gave them opportunities: like having the chance to look around the desert, noticing a lack of water, that they might cry out to Him and see His miraculous provision of water; or wondering where the bakeries were, crying out to Him, and seeing God give them heavenly bread—manna—day by day for forty years; or considering the lack of shoe stores in the wilderness and experiencing the miracle of shoes that didn't wear out in the hot desert sun or on the baked rocks and sand! On and on the list goes, as the fledgling nation learned of the amazing ability God had to provide all they needed—an important lesson for the nation designated to show God's goodness to all the world.

This was not a one-sided, vending machine, grumpy-request-automatic-answer sort of provision.

This was not a one-sided, vending machine, grumpy-request-automatic-answer sort of provision, however. We see in the book of Exodus an ongoing issue of relationship between the people and God. The people, who had just seen their miraculous deliverance from slavery, when confronted by a problem, began to whine and complain to Moses about how he had brought them into the wilderness to die. The Bible tells us that their complaints were not really against Moses but against God. Yet, despite the people's ungratefulness, He continued in His mercy and kindness to take care of them, while at the same time teaching them that He was not a "tame lion" (in the words of C. S. Lewis) that could be pushed and pulled at whim. Read the book of Numbers to discover some of the wild occurrences that happened in the wilderness, including the day that the earth "opened its mouth" and swallowed the leaders of a rebellion against Moses (Numbers 16). The people learned, experience by experience, that God was not mocked—"for whatever a man sows, that he will also reap" (Galatians 6:7).

The Ten Commandments

As part of His discipleship of the children of Israel, God led them to a place called the Wilderness of Sinai in the third month of their wanderings to make a formal, binding agreement, or covenant, with them.

> "You have seen what I did to the Egyptians, and how I bore you on eagles' wings and brought you to Myself. Now therefore, if you will indeed obey My voice and keep My covenant, then you shall be a special treasure to Me above all

Exodus 20:1–17

And God spoke all these words, saying:

"I *am* the LORD your God, who brought you out of the land of Egypt, out of the house of bondage.

"You shall have no other gods before Me.

"You shall not make for yourself a carved image—any likeness *of anything* that *is* in heaven above, or that *is* in the earth beneath, or that *is* in the water under the earth; you shall not bow down to them nor serve them. For I, the LORD your God, *am* a jealous God, visiting the iniquity of the fathers upon the children to the third and fourth *generations* of those who hate Me, but showing mercy to thousands, to those who love Me and keep My commandments.

"You shall not take the name of the LORD your God in vain, for the LORD will not hold *him* guiltless who takes His name in vain.

"Remember the Sabbath day, to keep it holy. Six days you shall labor and do all your work, but the seventh day *is* the Sabbath of the LORD your God. *In it* you shall do no work: you, nor your son, nor your daughter, nor your male servant, nor your female servant, nor your cattle, nor your stranger who *is* within your gates. For *in* six days the LORD made the heavens and the earth, the sea, and all that *is* in them, and rested the seventh day. Therefore the LORD blessed the Sabbath day and hallowed it.

"Honor your father and your mother, that your days may be long upon the land which the LORD your God is giving you.

"You shall not murder.

"You shall not commit adultery.

"You shall not steal.

"You shall not bear false witness against your neighbor.

"You shall not covet your neighbor's house; you shall not covet your neighbor's wife, nor his male servant, nor his female servant, nor his ox, nor his donkey, nor anything that *is* your neighbor's."

people; for all the earth is Mine. And you shall be to Me a kingdom of priests and a holy nation." Exodus 19:4–6

The people listened to these words, which Moses gave them, and readily agreed to obey the Lord. In that desert setting, with Egypt behind them and the unknown before them, the children of Israel gave themselves willingly, albeit imperfectly, to this Delivering God. At that moment He gave them, written on stone by His own hand, an understanding of His ways and His design for all people that has impacted the world ever since. We call it the Ten Commandments.

With Egypt behind them and the unknown before them, the children of Israel gave themselves willingly, albeit imperfectly, to this Delivering God.

Think about it. These commandments were not given in anger, as punishment for a disobedient people. They were not given by a killjoy God who only wanted the worst for His children. No! Stop for a moment and consider the setting, and contemplate the motivation. God offered to make them a special treasure, and they willingly said that was what they wanted. In that atmosphere of relationship, when One offered and the other responded, God gave the people a depth of understanding that no one since the Fall

Meses showing the people the Ten commandments (Gustave Dore, 1865)

of Adam had ever known. He told them aspects of how they were designed to live in relationship to Him (the first four commandments) and how they were designed to live in relationship with one another (the last six commandments). It was a gift, it was a communication of loving truth that would, if obeyed, give tremendous blessing to the people who lived it out. It would not make them righteous (Isaiah 64:6)—that belongs to God alone (Philippians 3:9)—but it would immeasurably bless them and teach them about how to live out their relationships.

After the giving of the Ten Commandments (Exodus 20), the people were so afraid of the awesome power and presence of God that they begged Moses to be the one who spoke directly to and heard directly from God. It was at that point that the precise details of how to live and how to worship were given to Moses to convey to the people. In the book of Hebrews, we are told that the Tabernacle, the priesthood, and the daily sacrifices were earthly symbols of the heavenly reality of what Jesus would later accomplish as the Savior.

> For if He were on earth, He would not be a priest, since there are priests who offer the gifts according to the law: who serve the *copy and shadow* of the heavenly things, as Moses was divinely instructed when he was about to make the tabernacle. For He said, "See that you make all things according to the pattern shown you on the mountain." But now He has obtained a more excellent ministry, inasmuch as He is also Mediator of a better covenant, which was established on better promises. Hebrews 8:4–6

The Tabernacle, the priesthood, and the daily sacrifices were earthly symbols of the heavenly reality of what Jesus would later accomplish as the Savior.

Moses spent forty days and nights on the mountain receiving specific instruction from God, while the people waited impatiently below. They reached a point where they assumed Moses had been consumed, or had forgotten about them, or had lost his mind and was wandering somewhere in the wilderness, or had somehow been incapacitated as their leader. This conclusion made them very insecure and very forgetful about the God who had delivered them out of Egypt. How do we know this?

> Now when the people saw that Moses delayed coming down from the mountain, the people gathered together to Aaron, and said to him, "Come, make us gods that shall go

> before us; for as for this Moses, the man who brought us up out of the land of Egypt, we do not know what has become of him." Exodus 32:1

This is just a few short weeks after telling God that they would obey Him! How quickly people seem to forget God's faithfulness, His goodness, His wisdom, and His provision. In my own life, I can think of many instances when, shortly after seeing God's mighty work in my life, I began to worry about the future. How foolish! The Bible tells us that God is the same yesterday, today, and forever. His character never changes. He never forsakes us. Never.

The ten spies

These fearful, complaining ones, whom God graciously forgave, made what possibly might have been their greatest failure at the border of the Promised Land. When Moses sent out leaders from each tribe of Israel to spy out Canaan and to bring back some of the fruit of the land, the men returned after forty days with tales of well fortified cities and fearsome giants. Though the land was "flowing with milk and honey," it was certainly too dangerous a place to think about calling home. When the people heard this, they began to weep and wail through the night. In addition to tearfully wishing that they had died before getting to this scary place, they determined to choose a leader to take them back to Egypt!

> Then Moses and Aaron fell on their faces before all the assembly of the congregation of the children of Israel. And Joshua the son of Nun and Caleb the son of Jephunneh, who were among those who had spied out the land, tore their clothes; and they spoke to all the congregation of the children of Israel, saying: "The land we passed through to spy out is an exceedingly good land. If the Lord delights in us, then He will bring us into this land and give it to us, 'a land which flows with milk and honey.' Only do not rebel against the Lord, nor fear the people of the land, for they are our bread; their protection has departed from them, and the Lord is with us. Do not fear them." And all the congregation said to stone them with stones... Numbers 14:5–10

Scripture shows again a marvelous depiction of God's mercy and patience.

This was not a pretty picture, was it? It seems somewhat reminiscent of man's rebellion after the Fall (with God's provision of mercy) and man's rebellion after the Flood (with, again, God's provision of mercy). Now, in the same way, we see man's rebellion after the Exodus. It is the same thread of the sinfulness of man which we saw in the first chapter, intertwined with the thread of God's purpose for redemption, woven throughout each page of history. Though the children of Israel were ready to throw away obedience and pursue rebellion, this Scripture shows again a marvelous depiction of God's mercy and patience. He did not destroy them (which would have been a reasonable, human reaction at that point!), but continued to call them His own and to lead them faithfully. Pay attention, though, to the fact that He did not let them go into the Promised Land at that moment in time, even though that had been His original intention. In fact, after Moses communicated God's displeasure with the people, they said they were now sorry and were ready to take the Promised Land after all. Too late. The die had been cast. God told them that all of the people who were twenty years old and above would eventually die in the wilderness (except for Joshua and Caleb who believed Him). Because of their unbelief and murmuring, they would wander in the wilderness one year for every day that the spies had been in Canaan—forty years in all.

Exodus, Leviticus, Numbers, and Deuteronomy contain the account of the wanderings in the wilderness, as well as the Law of the Old Testament. It is a fascinating read, filled with the wildest things you've ever heard. Can you imagine following a huge cloud by day and a towering pillar of flame by night? What would it have been like to travel for forty years with such a massive bunch of whiners and complainers? Do you suppose it gradually got better as far as attitudes were concerned? Or, perhaps things improved as the older ones who didn't believe God died off! One way or another, they managed to muddle along through the barren wastelands, eating daily from God's own hand.

Entering the Promised Land

Finally, after forty years of camping out in the desert, we read these words:

> "Moses My servant is dead. Now therefore, arise, go over this Jordan, you and all this people, to the land which I am giving to them—the children of Israel. Every place that the sole of your foot will tread upon I have given you, as I said to Moses. . . . Be strong and of good courage, for to this people you shall divide as an inheritance the land which I swore to their fathers to give them." Joshua 1:2–3, 6

Can you imagine following a huge cloud by day and a towering pillar of flame by night?

Yahoo! School's over! Passing grades for all! Out of the desert and into real living!

Crossing the Jordan River and entering the Promised Land must have been one of the most amazing sensations of having "arrived" that any traveler has ever known. The only cloud on the horizon was the necessity of convincing all of the inhabitants that God had given the land of Canaan to the Israelites. And it took one of the most amazing miracles of God recorded in the Bible to accomplish that.

The city of Jericho was situated at a strategic location, acting as a fortified guard post into Canaan. Archaeological discoveries show that, though the city never got larger than twelve acres in size, its position and fortifications made it a formidable defensive weapon against intruders. So, what plan of attack did God give the children of Israel? Catapults and sieges? Ramming poles and ladders? Snipers and decoys? No, none of the above. In His painstaking method of teaching them that the battle belongs to the Lord (1 Samuel 17:47), God told them that their battle plan was to march around the city once a day for six days, with seven priests blowing ram's horn trumpets as they marched. On the seventh day, they were to march around the city seven times, and at the end of it, to shout. This unorthodox strategy would result, so they were told, in the city's walls falling down. Fortunately, Joshua and the children of Israel believed God could do what He promised, so they did just what they were told. The results, as they say, are history!

From that very promising beginning, the Israelites gradually occupied the land of Canaan. During the life of Joshua and the elders who served with him, the people obeyed the Lord and followed Him. However, shortly after that generation had died out, the children of Israel began to revert to old tricks—worshipping other gods and forsaking the One who had chosen them. You can read about this three hundred-plus years in the book of Judges, which has some fascinating stories including ones about Gideon and Samson.

Eventually, though, the people had had enough of depending on God to lead them and take care of them. They looked around at the other nations surrounding them and saw that those nations had something more enviable than an invisible God—they had a human king! And the Israelites began to beg God, through the prophet Samuel, for a king of their very own.

Thus began the Kingdom Years, the time of King Saul, King David, and King Solomon. Their stories range from giant killing to Temple building, from godly wisdom to raving insanity, from careful obedience to flaunting disobedience. During the time of Solomon, though other nations were powerful in their own right, Israel became distinguished among the nations as a place of wealth, grandeur, and unsearchable wisdom. From this rags-to-riches pinnacle of success, Israel soon plummeted to the depths of captivity and enslavement. That story, however, belongs to the next chapter.

Phase 1

Key People

Joshua
Leader who brought Israel into Canaan

Gideon
An unlikely warrior

Deborah
A woman who judged Israel

Samson
The strong man

King Saul
First king of Israel

King David
A man after God's own heart

King Solomon
The wisest man on earth

King Rehoboam
A foolish son

King Jeroboam
Did not believe God's word

Listen to This

What in the World? VOL. 1

DISC TWO:

» Abraham through Moses (track 4)

» Joshua through David (track 5)

» Solomon through Jeroboam (track 6)

True Tales VOL. 1

DISC THREE:

» The Hittites (track 1)

Look at This

» The Walls of Jericho—Archaeology Confirms: They Really DID Come a-tumblin' Down (www.answersingenesis.org/go/jericho)

» False History—"Out with David and Solomon!" (www.answers-ingenesis.org/go/david-solomon)

Read for Your Life

The Holy Bible

» The Main Story: Short Version—Joshua 24; 1 Samuel 12, 16–17; 2 Samuel 7; 1 Kings 3, 11–12. Long Version—Joshua; Judges; 1 & 2 Samuel; 1 Kings; 2 Kings 1–14; 1 Chronicles; 2 Chronicles 1–27

» Other Helpful Verses: Psalms, Proverbs

Talk Together

Opinion Column

» What did you find to be the most interesting aspect, or the most fascinating person, you encountered in your introduction to the children of Israel?

» What do you think God's intention was for the children of Israel when He gave them the Ten Commandments? How do you think they function in our lives and our society today?

» Joshua was one of twelve men who had spied out the land promised by God to the children of Israel. But of the twelve, only Joshua and Caleb came back with an enthusiastic, God-fearing report. All of the others spoke glowingly of the natural resources but were terrified of the fierce people populating Canaan. They warned the people that if they tried to go into the land, they would be destroyed. If you had been one of those delivered out of Egypt, what would you have thought about these conflicting reports?

Critical Puzzling

» Considering the trade routes, which pass through the Kingdom of Israel, what do you think God had in mind when He chose that geographic location for His chosen people?

» Consider whether God's "military strategy" for Jericho was the normal strategy for besieging a city. What made it effective, and do you think that it is repeatable today?

» During the period of the Judges of Israel, why do you think the nation suffered so many difficulties?

» In 1 Samuel 16, we see Samuel anointing a young, unknown man as king over Israel. Verse 7 tells us something significant about the difference between how we see people and how God sees people. What can you learn from this about God's ways?

» In the Psalms, David shares everything from dark despair to exultant victory. How did David's attitude toward God make a difference in his various situations?

» Why do you think King Solomon turned away from God after having received so much? What can we learn from this for our own lives?

Resources for Digging Deeper

Choose a few books that look interesting, or find your own.

ISRAEL

Halley's Bible Handbook

Henry H. Halley • This book contains wonderful study helps and insights related to the Old and New Testaments. It includes archaeological explanations from a Biblical perspective. (However, the archaeologists' findings in the Fertile Crescent are interpreted to mean that the Flood was a localized event.) **UE+**

The New Unger's Bible Handbook

Merrill F. Unger, revised by Gary Larson • This is my preferred source for information and insight on the archaeological record from a Biblical perspective. It is filled with color pictures, timelines, notes, helps, and exciting tidbits! **UE+**

Victor Journey Through the Bible

V. Gilbert Beers • With photos, maps, and charts and brief articles, this book gives an excellent enhancement to the reading of the Bible. **UE+**

The Daily Bible

Harvest House Publishers • Reading this Bible was our basic introduction to the concept of studying ancient civilizations and the Bible. It is set up chronologically with wonderful insights into the history of the Scriptures. **UE+**

The Works of Josephus

Since one of Josephus's purposes was to explain the history of Israel, this is an excellent (although difficult) resource for studying this subject. **HS+**

A Family Guide to the Biblical Holidays

Robin Sampson & Linda Pierce • A wonderful resource for celebrating the feasts of Israel in your family. Many helpful ideas and suggestions—an excellent addition to this study. **AA**

Dance, Sing, Remember A CELEBRATION OF JEWISH HOLIDAYS

Leslie Kimmelman • Written and illustrated for children, this is a delightful book. Discover recipes, games, history and more. **E+**

Student Bible Atlas

Tim Dowley • A Bible atlas is an indispensable tool in understanding the history of the children of Israel. This particular one is excellent for students. **AA**

Then and Now

Stefania Perring & Dominic Perring • The ruins of ancient civilizations, including Israel, will come to life for your family as you see the artist's rendition of what it once looked like superimposed over the ruin that now exists. See Masada, Jerusalem and more! **UP+**

TRADE

Video Series: That the World May Know

Focus on the Family • Both an incredible introduction to the Holy Land and also valuable "faith lessons" from the history of this people. **AA**

Sold!—The Origins of Money & Trade

Runestone Press • Economics and trade routes had a mighty impact on cultures from earliest times. Learn more about how this worked, and then apply it to the country of Israel. **UE+**

What books did you like best?

____

____

____

____

____

For more books, use these Dewey Decimal numbers in your library:

Bible: #220

Ancient Palestine: #933

Judaism: #296

Also, look for biographies on the key people listed.

The Internet also contains a wealth of information about the children of Israel.

What sites were the most helpful?

____

____

____

____

Student Self-Evaluation UNIT 4, PHASE 1

Dates and hours:____________________

Key Concepts

Rephrase the five Key Concepts of this Unit and confirm your understanding of each:

- Strategic Location & God's Purpose

  Jericho and to enter the promiseland

- The Chronology

  Leaving egypt, 40 years in desert, finding Jericho

- The Glory waiting 40 years,

  God gave them the promise land

- The Divided Kingdom

  most people wanted to worship idoles

- Application

  ?

Tools for Self-Evaulation

Evaluate your personal participation in the discussions of this Phase. Bearing in mind that a good participant in a discussion is not always the most vocal participant, ask yourself these questions: Were you an active participant? Did you ask perceptive questions? Were you willing to listen to other participants of the discussion and draw out their opinions? Record your observations and how you would like to improve your participation in the future:

____

____

Every time period is too complex to be understood in one Phase of study. Evaluate your current knowledge of the time of the Children of Israel. What have you focused on so far? What are your weakest areas of knowledge?

____

____

Based on the evaluation of this introduction, project ahead what you would like to study more of in the following Phases:

____

Phase 2

Research & Reporting

Explore one or more of these areas to discover something significant!

The Ancient Kingdom

Find one of the books listed, or a book of your choice, for more information on the ancient kingdom of Israel. Report your findings.

Ancient Personalities

Compare and contrast Ruth and Rahab; Samson and Gideon; Samuel and Eli.

The Temple

Research the temple of Solomon. Report on the funding, the materials, the building of the temple, as well as the use or abuse of it in history.

Archaeology

Research and write about what archaeologists have uncovered in the digs of Jericho, Ebla, Jerusalem, and Tell el Amarna. Remember that there are differing interpretations of the actual finds.

Trade Routes

Research and report on the ancient trade routes of the Middle East. What modes of transportation were used in this area? What have archaeologists learned about trade goods imported and exported? What was used for money? How did this impact Judah and Israel?

Consequences

Explore in Scripture the consequences of obedience and disobedience in Israel's history. Can you extrapolate from this to your own society?

Phoenicia

Learn about Phoenicia, its cities, export, navigation, trade routes, and relation to Israel. What new process did the Phoenicians bring to writing? Hiram was king of Tyre during Solomon's reign. What did he do for Israel?

Timeline

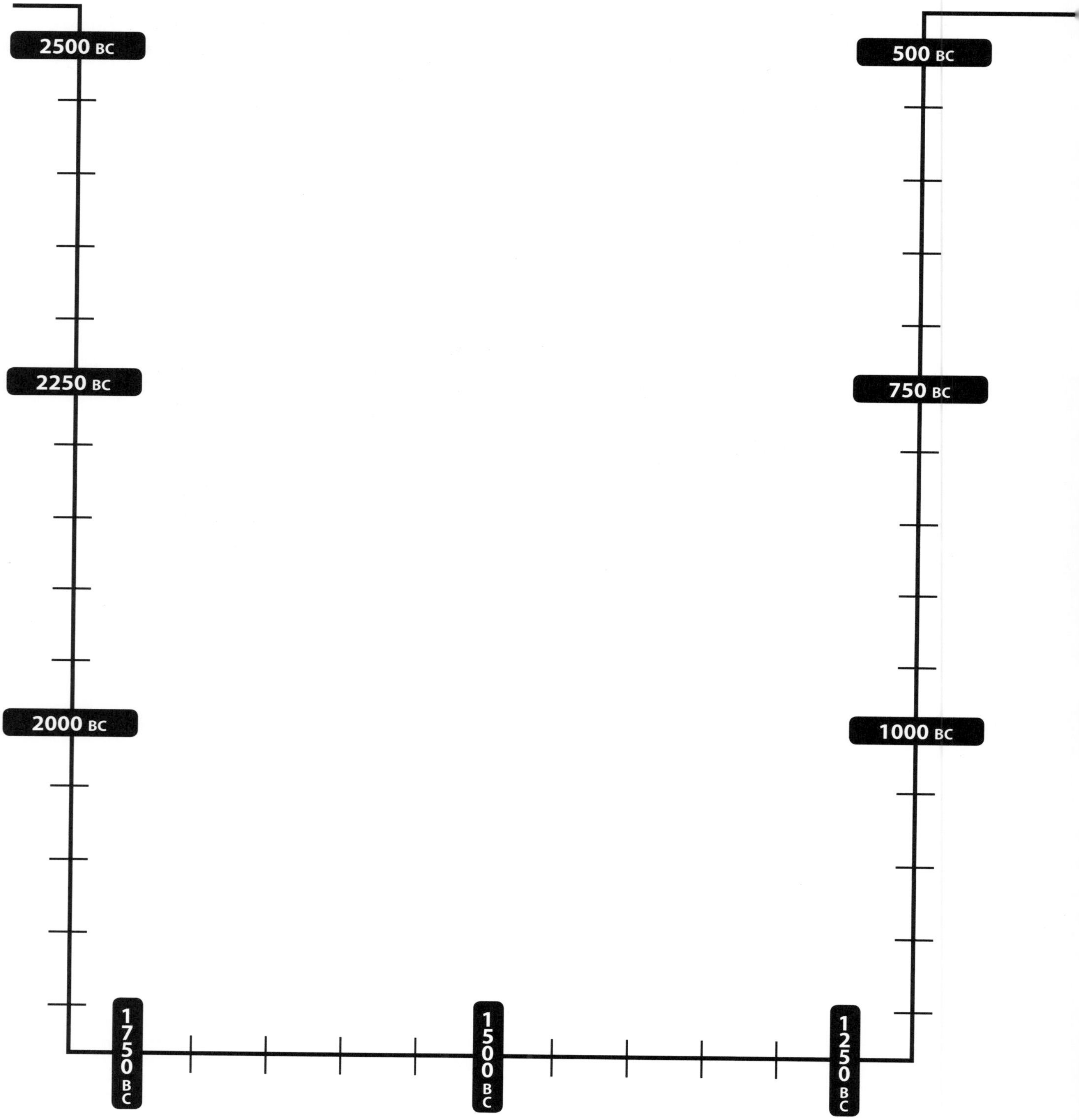
2500 BC
2250 BC
2000 BC
1750 BC
1500 BC
1250 BC
1000 BC
750 BC
500 BC

Consider this for your timeline

The historians and archaeologists who do not believe the Bible is without error see no evidence of the Conquest or even of King Saul or King David. As we discovered in the previous chapter, the archaeological evidence that has been considered lacking may, in fact, be widely available—if they look for it in a different archaeological time period than has been accepted up until now. With David Rohl's new Egyptian chronology, exciting possibilities have been suggested concerning correspondence found at Tell El Amarna written to the Pharaoh of Egypt by King Saul of Israel! That, along with the verification of the fall of Jericho in the exact manner described by the Scriptures (researched most extensively by Kathleen Kenyon who, unfortunately, did not recognize the involvement of the Hebrews in the destruction of the city due to the previously accepted dating of the fall of Jericho), give Bible students a whole new confidence in the accurate dating of what the Bible has so carefully described.

Key Events

- The Conquest
- Division of the Kingdom
- Kings of Northern Kingdom
- Kings of Southern Kingdom

Be sure to include the people listed in Key People in Phase 1.

Brain Stretchers

North versus South

Do a research paper with photos or illustrations on the differences between the northern kingdom of Israel and the southern kingdom of Judah. Include geographical, political, economic, and religious differences. Using the Scriptures, determine why there are differences. What is the biblical explanation?

The Neighbors

Discover the geographical boundaries of the neighboring countries (such as Phoenicia, Philistia, Moab, Edom, etc.). Who were the founders of these nations? What part did Egypt play in the politics of the area during the time of the Kingdom? Make a diagram showing the who, where, when, and how of these allies and enemies.

From Conquest to Current

Investigate, in the library or on the Internet, the history of Israel from the time of Joshua to the present. Use maps to show the dispersion throughout the world of the Hebrew people, and trace the persecution that often followed them. Consider what prophetic Scriptures have been fulfilled in their history.

Create Your Own Research Topic

____

____

____

Words to Watch

Remember—The easiest way to learn a subject is to master its terms:

conquest	temple	tabernacle	tribute
alliance	angel	monarchy	theocracy
prophet	anoint	Philistines	Jericho
Jerusalem	Jordan river	Gilgal	Gaza
Lachish	Canaan	idolatry	talent
shekel	Pentateuch	Talmud	Torah
tell (tel)	Ark of the Covenant		

Other words you need to look up:

____

____

____

____

Student Self-Evaluation UNIT 4, PHASE 2

Dates and hours:________________________

Research Project

- Summarize your research question:

  ____

  ____

- List your most useful sources by author, title, and page number or URL where applicable (continue list in margin if necessary):

  ____

  ____

  ____

Now take a moment to evaluate the sources you just listed. Do they provide a balanced view of your research question? Should you have sought an additional opinion? Are your sources credible (if you found them on your own)? Record your observations:

____

____

Evaluate your research project in its final presentation. What are its strengths? If you had time to revisit this project, what would you change? Consider giving yourself a letter grade based on your project's merits and weaknesses.

____

____

Letter grade: _____

You have just completed an area of specific research in the time of the Children of Israel. Now what would you like to explore in the upcoming Phases? Set some objectives for yourself:

____

Phase 3

Maps and Mapping

Physical Terrain

» Label and color the Jordan river.

» Label and color the Sea of Galilee and the Dead Sea.

» Draw in and color the mountain ranges, deserts, and green areas.

Geopolitical

» Place Jerusalem, Bethlehem, Jericho, Tyre, and Sidon on the map.

» What countries (both ancient and modern) are they located in?

» Color in the Valley of Jezreel, Jabbok River, Plain of Sharon, and the Golan Heights.

» Draw the boundaries of the northern Kingdom of Israel and the southern Kingdom of Judah.

Explore

» ***Dissemination:*** Israel is in a strikingly strategic geographic location when one examines the trade routes of antiquity. Consider together the different people groups who would travel through Israel. What would be the trickle down effect of the stories of the faithfulness and power of the God of the Hebrews disseminating throughout different lands? Who do you think would hear these stories? How far away could this news travel, given the trade routes?

» ***Christian Outreach:*** What is the unique position of Christianity to the people of Israel? What is the status of Christian outreach at this time? Discuss the difficulties and the potential solutions for Christians seeking to serve God in this land.

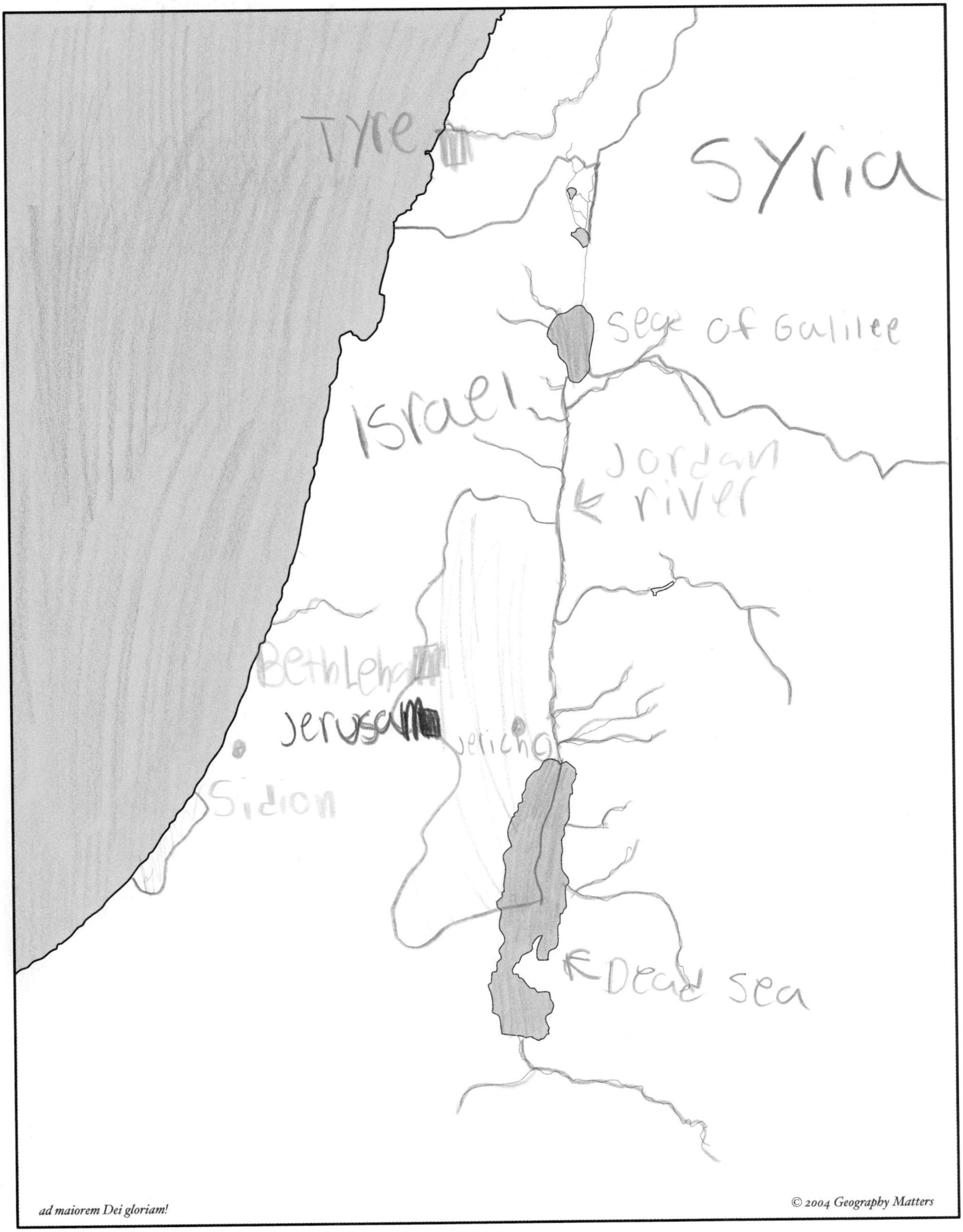
Tyre
Syria
Sea of Galilee
Israel
Jordan river
Jericho
Sidion
Dead sea
ad maiorem Dei gloriam!
© 2004 Geography Matters

CONSIDER:

Peter Paul Rubens (1577–1640 AD) was highly educated, and was considered to be one of the most intellectual artists of the seventeenth century. He worked both as an international diplomat and an artist—quite an unusual combination! A wealthy and influential painter of the Baroque style, Rubens was a master of communicating movement in art.

Art Appreciation

The Judgment of Solomon by Peter Paul Rubens

- » What does this painting communicate to you about Solomon?
- » How does the painting differ from your own impression of this historic event?
- » How would you describe Rubens's use of color and movement in this scene?

The artwork in the Tabernacle *(Read Exodus 25–27)* and Solomon's Temple *(Read 2 Chronicles 3–4)*

- » How would you describe the artistry of the Tabernacle or Solomon's Temple, including the colors, textures, and design?
- » What does this tell you about the value God places on beauty and artistic endeavors?

Architecture

The Temple in Jerusalem, which King Solomon built, was similar in its layout to the Tabernacle, but it was greatly increased in size and splendor. According to 2 Chronicles 3, the inside ceiling was fifty feet high, one hundred eighty feet long, and ninety feet wide. The tallest point on the Temple was twenty stories high! The structure itself was rectangular, surrounded by open courtyards. It had the inner "Holy of Holies," with a large outer hallway in front containing two huge columns of bronze. The inner sanctuary and altar were overlaid with gold, as were the carved doors. It was one of the most monumental and impressive buildings of that time period, but when Nebuchadnezzar invaded Jerusalem nearly four hundred years later, Solomon's Temple was utterly destroyed.

- » Look for an artist's rendition of Solomon's Temple online or in a book. How would you describe this amazing building?

Arts in Action

Select one or more, and let your artistic juices flow!

Imitation

Try your hand at imitating Rubens (trace, follow colors, etc.)

Costuming

Try making biblical costumes for your "reenacting" of Bible scenes. (I highly recommend *Bible Time Crafts for Kids* by Neva Hickerson, as it is filled with wonderful costumes, crafts, musical instruments, etc., that are easy to make!)

Psalm 23

Depict King David's Psalm 23 through art. What expression does the shepherd have on his face? Try to capture all of the elements of this Psalm.

Fabric Dying

The Phoenicians exported a purple dye that was extraordinarily expensive (one drop of dye from each mollusk!). Try dying fabric using a natural source, like beets or tea, for dye. Check the library for information.

Make the Temple

Make a model of Solomon's Temple. You could construct it from papier maché; fabric over a dowel; clay; bread dough; or whatever you prefer.

Working with Wool

- See if you can find someone who spins wool. After observing, you may want to ask to try it. (It's not as easy as it looks!)
- Once the wool is spun, it can be made into various articles of clothing through weaving, knitting, or crocheting. This is a great time to learn how to do any of these. Check the library for how-to books and start with a VERY simple project.

Papier-Maché Map

For an eye-opening adventure in geography, make a papier maché map of Israel including the Jordan River, the Sea of Galilee, the Dead Sea, the mountains and plains, plus the Desert of Zin, the Desert of Paran, and the Desert of Shur.

Science

Sheep

» Field Trip: Visit a farm with sheep, or a petting zoo. Ask lots of questions about the care of sheep, the way the wool is removed, what the wool can be used for, etc. If you can touch the fleece, rub the wool in your fingers for a few minutes. What ingredient is in the sheep wool, which makes your fingers soft?

Fermentation

» Chemistry: Learn how grapes are grown and then turned into wine or vinegar. What is the process? Try an experiment with some type of fermentation (make sure Mom knows what you left in the pantry!).

Music

Consider

» The Bible is filled with references to musical instruments and singing in ancient Israel, both of which were used in the joyful worship of God. The Psalms were all meant to be sung. Many even have comments telling which instruments were to accompany! There were professional musicians employed in the worship at the Temple, and Scripture indicates that these musicians were to be skilled.

» One of the most incredible stories in the Old Testament is found in 2 Chronicles 20:1–30. It tells of a very unique task for musicians—to go into battle, before the army, worshiping and praising God! Read this account out loud for the whole class or family, and then stand and sing together the Doxology.

DOXOLOGY

Praise God from whom all blessings flow,

Praise Him all creatures here below,

Praise Him above, ye heavenly host,

Praise Father, Son, and Holy Ghost.

Try This

» Do you know any worship hymns or choruses using Psalms? Have each student look through the Psalms, and when anyone recognizes the words to a familiar song, sing it. Some of you may know Psalm 125, Psalm 89, Psalm 63, or Psalm 34.

» You may also want to try singing a Psalm with your own melody, such as a folk tune or Christmas carol. Start with one line or verse.

» This is a family favorite (to the tune of "Short'ning Bread"):

- You have dealt well with Your servant,
O Lord, according to Your word. Psalm 119:65

Cooking

God told His chosen people that He was taking them to a land flowing with milk and honey. In order to really understand how wonderful milk and honey are, we are going to make Yogurt Cake with Honey Frosting. Thank you, Lord!

Yogurt Cake with Honey Frosting

1 cup butter
2 cups sugar
4 eggs, separated (room temp)
1 cup yogurt (plain)
3 cups flour
¼ tsp salt
4 tsp baking powder
3 tsp lemon extract

Cream butter and sugar together until light and fluffy. Add the egg yolks one at a time, beating until creamy and light. Stir in yogurt. Add flour, salt, baking powder, lemon extract. Mix well. Beat egg whites until stiff but not dry, and mix one-third into batter. Fold in remaining egg whites. Turn into a 10" tube pan and bake in preheated 350 degree oven for about 60 minutes, or until done.

Frosting

½ cup honey
2 egg whites, room temp.
¼ tsp salt
⅛ tsp cream of tartar

Bring honey to boil in saucepan. Beat egg whites until frothy, add salt and cream of tartar, continue to beat. When egg whites hold soft peaks, slowly add honey in a thin stream. Continue to beat until meringue is stiff and glossy. Frost cake when cool.

Student Self-Evaluation UNIT 4, PHASE 3

Dates and hours:____________________

Evaluate Your Projects

- List which of the activities listed in this Phase you did:

  ____

  ____

  ____

- Rate your enthusiasm: __________

  Explain: ____________________________________

  ____

- Rate the precision of your approach:__________

  Explain: ____________________________________

  ____

- Rate your effort toward the completion of the project: __________

  Explain: ____________________________________

  ____

Ask yourself what worked and what did not. What would you do differently in the future, and what would you repeat?

____

How specifically did these hands-on activities enhance your knowledge of the Children of Israel? What made them worthwhile?

____

In the first three Phases of this Unit, what aspect of the time period has most captured your imagination? What would you like to creatively pursue to conclude your study?

____

Phase 4

In Your Own Way . . .

We have seen the amazing way God cared for His people in the land of Israel, even when they walked in rebellion. Now, choose a selection of these activities, or create your own, which will best express what you have learned from this unit. Finally, pray for the peace of Jerusalem, and for your own nation.

LINGUISTICS

Journalism

Be a newspaper reporter for the *Desert Sun Times*, and give the exclusive inside scoop on the spies who came back from Canaan.

Prose

- Write a fictional account of an Israelite named "Benjamin the Skeptic" on the sixth and seventh day of the march around Jericho.
- Consider journaling in the style of the Psalms. Let God know what is on your heart, but remember, as David did, God's faithfulness.

Playing with Words

- The Alphabet Game: One person starts with the letter *A*.They must name a word that pertains to this unit beginning with *A* (such as "Ark of the Covenant".) The next person gives a word beginning with *B* (like "Benjamin"). Keep the game going through all of the letters, extra credit given for *X* and *Z*. How did you do? (Variation: In a family or small group of students, have each one use the same letter, and then everyone advances to the next letter.)
- Finish this limerick about Hiram:
  "There was a great king from Tyre,
  Who sent out his craftsmen for hire. . . ."

Poetry

In the style of David, compose a Psalm of thanksgiving to God. (Psalm 100 is a good example.)

Script writing

- Write a script that highlights the most important events during these 600 years of Israel's history, using vignettes of characters to tell the story.
- Write a funny monologue for Solomon, entitled "Life with Seven Hundred Wives."

ART

Painting/Drawing

Create an artistic rendering of the scene where Moses receives the Ten Commandments.

Political Cartooning

Show Rehoboam's decision to make life more difficult for the twelve tribes—and the unfortunate results.

Set Design

The Feast of Tabernacles is an incredibly artistic holiday! Make Succoth booths outside, prepare festive food, and invite your family, friends, and church over to help you celebrate God's wonderful provision for His people.

MUSIC

Compose

Write lyrics to a tune of your choosing about the Queen of Sheba coming to visit King Solomon. A good starting place might be the tune, "She'll Be Coming Round the Mountain."

Sing Ethnic

There are some wonderful Jewish songs, which could be learned and then sung. "Hava Nagila" is an example.

Performance Practice

With your teacher's help, select an appropriate piece of music written by a Jewish composer like Mendelssohn, or a piece with Jewish content. Prepare and perform the piece for an audience. Communicate with your audience the reason for your selection either in the program notes or in a short speech.

DRAMA

Comedy

Do a humorous skit about Gideon and his army.

Puppetry

Using puppets, act out the script listed above, using a narrator, worship songs, and quick scene changes.

Reality

Act out the story of the twelve spies. Use your imagination to create props, sets, and costumes. Be sure to include the results for the twelve and the results for the two!

Prop Needs

____

____

Costume Ideas

____

____

Role/Player

____

____

Set Suggestions

____

____

MOVEMENT

Pantomime

Pantomime the scene with King David bringing the Ark to Jerusalem.

Dance

Learn a Jewish folk dance, like the Horah.

Action

With a small group, design an action scene showing how Gideon was able to defeat the enemies of Israel. You may want to start from the scene where Gideon is in the winepress!

CONCEPTUAL DESIGN

Game Design

Design a board game to teach younger children about the history of Israel, from the time of Joshua through the division of the Kingdom. Your game board could show the geographic features of Israel, such as the mountains, the Jordan River, the Sea of Galilee, the Dead Sea, the Plain of Sharon, and whatever features would be useful in learning the history of this ancient people.

CREATE YOUR OWN EXPRESSION

Student Self-Evaluation UNIT 4, PHASE 4

Dates and hours:________________________

Evaluate Your Projects

- What creative project did you choose:

____

- What did you expect from your project, and how does the final project compare to your initial expectations?

____

____

- What do you like about your project? What would you change?

____

____

In Conclusion

Revisit the five Key Concepts from the beginning of this Unit. Explain how your understanding of and appreciation for each has grown over the course of your study.

____

____

____

____

____

____

Record your concluding thoughts on the Children of Israel:

____

____

____

Assyria & Babylon

UNIT 5

Key Concepts

- Jonah & Assyria
- Judgment of Israel
- Discovery of Nineveh
- Prophets & Babylon
- Babylonian Captivity

Winged bull of Assyria

Into captivity...

From the northeast part of Mesopotamia, on the banks of the Tigris River, arose a mighty nation of conquering warriors who would eventually become both a watchword among the nations for cruelty, as well as participants in the greatest revival ever witnessed.

In the southeast part of Mesopotamia, on the banks of the Euphrates River, came a king from a powerful empire both to triumphantly destroy Jerusalem and to discover God's power humbling the greatest of kings.

Two gentile nations, two conquering empires, both from the cradle of Mesopotamia: Assyria and Babylon take their place now on the stage of world history. Each find, in their own specific situation and moment of time, that the Hebrew God is more powerful than any god they have worshipped, and some willingly choose to worship Him.

5

Beginning in 2 Kings 15, we see the convergence of Israel with the Assyrians, and it is not a pretty picture, at least, not for the Israelites. How did they end up in such dire circumstances after having experienced the magnificence of Solomon's reign? What brought about such a complete reversal?

The answer lies in 1 Kings 11:9–13:

> So the Lord became angry with Solomon, because his heart had turned from the Lord God of Israel, who had appeared to him twice, and had commanded him concerning this thing, that he should not go after other gods; but he did not keep what the Lord had commanded. Therefore the Lord said to Solomon, "Because you have done this, and have not kept My covenant and My statutes,which I have commanded you, I will surely tear the kingdom away from you and give it to your servant. Nevertheless I will not do it in your days, for the sake of your father David; but I will tear it out of the hand of your son. However I will not tear away the whole kingdom, but I will give one tribe to your son for the sake of my servant David, and for the sake of Jerusalem which I have chosen.'"

Assyria and Babylon take their place now on the stage of world history.

Division of Israel

After the death of Solomon, his son Rehoboam very foolishly decided to ignore the counsel of his father's wise men, choosing to take the advice of his peers and show the people who was boss. Most of them responded by leaving him and following Solomon's former servant, Jereboam. Jereboam went north into the region of Galilee, while Rehoboam stayed with Jerusalem and the Temple. From this point, the nation was divided into Israel in the north and Judah in the south. Jereboam, fearing that his fickle followers would switch sides if they returned to offer sacrifices in the Temple, made two calves of gold and told the people they no longer needed to go to Jerusalem. They could stay in the north to worship because these calves were the ones that had brought them out of Egypt! Things went downhill for Israel from that point.

Though the people had turned away from God, He kept calling them back to Himself. Elijah and Elisha kept confronting the people with the preeminence of the Lord, in such momentous events as when Elijah called for a showdown between the prophets of Baal and the Lord. But even with that vivid demonstration of God's reality, the people would not permanently abandon their rebellion. The prophets Amos and Hosea brought the word of the Lord to the northern kingdom by warning them that impending judgment for sin was imminent. Along with the warning came the promise that God would turn from His wrath if they would quit offering themselves in worship to other gods.

> "I will heal their backsliding, I will love them freely, for My anger has turned away from him. . . . Ephraim shall say, 'What have I to do anymore with idols?'" Hosea 14:4, 8

As we shall soon see, however, the people of Israel did not take the warning of the prophets to heart. They continued to walk in disobedience and disregard of the God who had rescued and redeemed them from slavery.

> "I taught Ephraim to walk, taking them by their arms; but they did not know that I healed them. I drew them with gentle cords, with bands of love, and I was to them as those who take the yoke from their neck. I stooped and fed them. He shall not return to the land of Egypt; but the Assyrian shall be his king, because they refused to repent."
> Hosea 11:3–5

Though the people had turned away from God, He kept calling them back to Himself.

Beginning in 2 Kings 24, the southern kingdom of Judah comes into catastrophic contact with the other Mesopotamian empire, Babylon, as God's judgment on their sin unfolds. How was it that they did not learn the lesson of listening to God and obeying Him when they saw what happened to Israel? Much of the answer lies in the character qualities of their kings. In Judah, there were bad kings interspersed with good kings. Some of the kings, including Hezekiah and Josiah, served the Lord with gladness and the people followed them. Other kings encouraged the worship of false gods, even to the point of sacrificing their own children in hideous religious ceremonies, and the people followed them, as well. Since God's judgment is usually delayed, people begin to think they can do whatever they want without suffering consequences, especially when their leaders are leading the way.

Judgment of Israel

As in the case of Israel, God sent the people of Judah warning after warning over a period of more than a hundred years. He spoke of impending judgment through the prophets Joel, Isaiah, Micah, Zephaniah, Jeremiah, and Habakkuk. However, the people of Judah did not return to the Lord to serve Him alone. Because of the increasing apostasy of the nation, Jeremiah prophesied that King Nebuchadnezzar would take them captive to the land of Babylon. Mercifully, it was not to be a permanent removal from the land of Palestine:

> "For thus says the Lord: After seventy years are completed at Babylon, I will visit you and perform My good word toward you, and cause you to return to this place. For I know the thoughts that I think toward you, says the Lord, thoughts of peace and not of evil, to give you a future and a hope."
> Jeremiah 29:10–11

If you read any of these prophets, you will hear over and over again God's heart of yearning for His people. Though He can not let their rebellion and sin continue forever in the land, He longs for them to repent and be healed rather than face well-deserved judgment. Though they spit in His face by worshipping false and worthless gods, He still loves them and seeks their restoration. What an amazing God He is! The Scripture helps us understand this mystery a little better when it says,

> "For My thoughts are not your thoughts, nor are your ways My ways," says the Lord. "For as the heavens are higher than the earth, so are My ways higher than your ways, and My thoughts than your thoughts." Isaiah 55:8–9

His lovingkindness and mercy, and His wisdom and justice, go far beyond human ability or thought. At this particular moment in history, His mercy and His judgment allowed His people to be both warned and, eventually, punished. Even in punishment, though, there was hope for the future.

> "I will bring back the captives of My people Israel; they shall build the waste cities and inhabit them; they shall plant vineyards and drink wine from them; they shall also make gardens and eat fruit from them. I will plant them in their land, and no longer shall they be pulled up from the land I have given them," says the Lord your God. Amos 9:14–15

The people of Judah did not return to the Lord to serve Him alone.

So, who were these Mesopotamian conquerors, these nations used by God to accomplish His judgment on Israel and Judah? How did they rise to prominence in the earth? And what were their distinguishing characteristics?

The Assyrian people were warriors, hardened by the constant threat of attack from the mountainous tribes of the north, and made wealthy by their great conquests. Their greatest capital city, Nineveh, was the place of Jonah's message and the resulting revival. The Babylonians, by contrast, were the commercial center of the Near East, facilitating trade with the Middle East, Asia, and Africa through roads and the national "highway"—the Euphrates River. Great commerce brings great wealth, and Babylon—the most magnificent city of the ancient world—was visible proof of this.

Because both of these empires emerged out of Mesopotamia, birthplace to the earlier Sumerian and Akkadian nations, they share some characteristics, such as similarity in language and art. But, much as two brothers can struggle for the upper hand, so did Assyria and Babylon struggle for mastery over their lands and each other.

Here is a brief accounting of the most important Assyrian and Babylonian rulers and events, especially those who are mentioned in Scripture, or who connect archaeology to the Bible.

Old Babylonian Empire

- **Hammurabi** (reigned c. 1792–1750 BC): The most famous of Babylon's earliest rulers, this great king of the Old Babylonian Empire produced a code of 285 laws which dealt with everything from real estate to trade, from the family to personal property. There are modern scholars who, because they do not recognize the veracity of the biblical account, believe that Moses derived the Ten Commandments from Hammurabi's Code. This helps them explain away the profound wisdom of God's law. Hammurabi conquered the neighboring nations, forging an empire, which lasted just a short time after his death.

Assyrian Empire

- **Tiglath Pileser I** (reigned c. 1115–1077 BC): Assyria's rise to prominence began under this man. He was a fierce warrior and a terrifying enemy. He conquered not only Babylon but the Hittites, the Armenians, and forty other nations. Egypt sent him gifts, including a crocodile, to pacify and keep this conqueror out of their territory. He built many temples and palaces with the wealth of his conquests, but at the end of his reign, the Babylonians revolted and took his man-made gods back to Babylon.
- **Assunasirpal II** (884–859 BC): The Assyrians, after a few hundred years of decline, began a new campaign of conquest under this king. He restored the lands which had been lost to the Assyrian Empire and encouraged trade all the way to the Mediterranean.
- **Shalmaneser III** (858–824 BC): He continued to expand the Empire all the way to Damascus, killing 16,000 Syrians in one battle, and receiving tribute from lesser kings and nations.
- From 824 BC until 747 BC, there was a series of weak kings in Assyria, who could not prevent the empire from going into decline. It was during this time, in approximately 771 BC, that Jonah reluctantly went to Nineveh to take the word of the Lord to the Ninevites. Their reputation for cruelty to enemies was known to Jonah, and he loathed the thought of God forgiving them if they repented. However, God's mercy continued to shine out of the pages of the Old Testament, as He relented from destroying their city when they cried out to Him.
- **Tiglath Pileser III** (also known as Pul) (747–728 BC): The Assyrian king who brought the prophecies of Amos and Hosea to pass, he took most of the northern kingdom of Israel captive. The policy of the Assyrian kings was to remove the people of a land and replace them

The Assyrian people were warriors, hardened by the constant threat of attack from the mountainous tribes of the north, and made wealthy by their great conquests.

with foreigners from other conquered lands. This is described in 2 Kings 17:24:

> Then the king of Assyria brought people from Babylon, Cuthah, Ava, Hamath, and from Sepharvaim, and placed them in the cities of Samaria instead of the children of Israel; and they took possession of Samaria and dwelt in its cities.

- **Shalmaneser V** (728–717 BC): 2 Kings 17:3 says that Shalmaneser V, who has often been confused with an earlier king of the same name, came up against Hoshea, king of Israel in Samaria and Hoshea became his vassal, paying him tribute. Then, in 721 BC, he captured Samaria because Hoshea had stopped paying tribute. Shalmaneser had this inscribed at his royal palace in Khorsabad, "I besieged and captured Samaria, carrying off 27,290 of the people who dwelt therein." He also reconquered Babylon and defeated Egypt, leading his troops personally.
- **Sennacherib** (717–710 BC): The son of Shalmaneser, Sennacherib completely destroyed Babylon, burning it to the ground and killing nearly all of the inhabitants. In his conquests, he captured 80,000 oxen, 800,000 sheep, and 208,000 prisoners. With this infusion of capital, he renovated the city of Nineveh, which remained the premiere city in the empire until its destruction at the hands of the Babylonians and Medes.
- **Esarhaddon** (681–668 BC): One of the sons of Sennacherib, he invaded Egypt and made it a province of Assyria, and then went on to rebuild the city of Babylon, which made him popular with the inhabitants of that nation. Before his death, he made Assyria the master of the entire Near East.
- **Ashurbanipal** (668–648 BC): The prosperity of Assyria continued and grew during the reign of this king. When Ashurbanipal's palace was excavated in the mid-1800s, a library of unprecedented proportions came to light with more than 30,000 clay tablets dealing with such subjects as medicine, religion, history, and literature. With the end of Ashurbanipal's reign, the Assyrian Empire declined, until it was completely overthrown by the Babylonians in 626 BC with the destruction of the great city of Nineveh.

New Babylonian Empire

- **Nabopolassar** (626–605 BC): This conquering leader founded the New Babylonian Empire, as well as led the Babylonian army in the destruction of Nineveh.
- **Nebuchadnezzar II** (607–562 BC): Nebuchadnezzar served as viceroy with his father, Nabopolassar, for 20 months. This was the ruler who

brought the Babylonian Empire and the city of Babylon to their greatest heights. Jeremiah prophesied about the role of Nebuchadnezzar in history:

> "And now I have given all these lands into the hand of Nebuchadnezzar the king of Babylon, My servant; and the beasts of the field I have also given him to serve him. So all nations shall serve him and his son and his son's son, until the time of his land comes; and then many nations and great kings shall make him serve them. And it shall be that the nation and kingdom which will not serve Nebuchadnezzar the king of Babylon, and which will not put its neck under the yoke of the king of Babylon, that nation I will punish," says the Lord, "with the sword, the famine, and the pestilence, until I have consumed them by his hand." Jeremiah 27:6–8

God takes this reluctant prince turned shepherd and turns him into a powerful leader.

Nebuchadnezzar started his conquests in 607 BC as he commanded the Babylonian army against the Egyptians in the battle of Carchemish. He also came to Jerusalem and made King Jehoiakim his vassal, taking some of the most promising young men of Judah, such as Daniel, back to Babylon. He ascended the throne as sole king in 605 BC, and reigned for forty-three years. Though he preferred to stay in his capital city, he was not adverse to personally dealing with rebellious subjects. That is why he went back to Jerusalem in December 600 BC. The teenage king, Jehoiachin, was captured along with his mom, his wives, his officers, his craftsmen, and the mighty men of the land, and taken back to Babylon. Nebuchadnezzar placed a new king, Zedekiah, on the throne. Zedekiah, neither listening to the wisdom of the Lord in the prophets, nor learning a lesson from the previous king's experience, formed an alliance against Babylon with Egypt. When Nebuchadnezzar learned of this treachery, he determined to destroy Jerusalem and remove her last king. This was accomplished with a severe finality by 588 BC. Solomon's Temple was destroyed, the city walls were broken down, the houses of the rich and mighty were torched, and the rest of the inhabitants of Jerusalem were taken back to Babylon, leaving only a few of the poorest to farm the land.

This mighty ruler was a significant player in God's plan. In fact, it was Nebuchadnezzar who had the famous dream of a great statue, which Daniel then saw in prayer and interpreted. He told the troubled king that this image, with its "head of fine gold, its chest and arms of silver, its belly and thighs of bronze, its legs of iron, its feet partly of iron and partly of clay" described four kingdoms which would rule on the earth, with the first kingdom being his own:

> "You, O king, are a king of kings. For the God of heaven has given you a kingdom, power, strength, and glory; and wherever the children of men dwell, or the beasts of the field and the birds of the heaven, He has given them into your hand,

and has made you ruler over them all—you are this head of gold." Daniel 2:37–38

Daniel went on to describe three more conquering kingdoms in this dream, which we learn later in the book of Daniel are the kingdoms of the Persians & Medes, the Greeks, and finally, the Romans. These kingdoms are described with such detailed accuracy, that modern critics say it could not have been written in the mid-500s BC, but must have been written in 165 BC (after Antiochus Epiphanes desecrated the Temple in Jerusalem in 167 BC). In reality, however, God is able to give His servants wisdom and knowledge of the future. After all, God is the One, "declaring the end from the beginning, and from ancient times things that are not yet done, saying, 'My counsel shall stand, and I will do all My pleasure.'" Isaiah 46:10

This mighty ruler was a significant player in God's plan.

In the dream, these four kingdoms represented by the great statue were destroyed by a great stone, which then "became a great mountain and filled the whole earth" (Daniel 2:35). Daniel told the king: "And in the days of these kings the God of heaven will set up a kingdom which shall never be destroyed" (Daniel 2:44). By the end of this book, we will discover how truly this prophetic dream came true.

Evidently, Nebuchadnezzar agreed with God's assessment of him being a king of kings and a ruler over all, as most of the bricks which have been recovered from Babylon are stamped with these words: "I am Nebuchadnezzar, king of Babylon, son of Nabopolassar, king of Babylon." He went on to boast, "Is not this great Babylon, that I have built for a royal dwelling by my mighty power and for the honor of my majesty?" (Daniel 4:30). Scripture describes that at the moment of his greatest glory and pride, Nebuchadnezzar was humbled by going stark, raving mad for a period of seven years (most scholars agree that the time period mentioned was years.) When he came back to sanity, he began to praise and honor the God of the Jews. This experience has not been found in the official Babylonian records, but then, archaeologists have not recovered records for the last thirty-two years of Nebuchadnezzar's reign.

Assyrian royal guards from Nineveh

Beyond maintaining order in his empire and having dealings with the God of the Jews, Nebuchadnezzar finished the reconstruction of Babylon, which his father had envisioned and planned. The city of Babylon was in two sections, divided by the palm-fringed Euphrates River. Herodotus, the Greek historian who saw Babylon a hundred and fifty years after Nebuchadnezzar, said that the city was surrounded by an outer wall sixty miles in length, fifteen miles wide, 300 feet high, and 85 feet thick! Between the outer walls and inner walls was a wide moat, and people were only able to enter the city through eight huge bronze gates. It seemed impregnable, impossible to successfully invade. However, after the seventy years of captivity for the Jews was completed, the Persians took mighty Babylon in one night. How were they able to accomplish such a task? Though you can read the story in Daniel 5, the true reason behind the military success is this:

> "Blessed be the name of God forever and ever, for wisdom and might are His. And He changes the times and the seasons; *He removes kings and raises up kings;* He gives wisdom to the wise and knowledge to those who have understanding." Daniel 2:20–21

At the moment of his greatest glory and pride, he was humbled by going stark, raving mad for a period of seven years.

We have seen God's incredible mercy towards those who knew Him and towards those who did not know Him, His long-suffering towards Israel and Judah (and even Nebuchadnezzar!) with prophetic warnings of impending judgment so that they might repent, and His on-time delivery of His promises. What an awesome God!

Phase 1

Key People

Jonah
Reluctant Prophet to Assyria

Tiglath-Pileser III
Assyrian king who took part of Israel captive

Shalmaneser V
Assyrian king who took the rest of Israel captive

Sennacherib
Assyrian king who challenged God . . . and lost!

Hezekiah
Good king of Judah

Josiah
Good king of Judah

continued next page

Listen to This

What in the World? VOL. 1

DISC TWO:

» Jonah Goes to Nineveh (track 7)

DISC THREE:

» Assyria (track 1)

» Babylon (track 2)

True Tales VOL. 1

DISC THREE:

» The Discovery of Nineveh (track 2)

Digging Deeper VOL. 1

DISC TWO:

» The Seven Wonders of the Ancient World: Hanging Gardens of Babylon (track 3)

Look at This

» Evidentialism—The Bible and Assyrian Chronology (www.answersingenesis.org/go/assyria)

Read For Your Life

» The Main Story: Jonah; 2 Kings 17–18; 2 Chronicles 32:1–22; 2 Kings 20, 24–25; Daniel 1–5, 7–8.

» Other Helpful Verses: Nahum; Genesis 10:8–12; Isaiah 10:5–15; Isaiah 19:23–25; Isaiah 36–37; Micah 5:4–6; Zephaniah 2:13–15; Hosea 11:1–12; Psalm 137; Habakkuk, Micah.

Talk Together

Opinion Column

- What did you find to be the most interesting aspect, or the most fascinating person, you encountered in your introduction to Assyria and Babylon?
- Imagine you live inside Jerusalem during the reign of King Hezekiah. What will you think and what will you do when King Sennacherib of Assyria begins to threaten your city?
- Considering what you know about the life of Daniel and his three Hebrew companions, what do you think it would have been like to be one of the Judean captives taken to Babylon?
- Why do you think God kept showing King Nebuchadnezzar the future, and why did God allow him to see the three Hebrew children with the fourth "like a Son of Man" in the fiery furnace?
- When the prophet Jeremiah told the people to settle down in Babylon, build homes, and plant vineyards, they knew their time in captivity would not be short (Jeremiah 29:4–7). Imagine you are a Jewish mother or father of children born in Babylon. How would you describe what your homeland in Jerusalem had been like? What reasons would you give for the captivity?
- Why do you think that King Belshazzar ordered the vessels of gold from the Temple at Jerusalem to be used for his drunken party (Daniel 5)? What was the result?

Major & Minor Prophets
Warned Judah & Israel of coming destruction

Hammurabi
Early Babylonian king who reformed laws

Nebuchadnezzar II
Babylonian king who took Judah captive

Daniel
Hebrew advisor to King Nebuchadnezzar

Critical Puzzling

- » Why do you think God sent Jonah to Nineveh, and how did the revival at Nineveh impact the Assyrian nation?
- » Referring to Isaiah 7:17–20, what do you think God's purpose was at that time for the Assyrian people?
- » The relief sculptures on the palace walls at Nineveh show the king hunting lions. How is this similar to the biblical description of Nimrod? How might this indicate the attitude of the rulers towards their people?
- » Why do you think God called King Nebuchadnezzar, "My servant"? What does that tell us about the kind of people God can use for His purposes?
- » Read Habakkuk 3:16–19. What kind of response did Habakkuk have at the time of the invasion of Jerusalem, and how can you apply this to your life right now?
- » Babylon was the most magnificent city of antiquity, filled with the worship of false gods. What do you think it would have been like to be a worshipper of Jehovah living in this city?
- » Using the themes presented in Nahum 1:8 and Matthew 26:52, explain the connection you observe between Assyria's ways of warfare and its demise.

Resources for Digging Deeper

Choose a few books that look interesting, or find your own.

ARCHAEOLOGICAL FINDS OF ASSYRIA

Secrets of the Royal Mounds

Cynthia Jameson • This delightful book is the story of Austen Layard, a British adventurer in the mid-1800s, who was the first to discover the cities of Assyria. It's certainly worth the trouble to find, as it is written in a capture-your-interest style. **UE+**

Nineveh and Its Remains

Austen Henry Layard • Read a first-hand account of the unbelievable discovery of Nineveh in the mid-1800s. It is an amazing read for older students, and has recently been reprinted! **HS+**

The Assyrians

Elaine Landau • It is difficult to find books on the Assyrian time period which are appropriate for younger students. This is the best we have seen! **UE+**

Discoveries Among the Ruins of Nineveh

Austen Henry Layard • This is a fascinating first-person account of Layard's second dig at Nineveh. It was published in the mid-1800s, so it may be difficult to locate, but again, it's certainly worth the trouble. **HS+**

The Assyrians Activity Book

Lorna Oakes • Published by the British Museum, this is a book with great suggested activities, interesting articles to read, and fascinating pictures to color. **UE+**

Then and Now

Stefania Perring & Dominic Perring • One chapter of this great archaeological resource deals with Nimrud (known as Calah in the Bible), which was once the capital city of Assyria. **UE+**

POETRY

The Destruction of Sennacherib

Lord Byron • A poem showing the power of the Lord over the Assyrians. **RA**

ANCIENT WRITING

Scrawl! Writing in Ancient Times

Runestone Press • One of the most amazing finds in the archaeological digs of Assyria was the library of Asshurbanipal, containing 30,000 books! Learn more about early writing and the steps involved in deciphering it, using this and the following book. **UE+**

Ancient Scrolls

Michael Avi-Yonah, retold by Richard Currier • This is a very interesting book about a fascinating subject. "The pen [including the stylus] is mightier than the sword," has held true from the very beginning! **MS+**

BABYLON

Heroes & Warriors: Nebuchadnezzar

Mark Healy • This is a fairly detailed, fairly dry book about King Nebuchadnezzar of Babylon. However, it is the only book that we found about this important historical figure. **MS+**

Great Wonders of the World

Russell Ash • Dorling Kindersley books are filled with amazing full-color drawings and helpful information. This one is devoted to the Seven Wonders of the Ancient World. **UE+**

The Seven Wonders of the Ancient World

Robert Silverberg • The Hanging Gardens of Babylon was one of the wonders of the ancient world, along with the Pyramid of Cheops (Egypt), the statue of Zeus (Greece), the temple of Artemis (Ephesus), the Mausoleum of Halicarnassus (Asia Minor), the Colossus of Rhodes (Rhodes), and the Pharos Lighthouse (Alexandria, Egypt). This is an excellent introduction containing fascinating stories about these man-made marvels. **UE+**

POTTERY

Fired Up! MAKING POTTERY IN ANCIENT TIMES

Rivka Gonen • Pottery is the most basic "book" archaeologists read as they try to understand ancient civilizations. This book is filled with pictures and descriptions of the types of pottery found in archaeological digs. Fascinating! **UE+**

VIDEOS

Gateway to the Gods: Babylon

THE ANTHONY ROLAND COLLECTION

Probably available from a university or state library, this film gives an excellent understanding of the ruins of Babylon, the archaeological treasures, and the history of this city. Not as exciting as the following video, but this is still an informative, interesting resource on the history of Babylon. **AA**

Assurnasirpal, The Assyrian King

THE ANTHONY ROLAND COLLECTION

Probably available through your state or university library, this is a fascinating video of the Assyrians. One section is told from the viewpoint of Assurnasirpal, an Assyrian king. It utilizes the sculptures and artistic carvings on the now excavated palace walls to tell the stories of the culture. The video may seem long to younger children, but the entire family will benefit from seeing the surrounding terrain and amazing art. **AA**

The Sevens Wonders of the Ancient World

Questar • Absolutely captivating! This video really makes these wonders come to life, and helps us understand more about the geography, the history, and the cultures of the seven locations. **AA**

What books did you like best?

The Internet also contains a wealth of information about Assyria and Babylon.

What sites were the most helpful?

For more books, use these Dewey Decimal numbers in your library:

Bible: #220

Ancient Middle & Near Eastern: #930

Ancient Mesopotamia & Iranian Plateau: #935

Ancient Palestine: #933

Also, look for biographies on the key people listed.

Student Self-Evaluation UNIT 5, PHASE 1

Dates and hours:________________________

Key Concepts

Rephrase the five Key Concepts of this Unit and confirm your understanding of each:

- Jonah & Assyria

- Judgment of Israel

- Discovery of Nineveh

- Prophets & Babylon

- Babylonian Captivity

Tools for Self-Evaulation

Evaluate your personal participation in the discussions of this Phase. Bearing in mind that a good participant in a discussion is not always the most vocal participant, ask yourself these questions: Were you an active participant? Did you ask perceptive questions? Were you willing to listen to other participants of the discussion and draw out their opinions? Record your observations and how you would like to improve your participation in the future:

Every time period is too complex to be understood in one Phase of study. Evaluate your current knowledge of Assyria & Babylon. What have you focused on so far? What are your weakest areas of knowledge?

Based on the evaluation of this introduction, project ahead what you would like to study more of in the following Phases:

Phase 2

Research & Reporting

Explore one or more of these areas to discover something significant!

Assyria

Find one of the books listed, or a book of your choice, for basic information on the history of ancient Assyria. Summarize the factors that led to Assyria's far-reaching dominion and the factors leading to their decline. Report your findings as "The Rise and Fall of the Assyrian Empire."

Siege Warfare

The Assyrians were remarkably adept at capturing fortified cities. Research and report on what kind of techniques and machinery they used for this purpose.

Assyrian Conquest

Not much is known about the daily life of the common people in Assyria, though it appears that their lives were significantly controlled by the "government." However, there is much information about the captives and slaves of Assyrian conquest. Investigate what you can discover about this culture in regard to their treatment of other peoples. Be sure to include the issue of deportation.

Old Testament

- Investigate the books of Amos and Hosea in the Old Testament. Report on such questions as:
  - To whom were these prophets speaking?
  - What was the message?
  - How did the people respond?
  - How did God deal with them?
- Research and report on the lives of Isaiah and King Hezekiah. Use the whole of Scripture.
- Investigate the books of Micah, Zephaniah, and Habakkuk in the Old Testament. Report on such questions as:
  - To whom were these prophets speaking?
  - What was the message?
  - How did the people respond?
  - How did God deal with them?

Samaria

Research and write about the cause of Samaria's blended religion. Include comments regarding the impact this had on the conversation in John 4.

Cuneiform

Research and explain what cuneiform is, and how it was deciphered in modern times. Explain the significance of the discovery of the library of Ashurbanipal in Nineveh in understanding cuneiform.

Assyrian/Biblical Chronology

Compile a list of names, dates, and accomplishments of Assyria's key leaders. Make a chart that shows this list in comparison with the events listed in the Bible, including the time of Jonah, the captivity of Israel, the siege of Judah, and the destruction of Nineveh.

Assyria in Today's News/Babylon in Today's News

In the library or on the Internet, research any information from current events relating to the kingdom of Assyria or the kingdom of Babylon. (Hint: Especially, research the Persian Gulf War or the Iraq War.)

Modern Day Assyrians

There are Assyrian people today, from the land of Iraq, who have moved to various parts of the world. Research and report on their belief system, their cultural practices, and their integration into other cultures.

Sennacherib

Investigate Sennacherib in the history of Assyria. Report on his significance in Assyrian history and how the empire was affected by his death.

A Scriptural View

Summarize, either in written or verbal form, what you know about:

- the role of Jonah in Assyrian history;
- God's timing in sending Jonah;
- the effect of Israel not obeying God, nor receiving His correction;
- the truth of biblical prophecies in relation to Assyria's destruction.

Summarize, either in written or verbal form, what you know about:

- the disobedience of Judah;
- the warnings of the prophets;
- the chastisement delivered by Nebuchadnezzar;
- the confrontation by God in Nebuchadnezzar's life;
- the fall of the Babylonian Empire.

The Hanging Gardens

Research the Hanging Gardens of Babylon. How and why do archaeologists believe the Hanging Gardens were built? Compare and contrast the difficulty in normal irrigation and the type of irrigation the Hanging Gardens would have required.

Babylon

Find one of the books listed, or a book of your choice, for basic information on the two kingdoms of Babylon, both the early one under Hammurabi and the later under King Nebuchadnezzar. Summarize the factors that led to the far-reaching dominion of the later kingdom of Babylon, and the factors leading to its decline. Subtitle your report "The Rise and Fall of the Babylonian Empire." Be sure to include the importance of Daniel's role in the later government of Babylon.

Hammurabi

Research and report on King Hammurabi, the code of laws he gave, and his impact on the early city of Babylon.

Judah's Captivity

Investigate in Scripture the three stages of captivity Judah experienced. What were the causes of each stage? What was the effect of each stage? What was the final result?

Pottery

Read about pottery in antiquity, and how it is used in modern times by archaeologists to understand ancient cultures. Discover what some of the potential difficulties are with this system.

A Biblical View of Babylon

Babylon is mentioned from Genesis to Revelation. List the verses relating to this city, and chart what the Bible says about Babylon (chronologically).

Nebuchadnezzar

Research and report on the life of King Nebuchadnezzar. How significant was this leader in Babylonian history? How was that empire affected by his death? Be sure to include what Daniel says about the attitude of the king in his last days.

Archaeological Finds of Babylon

Research and report on Robert Koldewey, the German archaeologist who excavated Babylon from 1899–1913.

Brain Stretchers

Iraq & Israel

Compare and contrast the history of Iraq (Assyria & Babylon) and the history of Israel. What cultural distinctives continue throughout the centuries in each nation, (i.e., religion, war, politics, class structure)?

Assyria and Babylon to the Present

Investigate the history of Iraq from the time of Nimrod and the building of the city of Babel, through the time of the Assyrians and the Babylonians, and up to the present. Be sure to include Alexander the Great's use of Babylon. Report your findings.

Empires

We will be looking at five major empires over the next several units. Consider starting an ongoing project to uncover any universal factors contributing to the rise and fall of empires.

Create Your Own Research Topic

____

____

____

Timeline

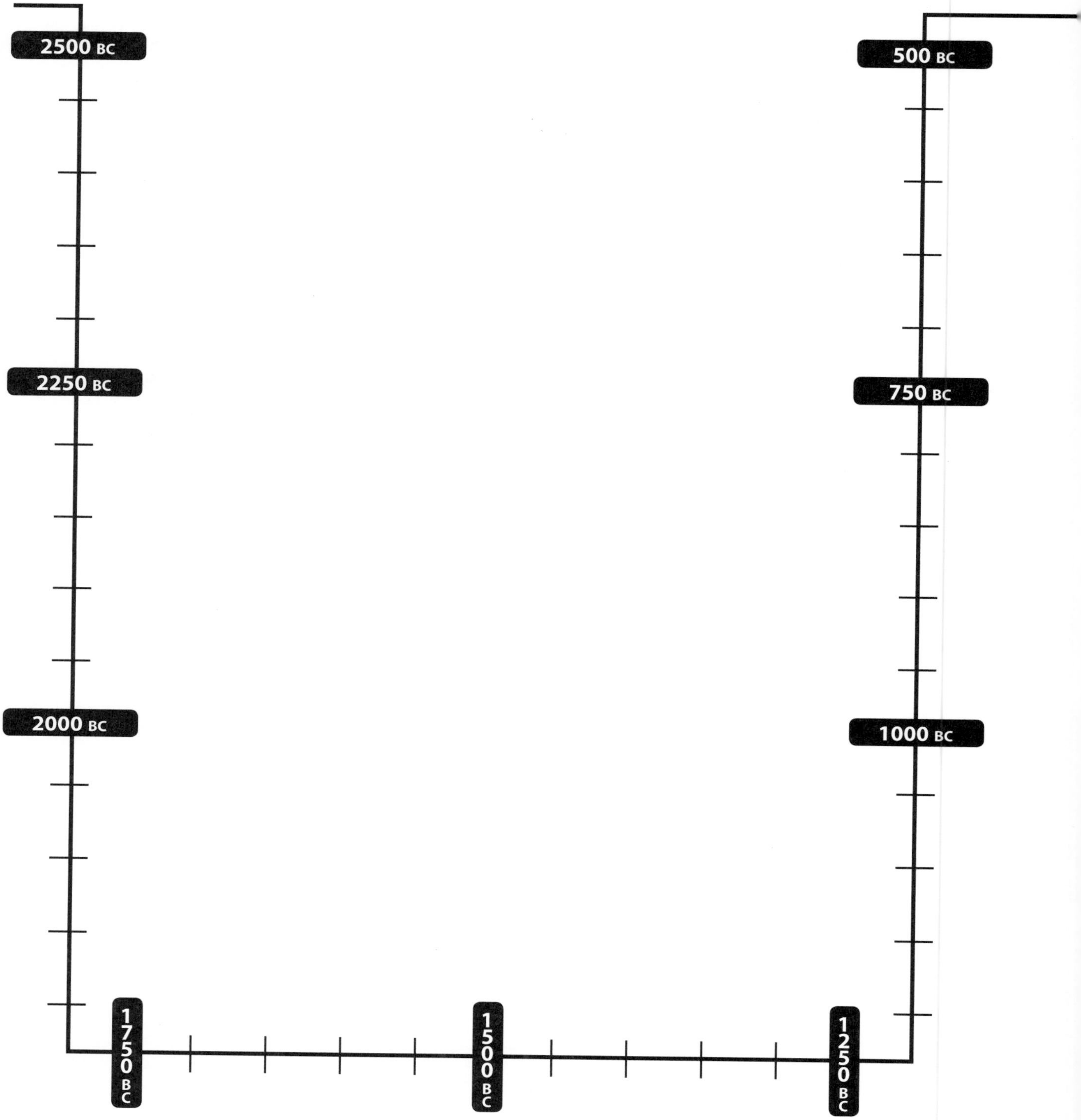
2500 BC
2250 BC
2000 BC
1750 BC
1500 BC
1250 BC
1000 BC
750 BC
500 BC

Consider this for your timeline

The timing of Jonah's mission to Nineveh is a significant factor in the purposes of God. He had spoken through the prophets to warn the northern kingdom of Israel that unless they repented, He would bring destruction into their midst. And, as is often the case, they didn't believe Him. Obviously, God was accomplishing many objectives at the same time, including: the preaching of Jonah to the people of Nineveh, the preparation of Assyria as a nation to bring judgment to Israel, and the object lesson for Judah of obedience to the Lord.

The amazing "coincidence" of Babylon's siege of Nineveh at the time when the Tigris River flooded, destroying part of Nineveh's outer wall, shows again the purposes of God, which exceed anything man can orchestrate.

Yet again, the overthrow of the Babylonians by the Persians & Medes occurs right at the perfect moment—the night that Daniel told King Belshazzar that his time was up! God's timing is never early and never late. Instead, He chooses the right moment in history to accomplish His purposes for nations and people.

Key Events

- Israel's captivity
- Destruction of Nineveh
- Code of Hammurabi
- Judah's captivity
- The fall of Babylon

Be sure to include the people listed in Key People in Phase 1.

Words to Watch

Remember—The easiest way to learn a subject is to master its terms:

deportation	irrigation	chastise	scourge
judgment	remnant	soothsayer	empire
administrator	siege	engines	bas-relief
lyres	tribute	cuneiform	stylus
pottery			

Other words you need to look up:

Student Self-Evaluation UNIT 5, PHASE 2

Dates and hours:________________________

Research Project

- Summarize your research question:

____

____

- List your most useful sources by author, title, and page number or URL where applicable (continue list in margin if necessary):

____

____

____

Now take a moment to evaluate the sources you just listed. Do they provide a balanced view of your research question? Should you have sought an additional opinion? Are your sources credible (if you found them on your own)? Record your observations:

____

____

Evaluate your research project in its final presentation. What are its strengths? If you had time to revisit this project, what would you change? Consider giving yourself a letter grade based on your project's merits and weaknesses.

____

____

Letter grade: ____

You have just completed an area of specific research in the time of Assyria & Babylon. Now what would you like to explore in the upcoming Phases? Set some objectives for yourself:

____

Phase 3

Maps and Mapping

Physical Terrain

- Label and color the Tigris and Euphrates rivers on the outline map.
- Color the Fertile Crescent.
- Locate and indicate the mountain ranges, deserts, and green areas.

Geopolitical

- Locate and label the land of Assyria. What is today's name of that country?
- Label Nineveh and Nimrud on the map. What modern day cities are close to these ancient cities?
- Discover the terrain and climate of ancient Assyria.
- Locate and label the region of Babylon on the map. What is today's name of that country?
- Label the city of Babylon on the map. What modern day city is close to this?
- Discover the terrain and climate of ancient Babylon.

Explore

- ***Christian Outreach:*** What is the status of Christian outreach to the modern countries where Assyria and Babylon were located? How has Christian outreach been affected by recent wars? Discuss the difficulties and remarkable opportunities facing Christians in that area of the world today.
- ***Babylonian Ecosystem:*** What kind of terrain and ecosystem is in the land of ancient Babylon? How did the Babylonians grow food? What does this indicate about the level of technology available to this ancient people? Contrast this with Assyria's terrain and ecosystem.
- ***Climate:*** What type of climate is typical in the Mesopotamian region? How would the terrain and climate have affected the Assyrian culture and the Babylonian culture? Does this give you any insight into God's purpose for it?

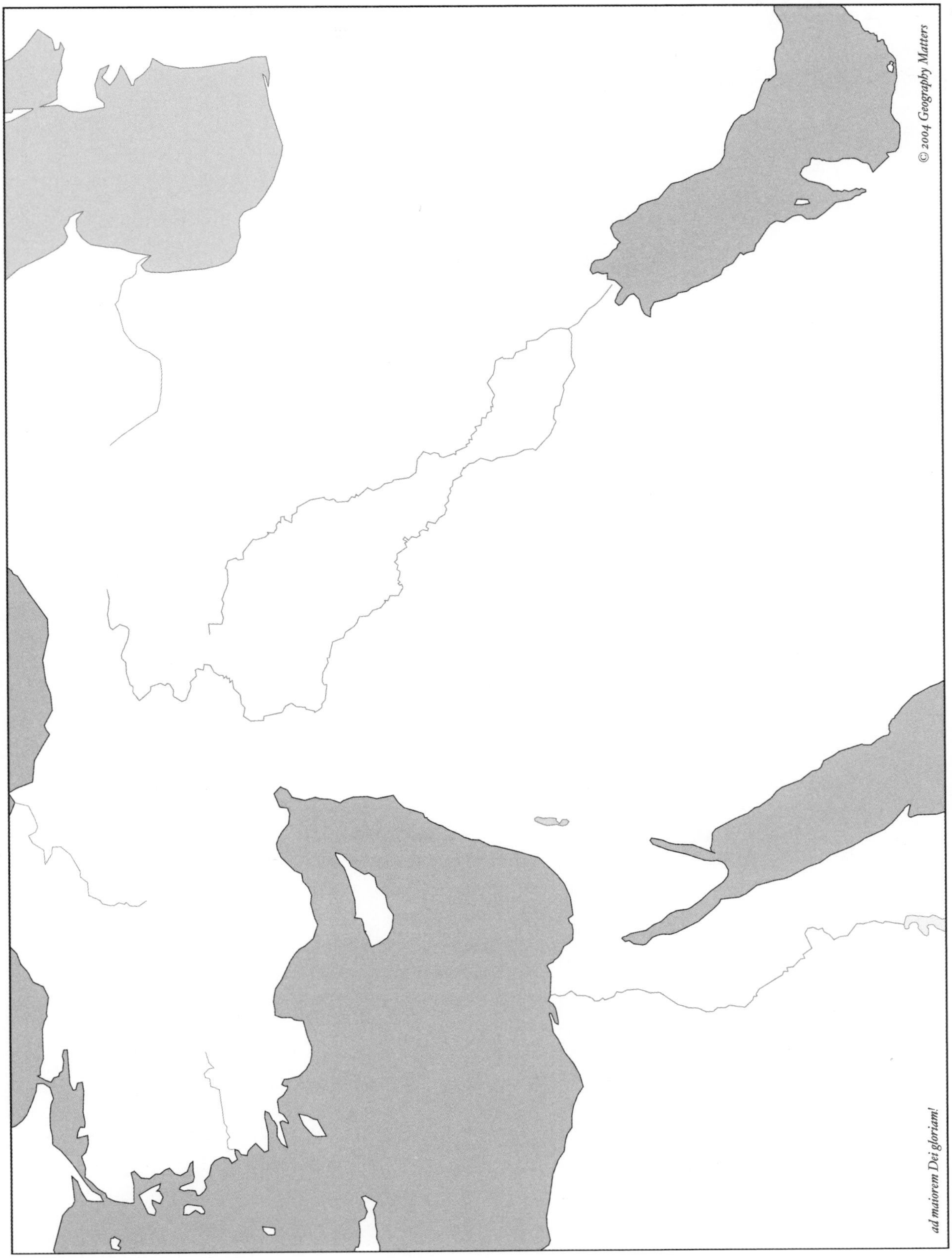
© 2004 Geography Matters
ad maiorem Dei gloriam!

Art Appreciation

Belshazzar's Feast by Rembrandt

» Do you think this painting reflects what the Bible describes?

» How does the painting differ from your own impression of this historic event?

» How would you describe Rembrandt's use of shadow and light in this painting?

Assyrian Bas-relief Sculpture in the British Museum

» How does this artwork help you understand more about the Assyrians?

» Do you think the people under siege by the Assyrians were frightened? How does this artwork inform your decision?

» How would you describe the animals depicted in Assyrian bas relief?

- Assyrian palaces were decorated with bas-relief pictures of battles, lion hunts, and other scenes intended to impress the viewer with the power and majesty of the king.

Architecture

The Hanging Gardens of Babylon were one of the Seven Wonders of the Ancient World. According to tradition, these gardens were created by King Nebuchadnezzar for his Medean queen, Amytis. No one knows exactly how the Hanging Gardens were built, or even where they were built. (A current theory is that the Hanging Gardens were actually built in Assyria!) However, it is possible to speculate that a well-watered garden, built on ascending levels, would provide a refreshing haven from the fierce Babylonian heat.

» Look for artists' renditions of the Hanging Gardens of Babylon. Are there any agreements about how this wonder was built?

Arts in Action

Select one or more, and let your artistic juices flow!

Imitation

Try your hand at creating a scene from the book of Daniel in the style of Rembrandt

Cuneiform

Try making your own cuneiform book. Items needed: modeling clay, "stylus," knife. Roll clay into flat "slates." Your "stylus" could be a drinking straw cut lengthwise, a wedge-shaped stick, or a pencil halved. Make up a simple code, then write a sentence. Show the code to your family or other students. Can anyone read the sentence? You could also imitate actual cuneiform markings by copying real examples from Assyria.

Repentant Prophet

Draw a picture of a large fish. Now draw a Jonah's-eye-view of a huge fish stomach! Can you draw the ribs of the fish? Is Jonah sitting, kneeling, lying down, standing up? What color is it inside the belly? What color is Jonah? (Consider: Many scholars believe that Jonah may have been bleached white inside the sea creature, and perhaps that is why the city of Nineveh took his message seriously!)

What do Jonah's clothes look like? Does the fish look puzzled?

Hanging Gardens

Try making a miniature version of the Hanging Gardens. You could make it with papier maché, LEGO bricks, wood, Styrofoam, or whatever your imagination suggests.

Relief Sculpture

Make a soft "stone" relief. Items needed: vermiculite, plaster of Paris, water, bucket, small board for each student, plastic spoon or old tool for carving, aluminum foil, masking tape. Make a "form" for each board with aluminum foil—bring the edges of the foil up ½" above the board, secure with masking tape. In a plastic bucket mix 3 scoops vermiculite, 2 scoops plaster of Paris, 2 scoops of water. Stir with a stick until very thick. Pour into aluminum foil form and wait 30 minutes or until hardened. Using a plastic spoon, carve a relief sculpture. Possibilities: an animal, a person, a chair, a mountain, a city… (Fact: Much of what is known about the Assyrian civilization was learned from the relief carvings on the walls of the archaeological ruins. Find some photos of these carvings. Do you think they were good artists? Do you think the Assyrians would enjoy Western art?)

The Four Empires

Draw a picture of Daniel's vision of the four empires. Using the interpretation given by Daniel in Daniel 2, portray the differing aspects of these four empires. Check what you learn about Babylon, Persia, Greece, and Rome with the biblical description.

Painted Babylonian Walls

Make a "wall" of bricks to paint: On a piece of wood, roll out clay, or bread dough, or plaster, etc. Mark lines in it while still soft to indicate bricks. After the wall dries, paint the wall blue using either tempera or acrylic to cover completely. After this layer dries, paint designs on selected bricks with bright colors. If you painted fierce animals, as the Babylonians did, would you be frightened to walk by this wall?

Science

Container Gardening

» Contact the local County Extension office to learn about gardening in different kinds of soil, different climates, and irrigation. Then plant at least two different mini-gardens in containers. One should be for plants that thrive in hot, dry climates, another should be for moisture-loving, shade plants. What kind of obstacles would the architect(s) of the Hanging Gardens of Babylon have had to overcome?

Evaporation

» One resource on the Hanging Gardens said that the rooms under the garden area were kept cool in the summer by the foliage of the plants and by the evaporating water. Discover what "swamp coolers" are, and how they function. Experiment with the cooling process of evaporation: 1) On a hot day, put room temperature water on your face and arms. As it evaporates, does it cool? 2) On a hot day, find some leafy trees or an arbor to sit under. 3) Try leaving one cup of room temperature water outside in direct sunlight and one cup in the cool leafy shade. See if there is a difference in the rate of evaporation. 4) Devise your own experiments.

Music

In the archaeological digs of Assyria, many pictures were found of musicians and various types of musical instruments. One can observe different instruments being played at the same time, such as harps and flutes. In fact, one scene from Assyria is that of a king and his queen reclining in their chairs in a lovely garden, while several musicians play (softly?) in the background. Though we do not know what the music sounded like, we can listen to the soothing sounds of the harp and the lilting voice of the flute today.

You might think, "Well, it's obvious!—A trumpet doesn't sound like a voice. And a guitar doesn't sound like a piano or a banjo." That's a very good observation, and what you have just noticed is one of the five major elements of music. Timbre (sounds like TAM-ber) is the name we give this element. Timbre is the uniquely different quality of sound produced by different instruments.

Listen:

» *Peter and the Wolf* by Prokofiev and *A Young Person's Guide to the Orchestra* by Benjamin Britten are musical pieces written to help students become familiar with the different instruments in the symphonic orchestra. These are highly regarded as an introduction to the element of timbre.

Try This

» To experiment with timbre, get your classmates or family and friends to gather as many musical instruments as you can find (piano, trumpet, recorder, violin, drum, etc.). Add some nonmusical instruments as well, such as metal pots and wooden spoons. While the rest close their eyes, let one person pluck, blow, or tap an instrument. Try to determine which instrument is being played just by its sound. Let everyone have a turn.

» Now listen to some recordings of various types of music. Can you identify any of the instruments being played? Listen for percussion, woodwinds, brass, and strings. If there are singers, listen for the differences in men's, women's, and children's voices.

Isn't it wonderful that God gave us more than one sound to use in music?

Thank you Lord, for giving us different ***timbres.***

Cooking

The Assyrians used barley as one of their primary grains. Though this recipe was not found in the ruins (!), it will give you a taste of the foods of this culture.

Barley Soup

1½ cups barley, soaked overnight in water
3 tbsp butter
1 tbsp flour
4 cups chicken broth
white pepper
1 egg, lightly beaten
2 cups water
1 tsp salt
1 cup onion, chopped fine
4 cups yogurt, plain
2 tbsp fresh coriander (or ½ tbsp dried)

Drain barley and place in saucepan with water and salt. Cover tightly and simmer until barley has absorbed all liquid, and grains are separated, about one hour. Add more water only if necessary. Cook onion in butter until soft but not brown. Stir in yogurt. Remove from heat. Mix egg and flour together and blend into the yogurt mixture. Bring the chicken stock to a boil in a large saucepan; stir in yogurt mixture and barley. Add pepper and salt. Pour into bowls and sprinkle with coriander. Serves 8.

Ezekiel's Many-Floured Bread

2 tbsp yeast
1½ cup warm water
1 egg
¼ cup oil (plus 1 tbsp to brush top of bread)
2½ tsp salt
¼ cup millet flour
2–2½ cups unbleached flour
1 tbsp coriander seed
¼ cup lentil flour
¼ cup barley flour
¼ cup fava (broad bean) flour
⅓ cup honey
2 cups whole wheat flour
1 tbsp cumin

Dissolve yeast in warm water. Mix in next 5 ingredients. Stir in all flours, except white flour, and beat well. Add enough white flour to make a dough that can be gathered into a ball. Turn onto lightly floured surface and knead 10 minutes. Place in greased bowl, turning over to grease surface. Cover with a cloth and let rise in a warm place until double in bulk, about 1½ hours. Punch down and let rise again about 1 hour. Shape into 2 round loaves and place on greased baking sheet. Cover and let rise 1 hour. Bake at 350 degrees for about 30 minutes. Remove, brush with remaining oil. Makes 2 loaves.

CONSIDER:

Those who were taken captive by Babylon had many changes to adjust to, including unusual and unfamiliar ingredients for basic food. It was undoubtedly a difficult time, but the routine of daily life had its own comforts. Try this unusual "comfort food" and rejoice in the goodness and dependability of the Lord!

Student Self-Evaluation UNIT 5, PHASE 3

Dates and hours:____________________

Evaluate Your Projects

- List which of the activities listed in this Phase you did:

____

____

____

- Rate your enthusiasm: __________

  Explain: ____________________________________

  ____

- Rate the precision of your approach:__________

  Explain: ____________________________________

  ____

- Rate your effort towards the completion of the project: __________

  Explain: ____________________________________

  ____

Ask yourself what worked and what did not. What would you do differently in the future, and what would you repeat?

____

How specifically did these hands-on activities enhance your knowledge of Assyria & Babylon? What made them worthwhile?

____

In the first three Phases of this Unit, what aspect of the time period has most captured your imagination? What would you like to creatively pursue to conclude your study?

____

Phase 4

In Your Own Way. . .

We have seen God's grace and mercy towards the Assyrians and the Babylonians, and how He used them in the kingdoms of Israel and Judah. Mercy and justice combined under the wisdom of God for His eternal purposes. Now, choose a selection of these activities, or create your own, which will best express what you have learned from this Unit.

LINGUISTICS

Journalism

- Be a newspaper reporter for the *Hebrew Times* and write an exposé on Sennacherib's defeat at Jerusalem.
- Be a newspaper reporter for the *The Babylon Babbler* and write the fast-breaking story of "Three Engage in Civil Disobedience, Come Out Smelling Like a Rose" or "Fourth Figure Found in Flaming Fiery Furnace!"

Prose

- Write a fictional account of Jonah's experience hiking across the desert to Nineveh.
- You are with Layard at the discovery of Nineveh. Write a letter "home" to tell your family about the happenings of the dig.
- Write a short story from the perspective of one of the slaves commanded to bring the holy vessels from Jerusalem to Belshazzar at his feast.
- Retell the captivity of Judah using modern names and terms.

Playing with Words

- Imagine you are one of those Israelites taken into slavery by Shalmaneser V. Write a coded message to your cousin in Jerusalem.
- Finish this limerick about Jonah's "pity party" after God forgave the Ninevites:
  There was a young man from Israel,
  Who honestly felt rather miserable . . .

Poetry

Discover the connection these words have to the Unit, and then write a rhyming poem using them: *irrigation, evaporation, deportation (Babylon); demonstrate, illustrate, appreciate (Daniel); weep, reap, leap (Judah)*

Painting/Drawing

Illustrate a book for young children showing Jonah's adventures.

ART

Graphic Design

Design a T-shirt that King Nebuchadnezzar would sell to tourists showing who REALLY is in charge of Babylon.

Sculpting

Using bas-relief sculpture, tell the story of Assyria's major events.

Cartooning

As a political cartoonist for the local *Jerusalem News* in 701 BC, draw your version of the Rabshakeh (messenger from Sennacherib), or of what recently transpired outside the city gates.

MUSIC

Compose

- Write a tongue-in-cheek Hymn of Tribute to King Nebuchadnezzar.
- In honor of Shadrach, Meshach, and Abednego, compose a song called, "Just the Three of Us," but add a historically surprising fourth part.

Performance Practice

With your teacher's help, select an appropriate piece of music, which expresses some element from this Unit. Prepare and perform the piece for an audience. Communicate with your audience the reason for your selection either in the program notes or in a short speech.

DRAMA

Comedy

- Do a humorous skit about scoffers in the 1800s being confronted with Layard's discovery.
- Do a humorous skit about Nebuchadnezzar, his pride, going crazy, and his eventual repentance.

Reality

- Act out the book of Jonah. Use your imagination to create props, sets, and costumes. (Good luck with the big fish!) Be sure to include realistic mourning and rejoicing!
- Perform the scene with King Hezekiah, the prophet Isaiah, and the people of Jerusalem as they are attacked by the Assyrians. Set up the surprise ending!

Tragedy

Act out God's heart as His people continually reject Him.

Puppetry

Put on a puppet show showing the young men with Daniel who refused the king's rich food. Be sure to show the effects of the rich diet on other young men!

Prop Needs

___

___

___

Costume Ideas

___

___

___

Role/Player

___

___

___

Set Suggestions

___

___

___

MOVEMENT

Pantomime

- Pantomime Jonah being swallowed, being spit out, and then walking for days across the desert.
- Pantomime Austen Layard's excitement when he discovered Nineveh. Include the huge mounds of sand, the excavations, and some of the surprising discoveries.

Dance

Choreograph a dance that portrays the incident of the handwriting on the wall in Babylon.

Miniature Action

Make a small "settlement" out of LEGO bricks or other building toys. Build a wall around the settlement. Now make a "siege engine" with a battering ram. Add soldiers to the scene. Now reenact either the captivity of Israel or God's deliverance of Judah.

CONCEPTUAL DESIGN

Irrigate an Elevated Garden

Design a hanging garden of the same basic dimensions as the original, which would use high-tech engineering currently available, or future-tech engineering that you dream up.

CREATE YOUR OWN EXPRESSION

____

____

____

____

____

Student Self-Evaluation UNIT 5, PHASE 4

Dates and hours:____________________

Evaluate Your Projects

- What creative project did you choose?

- What did you expect from your project, and how does the final project compare to your initial expectations?

- What do you like about your project? What would you change?

In Conclusion

Revisit the five Key Concepts from the beginning of this Unit. Explain how your understanding of and appreciation for each has grown over the course of your study.

Record your concluding thoughts on Assyria & Babylon:

The Persians & Medes:

UNIT 6

Key Concepts

- The Persian Empire
- Daniel's vision
- Rebuilding the Temple
- Esther and Purim

The ruins of the city of Persepolis, founded by Darius I in the sixth century BC

Repatriation to Jerusalem...

"Thus says the Lord to His anointed, to Cyrus, whose right hand I have held, to subdue nations before him and loose the armor of kings, to open before him the double doors, so that the gates will not be shut; I will go before you and make the crooked places straight; I will break in pieces the gates of bronze and cut the bars of iron, I will give you the treasures of darkness and hidden riches of secret places, that you may know that I, the Lord, who call you by your name, am the God of Israel. For Jacob My servant's sake, and Israel My elect, I have even called you by your name; I have named you, though you have not known Me. I am the Lord, and there is no other, there is no god besides Me. I will gird you, though you have not known Me, that they may know from the rising of the sun to its setting that there is none besides Me. I am the Lord and there is no other; I form the light and create darkness, I make peace and create calamity; I, the Lord, do all these things." Isaiah 45:1–7

A king named Cyrus came to the throne of Persia in 559 BC—about eighty years after Isaiah's prophecy. He immediately made preparations to throw off the yoke of the neighboring Median Empire, which had grown in size and power since the time of Nineveh's destruction. The Medes and Babylonians together had sacked Nineveh and had divided the Assyrian Empire between them. These two budding empires, along with Egypt and Lydia (who controlled most of Asia Minor), had maintained a balance of power until 590 BC, when the Median king, Cyaxares, decided to enlarge his kingdom by attacking Lydia. Though the war had lasted five years, Cyaxares was not successful. When his successor came to the throne, the Median Empire began to wane, and was held together only by a fragile thread of power which was to soon come undone when Cyrus gave it a tug.

In 548 BC, after waging war for three years, Cyrus triumphantly marched into the capital city of the Medes. We see his great statesmanship and wisdom displayed in the way he honored the defeated Medes, giving many of their nobles a place in his own court, taking their capital city as his second capital, by referring to the Persian empire as that of the "Medes and Persians," and by allowing their king to live to the end of his natural life in the royal court of Cyrus.

The Medes and Babylonians together had sacked Nineveh and had divided the Assyrian Empire between them.

With his formidable army, Cyrus next successfully attacked and conquered Lydia in 548 BC. Two down, two to go. Before he left the area, Cyrus decided to complete the conquest of the area by capturing the Greek cities of Ionia (on the eastern edge of the Aegean Sea) and subjecting them to both tribute and service in his army. Having nearly doubled the size of his empire, Cyrus entered Babylonia in 539 BC and in October the following year, defeated Nabonidus, the Babylonian king. Nabonidus's son and co-regent, Belshazzar, was killed and the city of Babylon was taken a week later by Cyrus's general, Gobryas. Cyrus actually entered the city in a triumphant procession on October 29, saying in his first official proclamation: *"I am Cyrus, king of the universe, Great King, mighty king, king of Babylon, king of Sumer and Akkad, king of the world quarters."*

This king was the ruler of the second kingdom in the great image Daniel had seen, the one with the chest and arms of silver. In Daniel 7:5, King Cyrus and the Medo-Persian Empire are described, not as a part of a statue, but as an animal:

> And suddenly another beast, a second, like a bear. It was raised up on one side, and had three ribs in its mouth between its teeth. And they said thus to it: "Arise, devour much flesh!"

Cyrus had just grabbed the third rib when he took Babylon and its empire. The first rib had been the empire of the Medes; the second, the Lydians. And from this beginning, the Medo-Persian Empire would go on to conquer many people and many lands—"much flesh." Isn't it incredible to know the One who knows it all?

Rebuilding the Temple

In the year after he captured Babylon, Cyrus announced a change. The prevailing custom followed by conquering armies had been to rip people away from their land and forcibly resettle them elsewhere. Instead, Cyrus began a new and humane policy of repatriation for the displaced peoples of his empire, specifically the Jews, when he made this proclamation:

> "All the kingdoms of the earth the Lord God of heaven has given me. And He has commanded me to build Him a house at Jerusalem which is in Judah. Who is there among you of all His people? May the Lord his God be with him, and let him go up!" 2 Chronicles 36:22–23

Among the Jews in Babylon there was a group of courageous and visionary people who responded to Cyrus's words and, with Zerubbabel as their leader, returned to the ruins of Jerusalem. They first erected an altar of sacrifice in 536 BC, and then began to build the Temple in 535 BC.

However, as they began the work, their neighboring enemies did everything possible to threaten and demoralize them:

> Then the people of the land tried to discourage the people of Judah. They troubled them in building, and hired counselors against them to frustrate their purpose all the days of Cyrus king of Persia, even until the reign of Darius king of Persia. Ezra 4:4–5

This king was the ruler of the second kingdom in the great image Daniel had seen.

Not only did they deal with nasty neighbors, the Jews also dealt with a desolated land, hard work, crop failure, and a sense of the paltry size of this Temple in comparison to Solomon's Temple.

> But many of the priests and Levites and heads of the fathers' houses, who were old men, who had seen the first temple, wept with a loud voice when the foundation of this temple was laid before their eyes; yet many shouted aloud for joy, so that the people could not discern the noise of the shout of joy from the noise of the weeping of the people. Ezra 3:12–13

Can you imagine? From the luxuries of Babylon to the ruins of Jerusalem . . . from the blessing of the king to the taunts of their enemies . . . from the magnificence of Solomon's Temple to the seemingly insignificant foundations of a new temple, all worked insidiously on the hearts and minds of these repatriated Jews. Within two years, work on the Temple ceased. The people lost their focus and began to worry about their own needs, building luxurious, paneled dwellings for themselves. As is often the case, when people quit obeying the Lord and focus on their own comforts and ease, the opposition of the enemy dies down. But, for the Jews, it did not bring the satisfaction that they expected:

> "You looked for much, but indeed it came to little; and when you brought it home, I blew it away. Why?" says the Lord of hosts, "Because of My house that is in ruins, while every one of you runs to his own house." Haggai 1:9

When people quit obeying the Lord and focus on their own comforts and ease, the opposition of the enemy dies down.

Shortly after King Darius I (521–485 BC) began his reign, God sent Haggai and Zechariah to prophesy to the Jews in Jerusalem and Judah. You see, God still sought primacy in His people's hearts. It wasn't that He selfishly wanted His house built before theirs, but that He knew if they did not serve Him first, they would be drawn away again into idolatry and rebellion. So, with great love and mercy, He got their attention through the prophets, who told the people in no uncertain terms to recognize that they had neglected God's temple. Zerubbabel and Joshua, the high priest, immediately responded to the Lord in obedience, and the people followed. From 520 until 515 BC, they labored to finish what they had begun, hopeful because God had promised them they would succeed:

> The hands of Zerubbabel have laid the foundation of this temple; his hands shall also *finish* it. Then you will know that the Lord of hosts has sent Me to you. For who has despised the day of small things? Zechariah 4:9–10

As soon as the Jews restarted their work on the temple, the appointed Persian governor of that satrapy, or region, wrote to King Darius I to let him know what was going on in Jerusalem, and to ask whether or not King Cyrus had actually made a proclamation for the rebuilding of the temple. This is part of King Darius I's reply:

> "Now therefore, Tattenai, governor of the region beyond the River, and Shethar-Boznai, and your companions the Persians who are beyond the River, keep yourselves far from there. Let the work of this house of God alone; let the governor of the Jews and the elders of the Jews build this house of God on its site. Moreover I issue a decree as to what you shall do for the elders of these Jews, for the building of this house of God: Let the cost be paid at the king's expense from taxes on the region beyond the River; this is to be given immediately to these men, so that they are not hindered...Also I issue a decree that whoever alters this edict, let a timber be

> pulled from his house and erected, and let him be hanged on it; and let his house be made a refuse heap because of this. And may the God who causes His name to dwell there destroy any king or people who put their hand to alter it, or to destroy this house of God which is in Jerusalem. I Darius issue the decree; let it be done diligently." Ezra 6:6–8,11–12

Isn't that just like God? Not only does He end the opposition of their enemies, but He sets it up so that the work is paid for with money collected by and under the control of these same enemies! And, in the Persian Empire, there was no arguing with the decision of the king. His decree was law. Disobedience meant death.

With great love and mercy, God got their attention through the prophets.

Esther and Purim

In about 519 BC King Darius I, who is also called Ahasuerus, held a huge feast for all his nobles and officials that went on for six months. To finish off the celebrations, he held a seven-day feast for all the people in Susa, and on the last day, called for his queen, Vashti.

> But Queen Vashti refused to come at the king's command brought by his eunuchs; therefore the king was furious, and his anger burned within him. Esther 1:12

In a moment of wrath, and with the advice of his counselors, Darius removed Vashti from her position, never to be seen by him again.

Darius was in no mood for going without his beautiful queen, but the law of the Persians and the Medes was that once the king had made an edict, it could not be revoked. His counselors suggested a scheme whereby he could choose the most beautiful girl in the kingdom to become his new queen. And that is how the Jewish beauty Esther was set at just such a moment in a place of influence and power.

The book of Esther tells how an enemy of the Jews, Haman, sought to completely eradicate them from the face of the earth. He did not know, nor did Darius, that Queen Esther was Jewish, and he never imagined that there was anything or anyone who could prevent their annihilation once King Darius signed the edict. But God keeps watch over His people, and He powerfully turned what was intended for evil and destruction to good for the Jews. Esther very literally risked her life to go before Darius without being summoned (according to the custom of Persian kings as reported in archaeological and historical records). God gave her favor with the king, though, which led to the exposure of Haman's evil plan and a new edict by the king allowing the Jews to arm and defend themselves. The celebration of this deliverance of the Jews under Esther in 510 BC is called the Feast of Purim.

King Darius I not only helped the Jews in several ways, he also solved a major problem within his far-flung empire: how to communicate quickly and efficiently with all of his governors (and spies) from India to Turkey, and Egypt to the Caspian Sea. He built and maintained roads, including the 1,500 mile "Royal Road" from Sardis to Susa, which had road stations to provide fresh horses for the king's messengers—a system of communication much like the Pony Express riders of the mid-1800s in America. Herodotus, the Greek historian, actually traveled on this road, saying, *"At intervals all along the road are recognized stations, with excellent inns, and the road itself is safe to travel by, as it never leaves inhabited country...The total number of stations on the road from Sardis to Susa is 111...Traveling at the rate of 150 furlongs [18 miles] a day, a man will take just ninety days to make the journey."*

Darius I became an absolute monarch. Not content with the size of his empire, he made his first strike at Europe in 512 BC, easily conquering Thrace at the northern rim of the Aegean Sea. He continued on to the steppes of southern Russia, seeking, without success, to defeat the Scythians. After much frustration in not conquering their armies, he returned to Persia.

> In the Persian Empire, there was no arguing with the decision of the king.

When the Greeks in the Persian Empire (from the Ionian coastline) saw that the mighty Persian Empire was not invincible, they took great hope that they might be able to throw off the Persian yoke. In 500 BC the Greeks of Ionia began to rebel against Darius, with the pledged support of Athens behind them. They actually set the Persian city of Sardis (in Lydia) ablaze, an act of aggression, which made the proud Darius more than willing for retaliation and retribution. He carefully prepared his army for war, and set out to teach the rebels (and their supporters) a lesson.

Thus, the stage is set for the Battle of Marathon in 490 BC. Though Darius was able to easily recapture the Ionian cities through the sheer might of numbers, this formula did not work when it came to the Athenians. As the Persian army of up to 300,000 soldiers landed on the plain of Marathon, they were confronted with a Greek army of less than ten thousand. To the amazement of the Persians, this small group of fierce Greek warriors was able to wreak havoc and destruction on the much larger Persian army. As the Persians began to flee from the battle, the Greeks chased them, capturing seven ships before the Persians were able to escape.

This defeat only strengthened Darius's resolve to destroy Athens. Herodotus tells us that, *"without loss of time he dispatched couriers to the various states under his dominion with orders to raise an army much larger than before; and also warships, transports, horses, and grain. So the royal command went round; and all Asia was in an uproar for three years, with the best men being enrolled in the army for the invasion of Greece."*

When he died in 485 BC, the duty of teaching Greece a lesson fell to his son, Xerxes (grandson of Cyrus the Great). The first item of business was to

Ezra 3:8–13

Now in the second month of the second year of their coming to the house of God at Jerusalem, Zerubbabel the son of Shealtiel, Jeshua the son of Jozadak, and the rest of their brethren the priests and the Levites, and all those who had come out of the captivity to Jerusalem, began *work* and appointed the Levites from twenty years old and above to oversee the work of the house of the Lord. Then Jeshua *with* his sons and brothers, Kadmiel *with* his sons, and the sons of Judah, arose as one to oversee those working on the house of God: the sons of Henadad *with* their sons and their brethren the Levites.

When the builders laid the foundation of the temple of the Lord, the priests stood in their apparel with trumpets, and the Levites, the sons of Asaph, with cymbals, to praise the Lord, according to the ordinance of David king of Israel. And they sang responsively, praising and giving thanks to the Lord:

"For *He is* good,
For His mercy *endures* forever toward Israel."

Then all the people shouted with a great shout, when they praised the Lord, because the foundation of the house of the Lord was laid.

But many of the priests and Levites and heads of the fathers' *houses,* old men who had seen the first temple, wept with a loud voice when the foundation of this temple was laid before their eyes. Yet many shouted aloud for joy, so that the people could not discern the noise of the shout of joy from the noise of the weeping of the people, for the people shouted with a loud shout, and the sound was heard afar off.

build a bridge across the stretch of water separating Asia from Europe—at the Hellespont. For this amazing endeavor, the engineers used boats that were anchored both upstream and downstream and held together by taut cables of flax and papyrus. Planks were laid down over the cables and then brushwood was laid on top of the planks, with a layer of soil over the brushwood. This soil was packed down to solid firmness. To finish off the bridge, a fence was put up on each side of the boats, high enough to keep the horses and mules from seeing over the edge and becoming frightened by the water!

Over this bridge in 480 BC, Xerxes marched the largest army ever assembled in antiquity. Though estimates differ, it was probably close to 1,500,000 soldiers marching to war against several thousand Greek soldiers. Incredibly, though Xerxes was finally able to revenge the burning of Sardis by burning Athens, his huge navy lost to the Greeks in the Battle of the Bay of Salamis. Xerxes left most of his land army to continue fighting the Greeks while he returned to Susa, believing that, in time, the Greeks would certainly fall to the greater strength and numbers of the Persian army. However, within a year, the Greeks had nearly decimated the Persians. Xerxes was forced to withdraw what was left of his army and end his European campaign.

This small group of fierce Greek warriors was able to wreak havoc and destruction on the much larger Persian army.

When Xerxes I died in 465 BC, his son Artaxerxes (465–425 BC) came fully to the throne—he had been viceroy with his father since 474 BC. In 467 BC Artaxerxes wrote a royal decree for Ezra the scribe, instructing him to take all who were willing and return to Jerusalem, receiving as much money and provision from the king's treasury as was necessary for beautifying the temple of the Lord. Isn't it amazing to consider that this was the *third* ruler of the Persian Empire to both support the policy of repatriation for the Jews and supply money for their temple?

In spite of the devious plotting of their enemies, Ezra received the bountiful favor and supply of Artaxerxes, and was allowed to take thousands more Jews with him to Jerusalem. In fact, Ezra had the opportunity to bear witness to Artaxerxes about the amazing goodness and power of God:

> "...The hand of our God is upon all those for good who seek Him, but His power and His wrath are against all those who forsake Him." Ezra 8:22

Thirteen years later, Artaxerxes' cupbearer came into his presence with obvious sorrow on his face. This official, with an extremely trusted and important post at the royal court, was a Jew by the name of Nehemiah. He had just learned that the walls of Jerusalem had been broken down and the gates were burned, leaving the city open to destruction at the whim of its enemies. Artaxerxes asked Nehemiah why he was so unhappy, and when he learned the reason, asked him to present his request. Nehemiah asked permission to go to Jerusalem and rebuild the walls, requesting even that the king would give letters of passage and supply. Artaxerxes readily agreed.

The story of the rebuilding of the city walls is as adventurous, dangerous and heroic as any best-selling epic novel.

So in 454 BC, Nehemiah and his Jewish compatriots went to Jerusalem, the third return of captives under the Persian kings. The story of the rebuilding of the city walls is as adventurous, dangerous, and heroic as any best-selling epic novel. Nehemiah, knowing that the enemy was watching his every move, went by night to survey the damage to the city. Then he gathered the people of Jerusalem and told them his mission from God (and from the king) was to rebuild the walls. As they gladly began the process, the wrath of their enemies was great. Knowing that an attack could come at

The Treasury of Athens, built to commemorate (and with the spoils of) the Battle of Marathon.

any time, Nehemiah instructed the builders that they should work with one hand at construction, and hold a weapon with the other. Though the enemy tried to draw Nehemiah into an ambush of assassination, he wisely stayed on the job. After fifty-two days, the wall was finished and Jerusalem was safe. Safe, but not obedient. The prophet Malachi, somewhere between 432 and 416 BC, brought the word of the Lord to the people of Judah and Jerusalem. He revealed the coldness of their hearts, the insincerity of their worship, their unfaithfulness in marriage, and their arrogant ways. But, as always, God's word was intended to bring them to repentance and renewed right relationship with Him. His last recorded words to His people prior to John the Baptist, brought hope for their future, prophetically foretelling the coming of the One who would be the Redeemer of Israel:

> Behold, I will send you Elijah the prophet before the coming of the great and dreadful day of the Lord. And he will turn the hearts of the fathers to the children, and the hearts of the children to their fathers, lest I come and strike the earth with a curse. Malachi 4:5–6

Just as the vision of Jerusalem fades from the pages of Old Testament Scripture, so fades the vision of Imperial Persia. The glory, renown, and power of Cyrus and Darius remained to Xerxes, but began to decline under the ineffectual rule of Artaxerxes. When he died, the struggle for the throne resulted in several kings being murdered shortly after taking the throne. Darius II (423–404 BC) was a degenerate, cruel king. When his son, Artaxerxes II, succeeded as king, the younger son, Cyrus, determined to seize the throne. Cyrus hired Greek mercenaries to supplement his own army, and in 401 BC marched against his brother. Shortly after the battle of Cunaxa began, Cyrus, the would-be usurper, was killed by Artaxerxes II. One of the Greek mercenaries fighting for Cyrus was Xenophon, known in history for his military tactics, his horsemanship, and his writings. Once Cyrus was killed and the Greek commanders serving him were murdered, ten thousand Greek soldiers tried to find a way out of an incredibly hostile Persian countryside, back to the safety of Greece. They were successful, but that story belongs to the next chapter.

Phase 1

Key People

Cyrus
King of Persia

Darius I
Persian king who lost battle of Marathon

Xerxes
Persian king who lost battle of Bay of Salamis

Esther
Hebrew queen who saved the Jews

Zerubbabel
Jewish leader who rebuilt the Temple

Ezra
Jewish priest of repatriation

Nehemiah
Jewish rebuilder of the walls of Jerusalem

Malachi
Last prophet of the Old Testament

Listen to This

What in the World? VOL. 1

DISC THREE:

» Cyrus the Great (track 3)

» The Persian Empire (track 4)

» Xerxes (track 5)

Read For Your Life

The Main Story

» Ezra, Esther, Nehemiah

» Other Helpful Verses: 2 Chronicles 36:22–23; Isaiah 13:17–19, 44:24–28, 45:1–7; Daniel 2:39, 5:30–31, 6:1–28, 9:1–11:2; Haggai, Zechariah, Malachi.

Talk Together

Opinion Column

» What did you find to be the most interesting aspect, or the most fascinating person, you encountered in your introduction to the Persians and Medes?

» Isaiah 44:28 and 45:2 speak of a man by the name of Cyrus whom God described as "a shepherd." Considering the fact that the book of Isaiah was written sometime between 740 and 680 BC, and King Cyrus appeared on the scene of history in the mid 500s BC, why do you think God would speak to Isaiah about a non-Jewish king one hundred-fifty years before he showed up?

» After reading the article at the beginning of this Unit, imagine you are one among hundreds of thousands of Xerxes' foot soldiers. When you are told to cross the bridge over the Hellespont, what is your reaction?

» Read Ezra 8:21–23. Imagine you are one of the people returning to Jerusalem with Ezra. Considering that it was extremely dangerous to travel through enemy territory, what are your thoughts as Ezra chooses to seek God for protection rather than ask the king for military escort? Have you and your family ever chosen to trust God in prayer in a specific situation, rather than rely on human wisdom? What was the outcome?

» Why do you think it was so death defying for Esther to present herself to the king?

Critical Puzzling

» The Persians followed a different policy of governing captured people than either the Assyrians or the Babylonians. Their policy was "repatriation," which allowed the people to return to their own lands. Why do you think they had this radically different policy than the Assyrians and Babylonians? What impact do you think this had on the Jews and what effect did it have on God's plan of redemption?

» Do you think Xerxes had any concept that he might be defeated by the Greeks at the Battle of the Bay of Salamis? Support your opinion.

Resources for Digging Deeper

Choose a few books that look interesting, or find your own.

PERSIA

The Persian Empire
Don Nardo • It is difficult to find books appropriate for children on the Persian Empire. This is the best one we have found. **UE+**

PERSIAN LEADERS

Cyrus the Persian
Sherman A. Nagel • This is a fascinating account of the life of Cyrus, written as historical fiction about the Babylonian, Persian, and biblical events. **UE+**

Behold Your Queen!
Gladys Malvern • Historical fiction concerning Esther, this wonderful book makes the details of the story of Esther come to life. **UE+**

Stories from Herodotus
translated by Glanville Downey • This book is a children's version of the writings of the ancient Greek historian Herodotus. It details the invasion of Greece by the Persians in 490 BC and 480 BC. We couldn't put it down. **UE+**

World Leaders Past and Present: Xerxes
Morgan Llywelyn • Written in a very interesting style, this is an excellent book about a fascinating leader! This gives a very thorough understanding of the most significant king of Persia. **MS+**

Within the Palace Gates
THE KING'S CUPBEARER
Anna P. Siviter • Originally published in 1932, it is a spellbinding story of Nehemiah, woven into the backdrop of the royal Persian Court. **UE+**

PERSIA VERSUS GREECE

The Lion in The Gateway

Mary Renault • A fictional account for children of the Persian invasion of Greece. The battles of Marathon, Thermopylae, and Salamis are described in rich detail. You will not understand the history of Persia or Greece without understanding these battles. **UE+**

Children of the Fox

Jill Paton Walsh • This book could be read either in this unit or the unit on Greece. It is another fictionalized story of the Persians invading Greece in 480 BC. Written as three short stories about Greek children, it includes a story about the aftermath of the invasion, which helps one understand the reason for the Peloponnesian wars between Athens and Sparta. **AA**

Exploits of Xenophon

Translated by Geoffrey Household • This is an incredible, riveting book! It is the true, autobiographical account of Greek mercenaries fighting for a Persian governor who wishes to usurp the throne and become king of Persia. **RA**

A MODERN DAY DANIEL

Imprisoned in Iran

Dan Baumann • A riveting true story about a Christian in Iran sharing the love of God while imprisoned and facing the death penalty in the land of ancient Persia. From YWAM Publishing. **UE+**

For more books, use these Dewey Decimal numbers in your library:

Bible: #220

Ancient Mesopotamia and the Iranian Plateau: #935

Ancient Palestine: #933

Also, look for biographies on the key people listed.

What books did you like best?

____

____

____

____

The Internet also contains a wealth of information about the Persians and the Medes.

What sites were the most helpful?

____

____

____

____

Student Self-Evaluation UNIT 6, PHASE 1

Dates and hours:____________________________

Key Concepts

Rephrase the four Key Concepts of this Unit and confirm your understanding of each:

- The Persian Empire

____

- Daniel's vision

____

- Rebuilding the temple

____

- Esther & Purim

____

Tools for Self-Evaulation

Evaluate your personal participation in the discussions of this Phase. Bearing in mind that a good participant in a discussion is not always the most vocal participant, ask yourself these questions: Were you an active participant? Did you ask perceptive questions? Were you willing to listen to other participants of the discussion and draw out their opinions? Record your observations and how you would like to improve your participation in the future:

____

____

Every time period is too complex to be understood in one Phase of study. Evaluate your current knowledge of the Persians & Medes. What have you focused on so far? What are your weakest areas of knowledge?

____

____

Based on the evaluation of this introduction, project ahead what you would like to study more of in the following Phases:

____

Phase 2

Research & Reporting

Explore one or more of these area to discover something significant!

Invasion of Greece

Find one of the books listed, or a book of your choice, for basic information about the Persian invasions of Greece. What was the short term impact of these invasions upon the Medo-Persian Empire? What was the long term impact upon Greece? Report your findings.

Old Testament Prophets

Investigate the books of Haggai, Zechariah, and Malachi in the Old Testament.

- To whom were these prophets speaking?
- What was the message?
- How did the people respond?
- How did God deal with them?

Persian Highway

Do a research paper on the Royal Road of Persia between Sardis and Susa.

Daniel's Vision

Using the vision of the four empires in Daniel 2, research the way that the Medo-Persian Empire fulfilled the biblical vision. Report your findings.

Floating Bridges

Discover the method used in creating Xerxes' floating bridge which spanned the Hellespont. What materials were used? How was it constructed? How stable would it have been? How many troops crossed it? What else crossed it? How long did it take? Was the bridge there when the army returned from Greece?

Purim

Research and write about the Feast of Purim, both the historical beginnings and the modern day celebration.

The Whole Story

Research and report on the "Rise and Fall of the Medo-Persian Empire." Who finally conquered this empire?

Persia to the Present

Investigate, using the library or the Internet, the history of Persia and Media from the time of King Cyrus to the present. What is the modern name of this nation? You may wish to interview adults who remember the deposing of the Shah in the 1970s. Report your findings.

Persian/Biblical Chronology

Compile a list of names, dates, and accomplishments of Media's and Persia's key leaders. How does this list compare with the events listed in the Bible?

Xerxes and His Army

Look up Xerxes in your history resources. How significant was this leader in Medo-Persian history? Discover more about the immense army of Xerxes. Where did his soldiers come from? Describe Xerxes' special fighting unit. How was Xerxes' army reprovisioned as they traveled? How many returned from the war in Greece? How was the empire affected by Xerxes' death?

Persian Law

Research and report on the way the ancient Persians viewed honesty. How is this magnified in the law of the kings? Can you make any modern comparisons or connections?

A Scriptural View

Summarize, either in written or verbal form, what you know about:

- King Cyrus;
- King Darius;
- Esther;
- King Xerxes;
- The invasions of Greece;
- Jews returning to Jerusalem;
- Rebuilding the Temple;
- Rebuilding the wall;
- Obedience to the commandments.

Rebuilding the Temple

Research and report on the rebuilding of the Temple. Make a chart showing the history of the Temple from the time of Solomon until the present.

Brain Stretchers

Compare and Contrast

Research the differences and similarities between Xerxes' bridge across the Hellespont and modern floating bridges. Report your findings.

Battle of the Bay of Salamis

Discover the tactics of the Greeks in fighting the Battle of the Bay of Salamis. Where did Xerxes' ships come from? How did he get them to Greece? How did Xerxes' navy lose the battle? Describe the differences between the Medo-Persian ships and the Greek ships.

Create Your Own Research Topic

____

____

____

Timeline

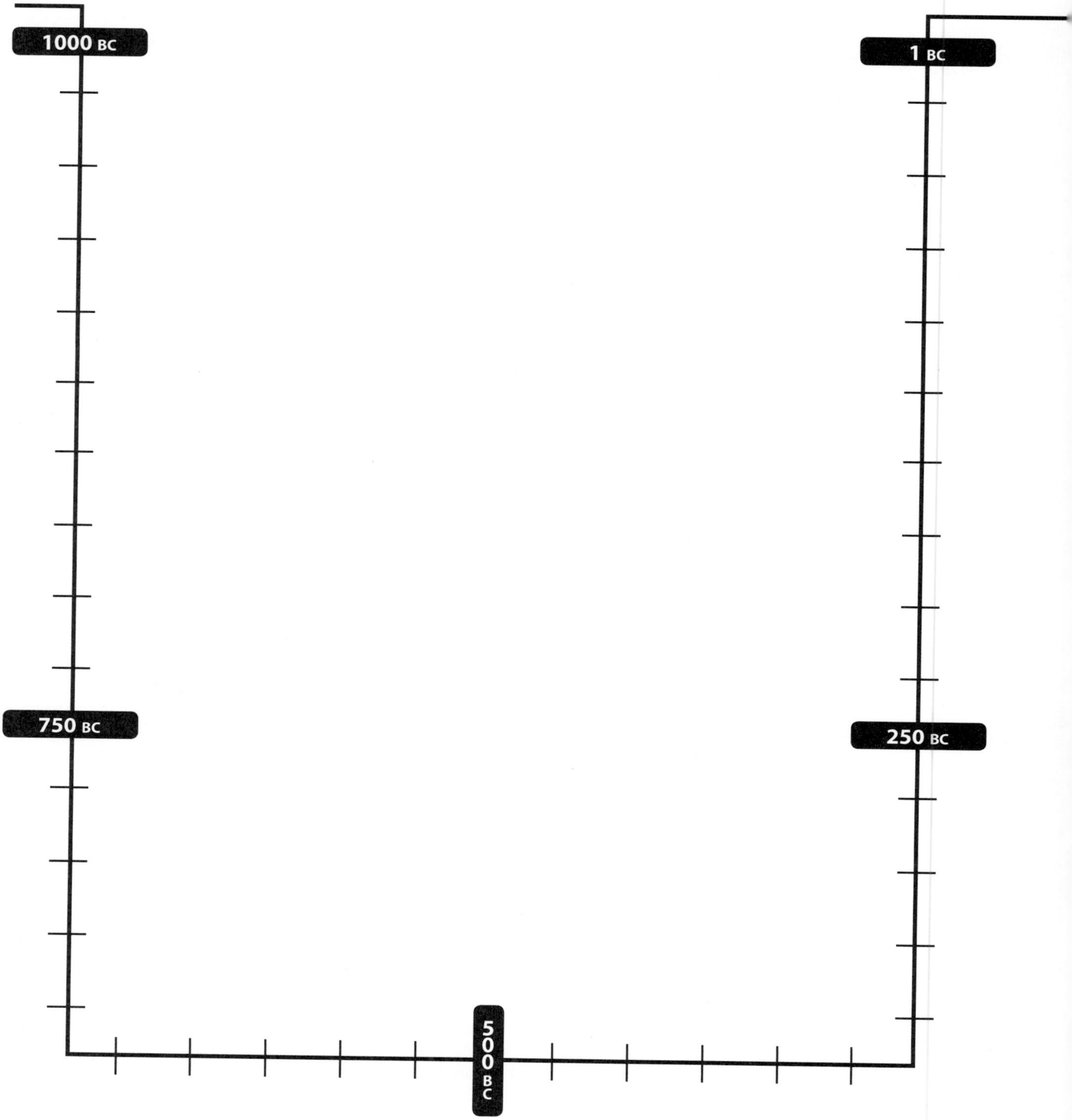

Consider this for your timeline

God's timing is perfect! He told Jeremiah that the time of captivity for the Jews in Babylon would last for seventy years, and the Medo-Persian army overthrew the Babylonian empire at exactly the right moment to accomplish the release and repatriation of the Jews back to Jerusalem to begin rebuilding the Temple in 536 BC—which was exactly seventy years from when they were taken captive in 607 BC. We must not grow indifferent to the remarkable faithfulness of God in the timeline of history!

The Book of Esther gives an awe-inspiring glimpse of the importance each of our lives has in history: *"Yet who knows whether you have come to the kingdom* ***for such a time as this****?"* (Esther 4:14). What does this mean to you? Reflect and consider how perfectly God has set you into your moment in history.

Key Events

- Cyrus's proclamation
- Return of Jews (three separate dates)
- Temple rebuilt
- Battle of Marathon
- Battle of Bay of Salamis

Be sure to include the people listed in Key People in Phase 1.

Words to Watch

Remember—The easiest way to learn a subject is to master its terms:

repatriate
Purim
gallows
invasion
Royal Road
trireme
Marathon
tactics
Persepolis

Other words you need to look up:

Student Self-Evaluation UNIT 6, PHASE 2

Dates and hours:____________________

Research Project

- Summarize your research question:

____

____

- List your most useful sources by author, title, and page number or URL where applicable (continue list in margin if necessary):

____

____

____

Now take a moment to evaluate the sources you just listed. Do they provide a balanced view of your research question? Should you have sought an additional opinion? Are your sources credible (if you found them on your own)? Record your observations:

____

____

Evaluate your research project in its final presentation. What are its strengths? If you had time to revisit this project, what would you change? Consider giving yourself a letter grade based on your project's merits and weaknesses.

____

____

Letter grade: ____

You have just completed an area of specific research in the time of the Persians & Medes. Now what would you like to explore in the upcoming Phases? Set some objectives for yourself:

____

Phase 3

Maps and Mapping

Physical Terrain

- » Label and color the Tigris and Euphrates rivers.
- » Locate and indicate the mountain ranges, deserts, and green areas of the ancient Medo-Persian Empire.
- » Shade and label the Persian Gulf.

Geopolitical

- » Draw the boundaries of ancient Persia and Media. What is today's name of those ancient countries?
- » Label the cities of Persepolis and Susa. What modern day cities are close to these ancient cities?
- » Discover the terrain and climate of Persia and Media.

CONSIDER:

Read Dan Baumann's book, *Imprisoned In Iran*, and discuss what his experience shows about the possibilities for Christian outreach in this nation.

Explore

- » ***Christian Outreach:*** What is the status of Christian outreach to the modern country where Persia was located? How has Christian outreach been affected in this country by the recent wars? Discuss the difficulties and remarkable opportunities facing Christians in that area of the world today.
- » ***The Geography of Esther:*** After reading the book of Esther, look in an atlas to discover where Shushan (Susa) was located. How far was it from Susa to Babylon to Jerusalem? How much territory was covered by the decree of the King of Persia to destroy the Jews?

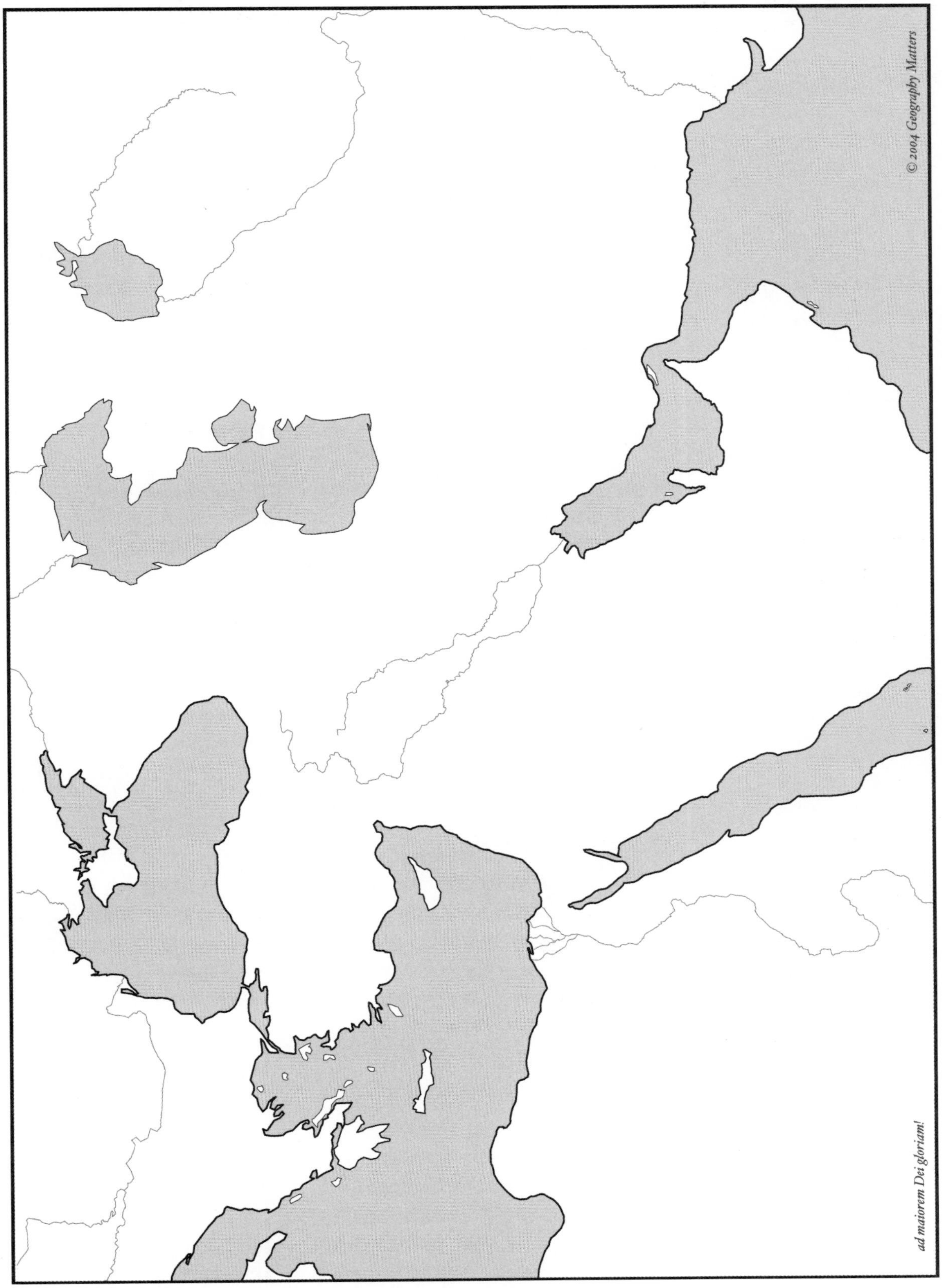
© 2004 Geography Matters
ad maiorem Dei gloriam!

CONSIDER:

Henry O. Tanner (AD 1859–1937) was the first African American artist to win international acclaim. He spent most of his professional career in France, avoiding the increasing hostility and racism of that time period in America. Tanner traveled twice to the Holy Land, which provided inspiration and insight into his many religious paintings.

Art Appreciation

Daniel in the Lion's Den by Henry O. Tanner

- Do you think this painting reflects what the Bible describes?
- How does the painting differ from your own impression of this historic event?
- How would you describe Tanner's use of shadow and light in this painting?

Glazed tile relief of ancient Persia

- How would you describe Persia's glazed tile relief artwork?
- Is it similar to other artwork we have previously observed?
- What can you learn about this culture from its art?
- From what you can discover, did the Persians and Medes create any art that was original to their culture?

Architecture

The magnificent architecture of the Persians can be glimpsed in the remains of the palace King Darius constructed at Persepolis, beginning c. 518 BC, which Alexander the Great later destroyed. It appears, from what can be seen of the ruins, that Darius intended the city of Persepolis to be the seat of government and the showplace of his fabulously wealthy empire. Alexander the Great, in 330 BC, allowed his soldiers to loot the city, carting away so much treasure that it took 20,000 mules and 5,000 camels to carry it all. He then set fire to Darius's palace, utterly destroying it, except for the ruins which can be seen today.

- Look for photos of the city of Persepolis, especially for the general staircase decorated with reliefs at Darius's palace. How would you describe these ruins? What are the similarities to Assyrian or Babylonian architecture?

Arts in Action

Select one or more, and let your artistic juices flow!

Imitation

- Try imitating Henry Tanner's use of light in the lion's den.
- Try creating something in the Persian style of art

Relief Carving

Try making a relief carving on wax or soap. Or, if you prefer, try using a slab of clay rolled flat onto a board and carve a relief of a simple animal, such as a fish. Let it dry and mount it.

Sand Cast Candle

A wonderful bronze head (cast, not sculptured) was found in the excavations of Persia. Make a sand cast candle by pouring hot wax into a form made in the sand. You can make a hollowed out space by packing the sand very firmly around a can, a ball, your hands, etc., then carefully removing the object. This creates the form. If you are very adventurous, try making a plaster cast. Check the library or an expert for more info.

Potato Stamp

In the Book of Esther, the king gives to Haman and then to Mordecai his signet ring. A signet ring was extremely important because it was stamped on official documents (much like a signature today). Create a stamp using a potato! Cut a potato in half, then use a toothpick to poke a design into the exposed surface on one half. Next, carefully carve away about ¼ inch of the rest of the potato half, letting the design stand out in sharp relief. Press the potato relief onto a rubber stamp ink pad, then stamp your relief design on paper.

Floating Bridge

Build a "floating bridge" out of balsa wood, LEGO bricks, Ivory soap bars, or other materials. Anchor ships across the span of a sink, wading pool, or small creek. Make miniature cables and string them across the tops of the ships. Build it up with planking, railing, etc., just as described at the crossing of the Hellespont.

Science

The cables used in supporting Xerxes' bridge across the Hellespont were made of flax and papyrus that were braided together. The first bridge he attempted also used cables of flax and papyrus, but they were not braided together, and the bridge came apart in a storm.

Braided Rope

Experiment with braiding various short ropes, each made with only one substance (thread, string, horse hair, human hair, etc.). Test their strength by hanging weights from the end until the ropes break. Now try braiding different substances together and hanging weights from the rope. Which ropes are the strongest? Does it improve the strength of a rope to use more than one material? Compare all of these to the strength of a spider's web.

» ***Variation:*** Try making a rope that is not braided, and one that is. Which is stronger? Read Ecclesiastes 4:12 and discuss it in light of your experiment.

» ***Space Age:*** Learn more about the new fibers and textiles used in space-age technology. Imagine the possibilities if Xerxes had had these materials!

Music

After the plot of Haman was uncovered, the Jews were allowed to defend themselves on the day of attack. Their defense was successful, and the Jewish nation survived this attempted annihilation. In response, the people celebrated with feasting and joy. Though the Bible does not describe the music of the celebration, we know that the Jews had used music in celebrations in the past. Do you think the music would have been loud or soft? Or, perhaps would it have been a combination of loud and soft? The term used to describe the loudness or softness in music is dynamics. Dynamics is another one of the fundamental elements of music. A piece of music can be played all at a loud dynamic level, or it can be played at a soft dynamic level, but most music has a combination of various dynamic levels.

Listen

» A wonderful example of strong dynamic changes is the *Surprise Symphony* by Franz Joseph Haydn. Haydn wrote strong contrasts of dynamics in this piece of music to address a problem. He was a diligent, hardworking, Christian composer who greatly respected the musicians in his orchestra. However, the rich people who came to hear the orchestra often fell asleep due to too much feasting and drinking. So he devised a solution! Listen carefully to the second movement, called the "Andante," to hear what he did. Imagine yourself sleeping like the rich patrons. Do you think his solution was effective?

Try This

» See how softly you can sing or tap or hum; then see how loudly you can sing or tap or hum; then determine how many different levels you can make. For instance, can you sing very, very soft? very soft? soft? medium soft? medium loud? loud? very loud? very, very loud? Musicians use Italian terms to indicate dynamic levels. "Piano" means soft, "forte" (FOR-tay) means loud.

Cooking

Our Unit examines the Medo-Persian Empire, the return of the Jews to Jerusalem, and the deliverance of the Jews recorded in the Book of Esther. When you learn about the climate of Persia, perhaps this soup will sound just right! (It is served cold.) And to help you celebrate Purim, we have included a delicious cookie recipe—Rejoice!

Persian Cucumber & Yogurt Soup

1 quart yogurt (plain)
1 cup buttermilk
½ cup walnuts, chopped
3 small cucumbers, peeled, seeded, chopped
½ cup fresh mint, finely chopped (or chopped green onions)

Beat yogurt and buttermilk together until well blended. Stir in mint and cucumbers; salt and pepper to taste. Serve very cold, sprinkle with chopped walnuts. Serves 8.

Hamantaschen Cookie Recipe (Purim)

1 cup whole wheat flour
1 cup white flour
2 tsp baking powder
½ cup sugar
¼ cup butter, softened
2 eggs, slightly beaten
1 tsp almond extract
¼ cup orange juice

(Traditional filling: poppy seed, prune. However, you can also use your imagination and come up with a sure-to-please-the-family filling.)

Combine and mix all dry ingredients. Cut in the butter. Add the eggs, almond extract, and juice. Mix dough into a ball, adding extra flour or water if needed for a workable dough. Roll out dough on a floured surface, ¼ in. thick. Cut with cookie cutter in 3 in. circles. Place 1 tsp filling in the center, and pinch dough up on three sides to form an open triangle. Bake at 350 degrees for 20 min., or until golden.

Student Self-Evaluation UNIT 6, PHASE 3

Dates and hours:____________________________

Evaluate Your Projects

- List which of the activities listed in this Phase you did:

  ____

  ____

  ____

- Rate your enthusiasm: ____________

  Explain: ____

  ____

- Rate the precision of your approach:____________

  Explain: ____

  ____

- Rate your effort towards the completion of the project: ____________

  Explain: ____

  ____

Ask yourself what worked and what did not. What would you do differently in the future, and what would you repeat?

____

How specifically did these hands-on activities enhance your knowledge of the Persians & Medes? What made them worthwhile?

____

In the first three Phases of this Unit, what aspect of the time period has most captured your imagination? What would you like to creatively pursue to conclude your study?

____

Phase 4

In Your Own Way…

We have seen God's amazing timing and redemptive purposes in the Medo-Persian Empire, and how He saved the Jewish people from extermination through Esther's intervention with the king. Praise the Lord for His perfect timing, perfect provision, and perfect purposes! Now, choose a selection of these activities, or create your own, which will best express what you have learned from this Unit.

LINGUISTICS

Journalism

Be a war correspondent accompanying Xerxes' invasion army. Write a series of news reports for *The Susa Sun* about the progress of the invasion of Greece.

Prose

- Write a fictional account of the journey from Babylon to Jerusalem, from the viewpoint of a sheep named "Baa-aa-aa-Hum-bug."
- Write a book for young children showing the events of Esther's life. Include her someday-to-be husband going off to conquer those cantankerous Greeks.

Playing with Words

Finish this limerick about Esther's uncle:
There once was an uncle named Mordecai
Whose enemies wanted to hang him high…

Poetry

- Write a poem with the first line, "From Babylon went good Zerubbabel."
- Write a poem of Esther, with her prayer to God the night before she went unbidden to the king.

ART

Painting/Drawing

Paint a scene from the rebuilding of the Temple. Focus on what colors best evoke the suppressed excitement and fear they would have felt as they worked in the midst of their enemies.

Graphic Design

- Create an advertisement for the second annual Feast of Purim, held in downtown Susa.
- Make an enlistment poster for soldiers to join Xerxes in his military invasion of Greece.
- Design a T-shirt for those who went with Ezra back to Jerusalem. Start with "We survived . . ."

Illustration

Illustrate the book for young children listed above.

Sculpting

Using materials you prefer to work with, sculpt the four empires of Daniel 2 as suggested in the vision.

Cartooning

- Draw a political cartoon showing the folks who were angry about the wall in Jerusalem being built (Nehemiah 4:7–9) and Nehemiah encouraging the Jewish wall builders to arm themselves against these angry folks.
- Make a multi-frame cartoon of Esther inviting the king and Haman to her house for a cozy meal, only to invite them again.

MUSIC

Compose

Create a jubilant song of praise about the dramatic deliverance of God's people from their enemies, focusing on Esther and Haman. You could use the songs of Miriam or Moses as your model, or one of the Psalms of David.

Performance Practice

With your teacher's help, select an appropriate piece of music, which expresses some element from this Unit, such as the joy of the repatriated Jews. Prepare and perform the piece for an audience. Communicate with your audience the reason for your selection either in the program notes or in a short speech.

DRAMA

Comedy

Create a humorous skit about Haman having to honor Mordecai.

Reality

Act out the rebuilding of Jerusalem's wall. Begin with Nehemiah's conversation with King Artaxerxes. Use your imagination to create props, sets, and costumes. Be sure to include realistic fear and rejoicing!

Celebrate

Celebrate the Feast of Purim. Learn about the traditions and rituals of this feast, prepare costumes and props to tell the story of Esther, and invite your family, friends, or neighbors to share this miraculous event.

Reader's Theater

Do a dramatic reading about the invasion of Greece by King Xerxes.

Prop Needs

___
___
___

Costume Ideas

___
___
___

Role/Player

___
___
___

Set Suggestions

___
___
___

MOVEMENT

Pantomime

Pantomime Esther's anxiety as she goes to the king, knowing that he may not extend his scepter.

Dance

Choreograph a dance that depicts the ending of seventy years of captivity, and the royal proclamation of King Cyrus for the willing Jews to return to Jerusalem.

Action

- Show the events of Haman's life in stylized action, including his swaggering pride.
- Act out the fights between the Jews and Persians, after the king's second proclamation. (What is the difference in mentality of the two groups? Consider representing this with different action styles.)

CONCEPTUAL DESIGN

Prefabricated Bridge

Using the concept of the prefabricated bridges used in World War II, design a prefabricated bridge with materials which would have been available in Xerxes' time. Improve the floating bridge used in the invasion of Greece at the Hellespont.

CREATE YOUR OWN EXPRESSION

___

___

___

___

___

Student Self-Evaluation UNIT 6, PHASE 4

Dates and hours:______________________

Evaluate Your Projects

- What creative project did you choose?

  ____

- What did you expect from your project, and how does the final project compare to your initial expectations?

  ____

  ____

- What do you like about your project? What would you change?

  ____

  ____

In Conclusion

Revisit the four Key Concepts from the beginning of this Unit. Explain how your understanding of and appreciation for each has grown over the course of your study.

____

____

____

____

____

____

Record your concluding thoughts on the Persians & Medes:

____

____

____

Greece & the Hellenists

UNIT 7

Key Concepts

- Golden Age of Greece
- Greek intellectual achievements
- Influence of Greek worldview
- Alexander the Great and his Empire
- Hanukkah's history

The third kingdom of Daniel's vision emerges . . .

Just before the defeat of the Babylonians at the hands of the Medo-Persian army in 539 BC, Daniel was given another startling, prophetic vision by God. In this vision, he saw a mighty, victorious ram that conquered to the west, the north, and the south, and was so powerful that no one could withstand it. Suddenly, from the west came a fierce male goat, which attacked the ram, and this furious goat trampled the ram to the ground. Daniel saw that "there was no one that could deliver the ram from his hand."

When Daniel sought the meaning of this vision, the angel Gabriel came to him and explained that, "the ram which you saw, having the two horns—they are the kings of Media and Persia. And the male goat is the kingdom of Greece. The large horn that is between its eyes is the first king" (Daniel 8:20–21).

Two hundred years before the event, God showed His people that a Greek king would topple the mighty Persian Empire. The name of this king was Alexander the Great, and he did exactly what Daniel saw in the vision. He was also the one described as "a leopard, which had on its back four wings of a bird" (Daniel 7:6), and his kingdom was the "belly and thighs of bronze" in the great statue dreamed by Nebuchadnezzar and interpreted by Daniel. But, before we study Alexander and the fruit of his conquests, we need to better understand the history of Greece prior to his advent.

A map of the terrain of Greece will show immediately that this area is rugged, mountainous, and coastal (no village or city is far from the sea). Because the land is mostly mountainous with few large plains, and because the sea is such a prominent feature, the ancient people of Greece developed a different style of living than the ancient farmers of Mesopotamia, including travel by boat rather than overland, because the sea was generally easier to traverse than the land. This familiarity with sea travel would prove significant in the areas of trade, warfare, and the spread of philosophic influence throughout the history of the Greeks.

Early Greece

Beginning in the 1200s BC with the invasion of southern Greece by the warlike Dorian tribe, the people of Greece scattered throughout the land. Small communities formed in isolated places, separated from each other by the mountains. These communities eventually became city-states, which included a city with its surrounding villages, farms, and countryside. These communities usually were set around a hill or rocky outcropping, and a fortress known as an *acropolis* was built at the summit, which could be easily defended if attacked. The best known of these city-states were Athens and Sparta, though there were many others throughout the land.

A map of the terrain of Greece will show immediately that this area is rugged, mountainous and coastal.

The people of this time did not think of themselves as "Greeks," but rather as Athenians, Spartans, Thebans, Corinthians, or whatever city-state they were from. This separation, which was both physical and philosophical, caused many difficulties for the Greek people and gave the Persian king, Darius, great assurance that he could pick off each querulous city-state one by one, rather than having to face a united enemy. In fact, in all of their history, it was only during periods of extreme duress, such as the Persian invasion by Xerxes, that the Greek city-states joined together to function as one group.

By the eighth century BC, the population was greater than this mountainous land could support, so many left to find new lands that would provide a more abundant life. These people traveled to many areas throughout the Mediterranean, including Italy, Sicily, France, north Africa, and up into the Black Sea region. Wherever they went, they set up Greek city-states similar to what they had experienced at home. These new settlements began trading with the city-states back in Greece, which brought about a tremendous influx of new resources for the Greek people. It also gave great wealth to those who controlled these resources, creating a prosperous middle class to compete with the wealthy, landowning aristocracy.

To fulfill their required duty to the city-state as soldiers, the newly enriched middle class developed weapons and armor in the seventh century BC, which could be used very successfully by foot soldiers. A new shield, called a *hoplon*, was developed, which put the weight of the shield on the soldier's shoulder rather than his wrist. Though this was an innovative and helpful design, it left the soldier's right side exposed. To protect this vulnerability, a new method of fighting was developed, which placed soldiers shoulder to shoulder in a tight formation know as a *phalanx*. The soldiers in formation behind the front line, pushed together towards the front, which gave the phalanx an incredible, indefatigable momentum. Not only were their right sides protected now, the structure of the phalanx made the armies efficient and powerful fighting machines. These well-outfitted, extremely proficient soldiers, known as *hoplites*, became the backbone of the various city-states' military force. In fact, they were nearly invincible, as King Darius learned to his dismay at the battle of Marathon.

The extreme differences between the wealthy and the poor brought the city to the brink of revolution.

By the mid-sixth century BC in Athens, the extreme differences between the wealthy and the poor brought the city to the brink of revolution. Plutarch, a Greek biographer of the first century BC, wrote about this time: "The disparity of fortune between the rich and the poor had reached its height, so that the city seemed to be in a truly dangerous condition, and no other means for freeing it from disturbances . . . seemed possible but a despotic power." However, rather than a revolution, a ruler named Solon provided a means for escape in 594 BC. In one move, he canceled all debt in Athens. All lands were released from mortgages, all people who had been made slaves due to debt were released, all sold into slavery abroad were brought home and freed. This one step had a remarkable effect upon Athens and its people. Just as God had told Moses to proclaim a Year of Jubilee every fiftieth year for the dismissal of debt and the blessing of the people, this Greek ruler saw wisdom in releasing the people from bondage.

Age of tyrants

Though Solon brought reform to the people of Athens, it wasn't long after his departure from Athens that the historical struggle between the wealthy and the poor again appeared to trouble the city. This time, a man seized power and became a *tyrant*. This Greek word meaning "ruler" did not have the same connotation at that time as it has today. In fact, the period of Greek history from about 650 BC to about 500 BC was known as the "age of tyrants," because many rulers of Greek city-states during this time had come to power not by royal birth nor by the will of the people, but through military power. Some ruled well, others did not, some ruled for long periods while others were quickly overthrown. In Athens, the man who seized control was named Pisistratus, and he basically enforced the laws of Solon. Under his rule, the Athenians became used to living with good laws, great public works (such as the building of temples and aqueducts), a powerful army that protected their peace, and economic improvement for all. As Will Durant wrote in *The Life of Greece*, "The poor were made less poor, the rich not less rich." After thirty-three years of this kind of peaceful rule, though, everything changed. The son of Pisistratus, who had ruled quietly for the previous thirteen years, suddenly changed his policies and subjected the Athenians to a reign of terror. He and his family were driven out of Athens in 510 BC, and the city was plunged into two years of civil war. But in 508 BC, Cleisthenes came to power. Finally, under this man, a new form of government called *democracy* was established in Athens. He demolished the power base of the aristocratic ruling families by dividing Athens into "tribes" composed of an equal number of districts from the city, the coast, and the interior. This gave the new democracy a broader base of support from geographic regions. Regardless of wealth, each citizen now had the right to vote on laws, to speak at governmental assemblies, to participate in the government if they were selected, and to fulfill their duty by volunteering at times to be on a legal jury.

To be a citizen in Athens, men who were at least eighteen years old had to show that they were eligible by:

1. proving that both parents were born in Athens;
2. proving that both parents were of the citizen class;
3. proving that the parents were legally married.

Many rulers of Greek city-states during this time had come to power not by royal birth nor by the will of the people, but through military power.

Those who became citizens were then expected to devote their time to the affairs of the city, learning all they could about politics and the issues of the day, and serving the system as needed. They were also expected to be prepared for military service, if necessary. However, doing physical labor or being involved in any form of business, apart from managing one's estate, was not considered proper for a citizen.

Those who were not citizens made up two other groups: the *metic*, who were the foreigners that traded, kept shops, made crafts, and owned ships; and the *slaves*, who did the manual labor in homes, markets, workshops, and the silver mines.

Shortly after this system of democracy began to function in Athens, the Persian Empire attacked the Athenians in 490 BC at the Plain of Marathon. Though the Persians were defeated in that battle, it was obvious to many that someday soon they would return, and they would be ready to take vengeance when they came.

Sparta

While Athens was struggling through various types of rule, Sparta developed a completely unique form of government. Sparta also had citizens, but only a very few could obtain citizenship. The requirements were:

1. prove that both parents were descended from the original Dorian invaders;
2. complete every stage of the Spartan school system (which had one main subject—warfare!);
3. belong to one of the military clubs, providing a certain amount of food and drink for it.

Those who became citizens were then expected to devote their time to the affairs of the city,

If you could meet these requirements, and were thirty years of age, you could be a citizen of Sparta. Now for the bad news: all Spartan citizens were full-time professional soldiers and were forbidden to do any other form of work from the ages of eighteen to sixty. If soldiers were not actually in battle, they were subjecting themselves to the harsh rigors of the Spartan soldier's lifestyle. They were expected to give total loyalty to the state, to obey those in authority, to prepare themselves at all times for war, and to prefer death to defeat in battle.

Those who were not citizens and yet were not slaves performed the function of craftsmen, fisherman, tradesmen, and sailors. The slaves were the conquered people from the neighboring land of Messenia, which now belonged to the Spartan city-state. They had no chance for freedom unless they successfully revolted (which happened only a few times). They were forced to farm the land of Sparta and the land of Messenia for the Spartan citizens, who were given an allotment of land and a certain number of slaves by the government.

When a baby boy was born to the soldier-class in Sparta, he was examined to make sure he was not weak or blemished. If he passed inspection, he was allowed to live. When this boy was seven years old, he was taken from his home to a barracks-school where he learned to fight and survive harsh treatment. When he finished school, each boy had to join the Spartan army where he would live in the austere barracks until old age. Though he was supposed to marry by age thirty, a Spartan soldier would not stay with his wife for more than a short time before going back to the barracks. This military mindset, and its efficient system of producing tough soldiers, made Sparta the greatest military power in Greece. The Spartans rarely left home, however, since they were always concerned about the very real threat of a slave revolt on their native soil.

The Persians attack

In 480 BC the Spartans were motivated to join with other Greek city-states. Why? The largest army ever assembled at that point in history was on the march against Greece. Led by the Persian king Xerxes, this army of more than a million soldiers was threatening the Greeks with the loss of all their freedom and much-desired independence. King Leonidas of Sparta took control of the 4,000 troops at Thermopylae, a narrow pass through which

Xerxes' huge army had to travel. An incredulous Xerxes watched his men suffering a tremendous defeat as they were repulsed again and again by this tiny army of Greeks. Who knows how long this would have continued if a traitor had not shown Xerxes a way to get behind the enemy position. Once Xerxes had annihilated King Leonidas and three hundred of his men (the rest being ordered by Leonidas to retreat), he marched on Athens.

The Athenians, after the Battle of Marathon, wisely listened to the counsel of a leader named Themistocles, who encouraged the people to build a proper seaport and a large fleet of warships. So as Xerxes came to Athens, the people fled the city, boarded boats at the harbor, and were taken out of harm's way. Xerxes, as we saw in the last unit, retaliated against the Greeks for the burning of Sardis during his father's reign by burning the city of Athens. But that was not sufficient punishment for these rebellious Greeks, so, when he was told that the Greeks had warships in the Bay of Salamis, he called for the Persian fleet to annihilate them. Aeschylus, a Greek playwright who described this battle from the viewpoint of the Persians, wrote,

This military mindset, and its efficient system of producing tough soldiers, made Sparta the greatest military power in Greece.

> A Greek ship charged first, chopped off the whole stern of a Phoenician galley. Then charge followed charge on every side. At first by its huge impetus our fleet withstood them. But soon in that narrow space, our ships were jammed in hundreds; none could help another. They rammed each other with their prows of bronze and some were stripped of every oar. Meanwhile, the enemy came around us in a ring and charged. Our vessels heeled over. The sea was carpeted with wrecks and dead men; all the shores and reefs were full of dead. Then every ship we had broke rank and rowed for life.

The Persian fleet was soundly defeated, and Xerxes went home. Many of the Greek city-states were concerned, however, that the Persians might return yet again, so they banded together into the Delian League with a common treasury held on the island of Delos. Athens was the leader of this league, contributing ships rather than money. This gave the Athenians an edge over their allies (who lacked sea power), creating eventually an Athenian Empire. In the mid-400s BC the Athenian leader, Pericles, realized that the accumulated treasure of the Delian League was lying unused and relatively unprotected on Delos, and suggested that the Athenians take the money back to Athens. Any money beyond what was absolutely necessary for the defense of the League could then be used by the Athenians to rebuild and beautify their city. Quite a good idea for Athens, not as good an idea for its allies in the Delian League, but who was going to argue with them? None of their allies had the power of Athens.

Classical Period

The Classical Period of Greek history (480–323 BC), began with the defeat of Xerxes and lasted until the time of Alexander the Great. The first fifty years of this period are known as the *Golden Age*, since this was the time when the arts (such as architecture, literature, philosophy, sculpting, and theater) flourished in Athens. This is the time of Socrates, the philosopher who asked questions; Aeschylus, the founder of Greek tragedy and writer of ninety plays; Pheidias, the sculptor who created the statue of Zeus (one of the Seven Wonders of the Ancient World) as well as the statue of Athena in the Parthenon; Herodotus, the Greek traveler and writer who became known as the *Father of History*; and many other influential people. However, the Golden Age came to an abrupt halt in 431 BC when Sparta and its allies went to war against Athens and its allies.

The war between Sparta and Athens was called the Peloponnesian War, and it lasted for twenty-seven years, devastating Greece. Since Sparta had a nearly invincible land army, and Athens had a superior navy, Sparta was able to invade the land surrounding Athens, but Athens was able to import food with its ships. This prolonged the struggle for many years. There was a short time of peace after a treaty was signed in 421 BC, but war soon broke out again. Eventually, Persia gave the Spartans a loan of money so that they were able to build a navy and destroy the Athenian fleet. This meant that Athens could no longer be resupplied with food, and in 404 BC, the starving Athenians surrendered to the Spartans.

None of their allies had the power of Athens.

Though the war was over, peace was not forthcoming. The weakened city-states continued to struggle for supremacy over each other, with constant battles and small wars. During this troubled time, Xenophon and thousands of other Greek mercenaries (soldiers for hire) went to work for Cyrus, the brother of the Persian king. In the last Unit, we learned that, after the death of Cyrus, who had been battling to to usurp the throne, ten thousand Greek soldiers had to battle their way out of a hostile Persian land. They elected the Athenian cavalry officer and former student of Socrates, Xenophon, to lead them safely home. Against overwhelming odds, Xenophon and his troops battled their way along the Tigris and north to Kurdistan and Armenia, all the way to the Black Sea—a journey of two thousand miles—contested every step of the way. It was in this epic struggle that the lesson was learned that a small Greek army could successfully war against a massive Persian army on its own terrain. This lesson would be studied and applied by one who was yet to come.

In 359 BC Philip II came to the throne of Macedonia, an area northeast of Greece. The country was in turmoil at this point due to constant invasions and civil war. However, Philip brought a brilliant military mind and a diplomatic tongue to bear on the chaotic state, and within twenty years he had turned Macedonia into the most powerful military state of the day. In 338 BC he won the battle of Chaeronea, conquering Athens, Thebes, and their allies, allowing Philip to take control of Greece. A year later he united Greece and Macedonia by planning a joint war against Persia. Though he was assassinated soon after, the war effort was continued by his son, Alexander.

Alexander the Great

At last we have arrived at the point where we started this story! Alexander took control of his father's military forces when he became king of Macedonia in 336 BC, and within two years subdued the entire country of Greece to his will. In 334 BC Alexander invaded Persia with 30,000 infantry and 5,000 cavalry, a paltry number compared to the size of army the Persians could muster. However, just as Xenophon had proved, the Greek army was more than capable of defeating the Persians. The battle of Issus in 333 BC was the first battle between the Greeks and Persians, and through Alexander's brilliant strategy it was won decisively. From there, Alexander turned toward Egypt to secure his flanks. On the way, he captured and destroyed the heretofore impregnable city of Tyre. As he journeyed onward to Egypt, he came to the land of Palestine. He destroyed the recalcitrant city of Gaza, and then turned his eye toward Jerusalem. The Jewish historian, Josephus, describes what happened next:

> Now Alexander, when he had taken Gaza, made haste to go up to Jerusalem; and Jaddua the high priest, when he heard that, was in an agony, and under terror, as not knowing how he should meet the Macedonians, since the king was displeased at his foregoing disobedience. He therefore ordained that the people should make supplications, and should join with him in offering sacrifice to God, whom he besought to protect that nation, and to deliver them from the perils that were coming upon them; whereupon God warned him in a dream, which came upon him after he had offered sacrifice, that 'he should take courage, and adorn the city, and open the gates; that the rest should appear in white garments, but that he and the priests should meet the king in the habits proper to their order, without the dread of any ill consequences, which the providence of God would prevent.' Upon which, when he rose from his sleep, he greatly rejoiced; and declared to all the warning he had received from God. . . . And when the Phoenicians and the Chaldeans that followed him, thought they should have liberty to plunder the city, and torment the high priest to death, which the king's displeasure fairly promised them, the very reverse of it happened; for Alexander, when he saw the multitude at a distance, in white garments, while the priests stood clothed with fine linen, and the high priest in purple and scarlet clothing, with his mitre on his head, having the golden plate whereon the name

Portrait bust showing Alexander the Great wearing a lion head-dress

> of God was engraved, he approached by himself, and adored that Name, and first saluted the high priest. The Jews also did altogether, with one voice, salute Alexander, and encompass him about; whereupon the king of Syria, and the rest, were surprised at what Alexander had done, and supposed him disordered in his mind. However, Parmenio alone went up to him, and asked him, 'How it came to pass, that when all others adored him, he should adore the high priest of the Jews?' To whom he replied, 'I did not adore him, but that God who hath honored him with the high priesthood; for I saw this very person in a dream, in this very habit, when I was at Dios in Macedonia, who, when I was considering with myself how I might obtain the dominion of Asia, exhorted me to make no delay, but boldly to pass over the sea thither, for that he would conduct my army, and would give me the dominion over the Persians.' And when the book of Daniel was shown him, wherein Daniel declared that one of the Greeks should destroy the empire of the Persians, he supposed that himself was the person intended: and as he was then glad, he dismissed the multitude for the present, but the next day he called them to him, and bade them ask what favors they pleased of him; whereupon the high priest desired that they might enjoy the laws of their forefathers, and might pay no tribute on the seventh year. He granted all they desired.

The country was in turmoil at this point due to constant invasions and civil war.

Alexander, over the next ten years, conquered every place he and his army came to, from Egypt to India. He was the first European to conquer Asia, and his empire was larger than any empire had ever been. When he died suddenly, at the age of thirty-three, his empire was forcibly broken up by four generals. By 281 BC the Hellenistic (or Greek) Empire of Alexander the Great was divided into three kingdoms: Egypt, ruled by the Ptolemies; Asia Minor to India, ruled by the Seleucids; and Macedonia and Greece ruled by the Antigonids.

Read the words of Daniel 8:8 and discover how perfectly God described Alexander and his empire:

> "Therefore the male goat grew very great; but when he became strong, the large horn was broken, and in place of it four notable ones came up toward the four winds of heaven."

The Hellenistic Empire brought the Greek language and culture to much of the known world. The permeating influence of Greek thought and Greek ways settled into the very fabric of most cultures from Rome to Egypt, and from Babylon to Jerusalem. Though many people welcomed what they considered the civilizing effect of the Greeks, there were some who fought to keep Hellenism at bay.

Judea had been under the benevolent control of the Ptolemies for many years and given the same consideration for their religious beliefs and ceremonies as Alexander the Great had provided. However, when Antiochus Epiphanes (a Seleucid ruler) came to power in Syria, he decided that the

Jews needed a good dose of hellenization in order to be freed from their ancient and obsolete religion. In 167 BC he sacked Jerusalem on the Sabbath, and set up a statue of Zeus in the Temple on the altar, where pigs were then offered as sacrifices. Next, he outlawed on pain of death the practice of circumcision, observing the Sabbath, or celebrating the Jewish holy days.

Many others who were committed to following the God of their fathers joined Mattathias in the hills.

The country erupted into revolution when Antiochus Epiphanes' officer arrived in the village of Modin. He expected the old priest, Mattathias, to meekly cooperate with the projected program of offering a pagan sacrifice, but Mattathias refused. When another Jew willingly came forth, Mattathias was enraged and he killed both the traitor to Judaism and the king's officer, along with destroying the pagan altar. Mattathias and his five sons then fled to the hills. Many others who were committed to following the God of their fathers joined Mattathias in the hills. They began to wage guerilla warfare on both the Syrians and the Hellenistic Jews who supported them. When Mattathias died, shortly after starting this revolt, his third son, Judas was chosen to be the military leader of the guerilla army. He was given the name "Maccabaeus" which means "the hammer." Judas Maccabaeus was a good choice as he proved to be a phenomenally successful general. Both Josephus and the Book of First Maccabees in the Apocrypha describe Judas Maccabaeus as one who trusted in the Lord and looked to Him for deliverance of his nation. God enabled the outnumbered Maccabean army to recapture Jerusalem three years after Antiochus Epiphanes had sacked it. They purified the Temple, grinding the statue of Zeus into dust, and then celebrated with an eight-day Feast of Dedication, known as Hanukkah, the Festival of Lights.

We have studied three empires that have come and gone since Daniel's dream. One remains.

Phase 1

Listen to This

What in the World? VOL. 1

DISC THREE:

» Daniel's Vision (track 6)

» Athens & Sparta (track 7)

» Alexander the Great (track 8)

DISC FOUR:

» The Hellenistic Empire (track 1)

Digging Deeper VOL. 1

DISC TWO:

» The Seven Wonders of the Ancient World: Colossus of Rhodes, Temple of Artemis, Lighthouse of Alexandria, Mausoleum at Halicarnassus, Statue of Zeus, Conclusion (tracks 4–9)

Read For Your Life

The Holy Bible

» The Main Story: Daniel 8:5–8, 21, 11:3–4, Acts 17:16–34, Acts 19:23–41

Key People

Pericles
Architect of the Golden Age of Greece

Herodotus
The first historian

Socrates
The Greek philosopher

Plato
The disciple of Socrates

Aristotle
Plato's disciple and Alexander the Great's tutor

Alexander the Great
Conquered the world in 10 years

Judas Maccabaeus
Leader of the Maccabean revolt

continued next page

Antiochus Epiphanes
Syrian ruler who stirred up the Jews

Ptolemy II
Ordered the Hebrew Scriptures translated into Greek—the Septuagint

Talk Together

Opinion Column

- What did you find to be the most interesting aspect, or the most fascinating person, you encountered in your introduction to Greece and the Hellenistic Empire?
- Why do you think God gave Daniel such a clear vision of a Greek king who would quickly sweep through the world, and then be gone just as quickly?
- Imagine you are an Athenian. How would you describe Sparta to a foreigner?
- The statue of Zeus at Olympus was built about 430 BC as an object of worship. After reading Acts 17:29, imagine you were an Athenian, had seen the statue of Zeus, and were listening to Paul. How would Paul's words affect you? What response would you give?

Critical Puzzling

- Why do you think the Greek soldiers were so effective? What application of this can you make in your own life? (Ephesians 6:10–17)
- The Greek philosopher and teacher, Aristotle, was Alexander the Great's tutor, prior to Alexander's conquests. What kind of impact do you think this famous Greek thinker would have had upon this Macedonian prince?
- Paul, in Acts 17, built a bridge of communication to the Greeks, using familiar things from their culture (statues, poetry, etc.) Consider, in light of his example, what our response should be to people who are outside of the Christian worldview.
- Why do you think that four generals were needed to take over Alexander's empire, rather than just one?
- About 270 BC, the Pharos (or Lighthouse) of Alexandria was built, and was considered to be one of the ancient wonders of the world. The Great Wall of China was finished about 220 BC. Why do you think this wasn't selected as one of the Seven Wonders of the Ancient World?
- Ptolemy II had the Old Testament translated from Hebrew to Greek. Why do you think he was so interested in the holy book of the Jews? What benefit do you see that this might have had for the Jewish people?

Resources for Digging Deeper

Choose a few books that look interesting, or find your own.

ANCIENT GREECE

The Greeks—Usborne Illustrated World History

Susan Peach & Anne Millard • Filled with short descriptions and great pictures, this is a wonderful, concise, fact-filled book about ancient Greece. **UE+**

Ancient Greece

Pamela Bradley • This Cambridge Junior History book is an excellent introduction to ancient Greece for pre-high school students. **UE+**

Growing Up in Ancient Greece

Chris Chelepi • Great overview! This series really helps explain many different aspects of life in ancient times. **E+**

Focus on Ancient Greeks

Anita Ganeri • If you can find it, this book is an excellent, multifaceted look at Greece. **E+**

Famous Men of Greece

John H Haaren & A. B. Poland • An excellent, brief introduction to the important historical figures of Greece, written in biographical style. **UE+**

Golden Days of Greece

Olivia Coolidge • This is one of the best authors of short biographies that I've found. Her books are uniformly interesting and filled with the kinds of tidbits that make history memorable. **UE+**

BIOGRAPHIES

Alexander the Great

Robert Green • This is a wonderful, short biography of the man who conquered the known world in ten years. **UE+**

Pericles (World Leaders Past and Present)

Perry Scott King • This was the Greek leader who masterminded the Golden Age of Greece after the victory over Xerxes. This series of books is absolutely fantastic reading! **MS+**

Alexander the Great (World Leaders Past and Present)

Dennis Wepman • One of the most significant military leaders in world history, Alexander the Great was also a fascinating historical figure. **MS+**

Judas Maccabaeus: Jewish Leader (World Leaders Past and Present)

E. H. Fortier • This is a riveting look at the Maccabean Revolt which occurred during the Hellenistic period. Skip Chapter Three, which deals with the history of Israel, because the author does not have a Biblical worldview. However, apart from that chapter, the book is fascinating, filled with historical details, and reads like fiction. **MS+**

In Search of Troy

Piero Ventura & Gian Paolo Ceserani • Piero Ventura is a masterful artist, and his books are always worth searching for. This is the intriguing story of Heinrich Schliemann, the amateur who discovered Troy. (Probably, the war between Troy and Greece took place during the time of the Mycenaeans.) **UE+**

TRAVELOGUE

The History: Herodotus

Translated by Henry Cary • This Greek historian was the first world traveler who kept track of the places he visited. Herodotus is one of the most important writers of antiquity, and his writings are still fascinating. **HS+**

MACCABEAN REVOLT

Apocrypha

The book of First Maccabees is one of the major historical accounts of the Maccabean revolt. It, along with Josephus, contains the best record of these events. **UE+**

The Works of Josephus

Book XII, chapters V–VIII, contains the account of Antiochus Epiphanes and his desecration of the Temple in Jerusalem. The resulting rebellion on the part of the pious Jews was led first by Mattathias Maccabaeus and then by his son Judas. It is an incredible tale of courage, of military shrewdness, and of God's blessing. **RA**

SCIENCE & MATH

Discoveries, Inventions & Ideas

Jane Shuter • This is an excellent introduction for younger students to the achievements of the Greeks, including astronomy, medicine, democracy, even the first fire engine! **E+**

Science in Ancient Greece

Kathlyn Gay • If you skip the second chapter on evolution, the remainder of the book is wonderful! Learn about many different areas of science which were "pioneered" by the Greeks. **UE+**

Make it Work! Ships

Andrew Solway • All of the books in this series are absolute wonders, especially because they truly create an environment for the whole family to discover science, history, etc. This book is great because it demonstrates the displacement of ships in water. That is the principle of buoyancy, which was discovered by Archimedes. **AA**

Make it Work! Machines

David Glover • One more experiment to show an invention of Archimedes. He invented the water screw, which still has many functions and is used in many parts of the world. A fabulous book! **AA**

Mathematicians are People, Too

Luetta Reimer & Wilbert Reimer • Three of the earliest named mathematicians in history were Greek. This fascinating book tells the story of these men as well as mathematicians from later times. **UE+**

COOKING

Greek Food and Drink

Irene Tavlarios • One of the best Greek cookbooks I've seen, this delightful book also describes some of the history of Greek cooking, lots of delectable pictures of food, and more. **UE+**

WARFARE AND WEAPONRY

The Greek Hoplite (Soldiers Through the Ages)

Martin Windrow • An excellent look at the Greek soldiers, who were among the best fighters of history. **UE+**

Digging Up the Past: Weapons and Warfare

Rivka Gonen • It's amazing how much we can learn about ancient cultures through their wars and weapons, both the winners and losers. **UE+**

Warfare in the Classical World

John Warry • An absolutely incredible book for those interested in following world history through warfare and weaponry. This book contains the best timeline I've ever seen for ancient civilizations. It is certainly worth the search. **MS+**

Charge! Weapons and Warfare in Ancient Times

Rivka Gonen • Filled with pictures, this book also details ancient history through warfare. Excellent for the younger students interested in this aspect of history. **UE+**

Military History of the World—Volume One

J. F. C. Fuller • For those who really want to dig into this subject, this is the book to get. It includes some fascinating accounts of Alexander the Great. **HS+**

What books did you like best?

____

____

____

____

____

The Internet also contains a wealth of information about ancient Greece and the Hellenistic Empire.

What sites were the most helpful?

____

____

____

____

____

For more books, use these Dewey Decimal numbers in your library:

Ancient Greece: #938

Classical Literature: #880

Also, look for biographies on the archae-ologists listed.

Student Self-Evaluation UNIT 7, PHASE 1

Dates and hours:____________________

Key Concepts

Rephrase the five Key Concepts of this Unit and confirm your understanding of each:

- Golden Age of Greece
- Greek intellectual achievements
- Influence of Greek worldview
- Alexander the Great & his empire
- Hanukkah's history

Tools for Self-Evaulation

Evaluate your personal participation in the discussions of this Phase. Bearing in mind that a good participant in a discussion is not always the most vocal participant, ask yourself these questions: Were you an active participant? Did you ask perceptive questions? Were you willing to listen to other participants of the discussion and draw out their opinions? Record your observations and how you would like to improve your participation in the future:

Every time period is too complex to be understood in one Phase of study. Evaluate your current knowledge of Greece & the Hellenists. What have you focused on so far? What are your weakest areas of knowledge?

Based on the evaluation of this introduction, project ahead what you would like to study more of in the following Phases:

Phase 2

Research & Reporting

Explore one or more of these areas to discover something significant!

Greece

- In the library or on the Internet, research any information related to Greece. (Look at newspapers, magazines, books, videos, etc.) Write to the Greek Embassy to request information about the history, terrain, climate, agriculture, etc., of Greece. Give your overview from ancient Greece to the present.
- Compile a list of names, dates and accomplishments of Greece's key leaders. Include Themistocles and Xenophon, though they were studied in Persia.
- Research and report on the Golden Age of Greece. Discover the answers to these questions: Why was it considered the Golden Age? What was accomplished during this time? Who were the important and influential people? How has the Golden Age continued to influence the world?
- Research and discover the attitude of ancient Greeks in regard to their treatment of other people groups. What purpose did the slaves fulfill? How did that impact the culture and lifestyle of the Greeks? Report your findings.
- Summarize the major events during this time period from approximately 800 BC to 200 BC. Draw a chart to show these events, their location, dates and participants.

Alexander the Great & His Empire

- Do a research paper with diagrams showing Alexander the Great's military conquests. Discover such issues as: Where did he start? Where did he go before Persia? Where did his armies stop? What were his provisioning needs? What were the attitudes of his soldiers and his officers toward him?
- Research and report on the "Rise and Fall of Alexander's Empire."
- Research Alexander's conquest of Tyre. Read Zechariah 9:1–4 and explain how this prophecy from 150 years earlier was fulfilled.
- After Alexander's death, his empire was divided between four generals. Research and report on what you discover about these generals. Answer such questions as: What country were the generals from? What did the Greeks think about "foreign" people? Who did the Greeks consider to be "barbarian"? Why? What opinion did the ruling generals have of foreigners in their lands? How does ethnocentrism fit this picture? Do you find evidences of racism as well?
- Research and report on the "Rise and Fall of the Ptolemies and the Seleucids."

Peloponnesian War

Find out who the Peloponnesian war involved, what issues were at stake, and the results (both short term and long term). Report your findings.

Compare & Contrast

- Research and report on the differences between the Greeks and the Jews during the Hellenistic period. (**Hint:** Find out about the forms of education, recreation, religion.)
- Research and report on the treatment of the Jews by the Ptolemies. How did the Seleucids differ? Does your research indicate any reason for this difference?

Science & Math

- Research and write about how science and mathematics were explored by the Greeks. What branches of science did the Greeks develop? What mathematical properties and concepts were discovered by the Greeks? Investigate the scientific and mathematical discoveries of Archimedes, Euclid, and Eratosthenes.
- Discover the beginnings of medical practice, including Hippocrates and the Hippocratic Oath. How has this influenced medical practice over the centuries? Report your findings.
- Research and explain who Pythagorus was, including his impact upon mathematics and music.

A Scriptural View

Read the eighth and eleventh chapter of Daniel, and then look in a Bible handbook or commentary to discover more information. How were the prophecies fulfilled? Report your findings.

Redemptive History

The hellenization of the known world had a unifying effect on the trade languages. Research and report on the effect this had upon the spread of the gospel of Jesus Christ.

The Maccabean Revolt

- Find one of the books listed, or a book of your choice, for basic information on the Maccabean revolt. Discover the short term result of Antiochus Epiphanes' desecration of the Temple, as well as the long term result. Report your findings.
- Do a research paper on Hanukkah, its beginning, and the subsequent developments in its celebration.

Alexandria

Look up and write about the people and events that contributed to Alexandria becoming a center of learning and influence.

Syria

In the library, or on the Internet, research any information related to Syria (newspapers, magazines, books, videos). Give an overview from the time of the Seleucids to the present.

Seven Wonders

Find out more about the Wonders of the Ancient World that were built during the Hellenistic period. How long did they last? Were they still standing in New Testament times? Were they seen by any New Testament figures?

Brain Stretchers

Compare & Contrast

Compare and contrast the events in the Middle East during this time with the events in China and India.

Science

Aristotle was not only Alexander the Great's tutor, he was one of the most influential scientists in world history. Research and report on Aristotle, his views on science, his long-lasting impact on medicine and other branches of science, and how the Scientific Revolution finally eradicated many of his theories.

Greek Education

Plato wrote in his *Republic* about his utopian views of education. Research and report on the impact his influence had on educational practice in the Middle Ages through the *Trivium* and *Quadrivium*, and the extent of his influence on education today. Do you feel these are positive or negative foundations?

Western Civilization

After reading about the Greek victories over the Medes and Persians, research the history of Western civilization. Make a simple chart showing the flow of Western civilization from the time of the Greeks to the present. Make another chart showing the history of the Middle East from the time of the Medes and Persians. Show the differences between the two charts, and explain what the impact of a Medo-Persian victory at Salamis would have had upon history.

Empires

Continue your work begun in Unit Five on the universal factors contributing to the rise and fall of empires.

Create Your Own Research Topic

____

____

____

Timeline

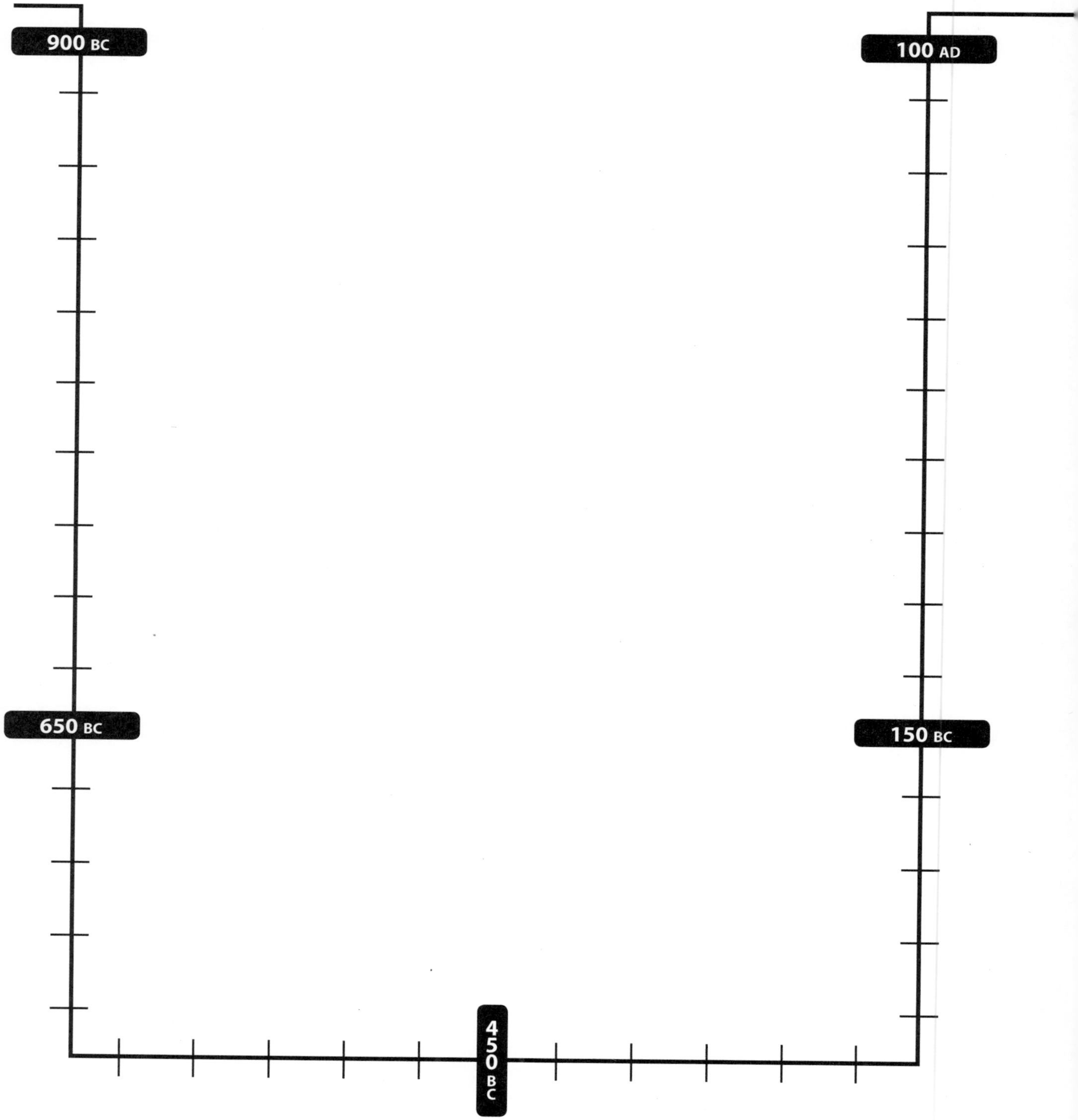

Consider this for your timeline

The Golden Age of Greece was very short-lived, though its influence continues to be felt. As you look up the dates for the different time periods in ancient Greece and the Hellenistic Empire, think about God's purposes being fulfilled in history. How did He use these events and these people for His own plans for redemption?

Key Events

- Golden Age of Greece
- Peloponnesian wars
- Alexander the Great's conquests
- Ptolemy II and the Septuagint
- Antiochus Epiphanes and the Maccabean Revolt
- Archimedes, Eratosthenes, Euclid
- Construction of the Pharos of Alexandria
- Construction of the Great Wall of China

Be sure to include the people listed in Key People in Phase 1.

Words to Watch

Remember—The easiest way to learn a subject is to master its terms:

democracy	sculpture	acropolis	conquest
barbarian	mathematics	spartan	philosopher
debate	architecture	column	capital
pedestal	circumference	geometry	buoyancy
fulcrum	desecrate	guerrilla	warfare
library	translate	Menorah	colossal
hellenize	assimilate		

Other words you need to look up:

Student Self-Evaluation UNIT 7, PHASE 2

Dates and hours:____________________

Research Project

- Summarize your research question:

____

____

- List your most useful sources by author, title, and page number or URL where applicable (continue list in margin if necessary):

____

____

____

Now take a moment to evaluate the sources you just listed. Do they provide a balanced view of your research question? Should you have sought an additional opinion? Are your sources credible (if you found them on your own)? Record your observations:

____

____

Evaluate your research project in its final presentation. What are its strengths? If you had time to revisit this project, what would you change? Consider giving yourself a letter grade based on your project's merits and weaknesses.

____

____

Letter grade: ____

You have just completed an area of specific research in the time of Greece & the Hellenists. Now what would you like to explore in the upcoming Phases? Set some objectives for yourself:

____

Phase 3

> **CONSIDER:**
>
> What was the type of warfare used by the Jews in the revolt, and how were such small numbers able to succeed over the larger Syrian army?

Maps and Mapping

Physical Terrain

» Label the mainland and islands of ancient Greece.

» Label the countries of ancient Macedonia, Crete, and Rhodes, and the island of Cyprus.

» Label the Tigris River, Euphrates River, Nile River, and Indus River.

» Shade and label the Mediterranean Sea, Aegean Sea, Caspian Sea, Aral Sea, Red Sea, and the Persian Gulf.

Geopolitical

» Label the cities of Ephesus and Athens.

» Draw the boundaries of Alexander's empire. What modern day countries are located within this area?

» Draw the boundaries of Ptolemaic Egypt (including the conquests), Syria (including the conquests), and Israel.

» Label the cities of Alexandria, Damascus, and Jerusalem.

» Locate and label each of the Seven Wonders of the Ancient World.

Explore

» ***Christian Outreach:*** What is the status of evangelical outreach to Greece and the former Hellenistic Empire today? What opportunities and what difficulties face those who share the gospel from an evangelical perspective in these nations?

» ***Greek Terrain:*** How would the geographic location of Greece, the terrain, the climate, and the Mediterranean Sea have affected the Greek culture and God's purpose for it?

» ***Palestinian Terrain:*** How would the terrain and climate of Israel have affected God's purposes as seen in the Maccabean revolt?

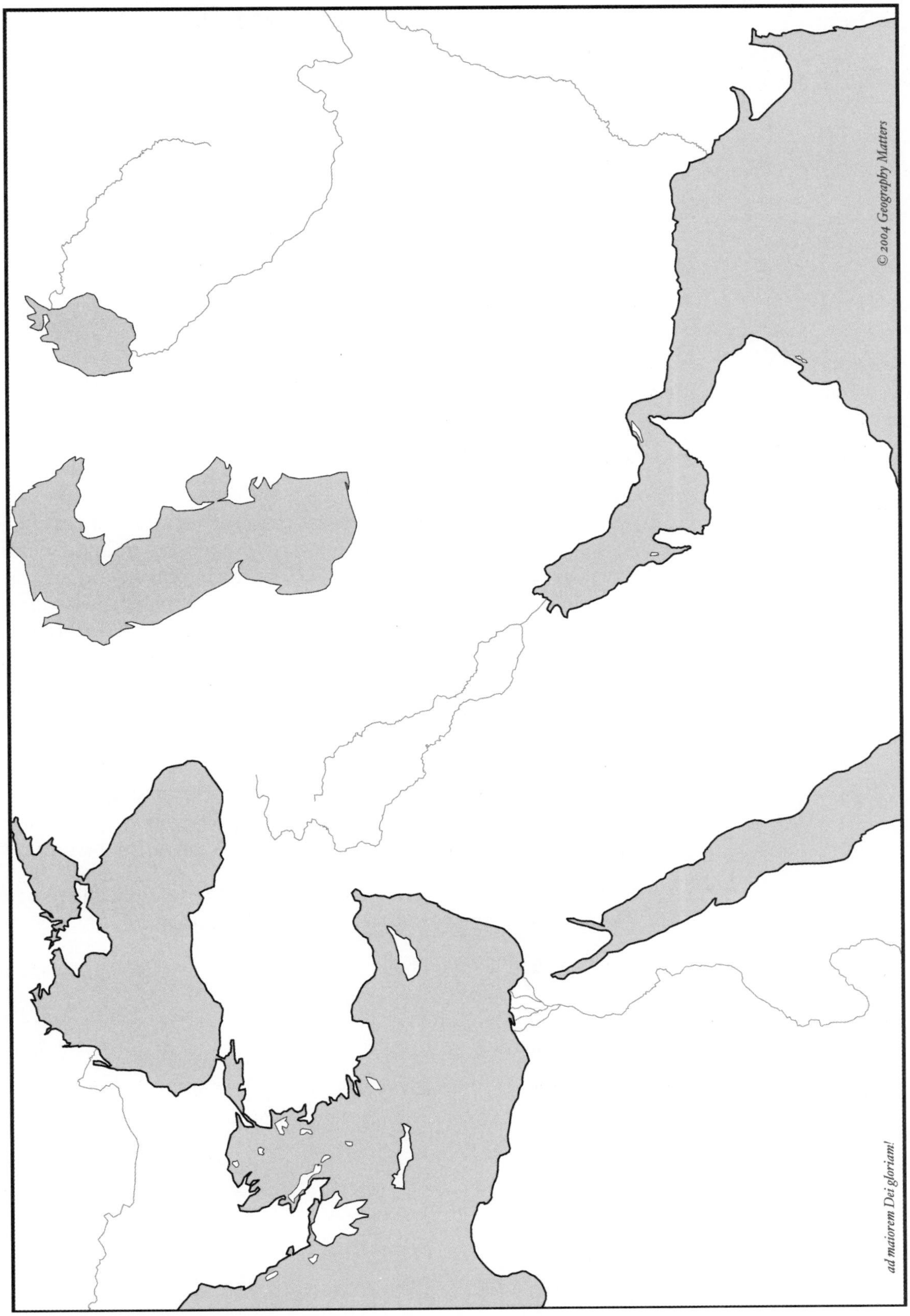
© 2004 Geography Matters
ad maiorem Dei gloriam!

CONSIDER:

Raphael (1483–1520 AD) was one of the giants of the High Renaissance period. Leonardo da Vinci and Michelangelo were his principal teachers when he moved to Florence as a twenty-one year old—quite an amazing pair of teachers! Pope Julius II requested Raphael to come to Rome in 1508 in order to paint frescoes in his Papal apartment. In this setting, Raphael, the "prince of painters," created two of the masterpieces of Renaissance art and philosophy—the *Disputa* and the *School of Athens*.

Art Appreciation

Philosophy (popularly known as the *School of Athens*) by Raphael

» At the center of this painting, two figures are shown walking together. They are Plato, who points heavenward, and Aristotle, who gestures towards the earth. Other philosophers are seen in this painting as well, including Euclid and Heraclitus. Why do you think he focused on Plato and Aristotle?

» How would you describe this painting?

» Notice the use of perspective. Have you seen other paintings in this study that convey the same sense of perspective?

Architecture

The Parthenon in Athens, Greece was constructed after the destruction of the city by Xerxes in 480 BC. It is one of the most famous buildings in history, built between 447 and 432 BC. The architects, Kallicarates and Iktinos, used meticulous measurements to create the appearance of exact alignment. All the horizontal lines are actually raised slightly in the middle in order to correct for the "sag" we would normally see in a long horizontal structure. They also made the columns bulge slightly outward one-third of the way up from the base. This was an amazing achievement for both the architects and the craftsmen, and it gave the Parthenon that particular sense of elasticity and life. Built entirely of marble, this Doric temple was dedicated to the goddess Athena. Her statue was sculpted in gold and ivory by Pheidias, the same sculptor who created the statue of Zeus at Olympia (one of the Seven Wonders of the Ancient World).

» Look for a photo of the Parthenon in Athens. What still remains in this ruin? How would you describe this building?

Arts in Action

Select one or more, and let your artistic juices flow!

Imitation

Try creating a vignette in the style of Raphael's *School of Athens*

Greek Vase Art

Buy a cheap white vase or try making a papier maché bowl. Paint a solid color, then when it is dry, paint your family on the vase. The only portraits done by Greeks were on vases!

Greek Columns

Draw or construct examples of the different Greek columns: Ionic, Dorian, and Corinthian.

Soft Stone Sculpting

Chisel a sculpture made of soft stone: 3 scoops vermiculite, 2 scoops plaster of Paris, 2 scoops water. Stir in bucket until it is very thick. Pour into small carton to harden for 30 minutes. Peel off carton and chisel with a plastic spoon or knife. How is this different from the casting process?

Candle Making

The Festival of Hanukkah is also known as the Festival of Lights. To illustrate this, try making your own candles. Since melted wax can be dangerous (it is VERY hot!), adult supervision is required. Consult your library or local expert for more info. After they are made, light one candle in a dark room. Then read John 8:12 out loud.

Make a Lighthouse

Make a model of the Pharos (Lighthouse) of Alexandria. LEGO bricks would be a great building material, or papier maché, or modeling clay. Try setting up the Pharos on a harbor of blue construction paper, showing that the lighthouse was on an island and that Alexandria was on the mainland.

The Great Wall of China

If you have a young friend or sibling with a sandbox, conquer it for an afternoon. Then build a Great Wall to keep out the barbarians. Use a map of the Great Wall to get some of the contours.

CONSIDER:

Thales (thay-leez) was another Greek scientist and philosopher. He figured out how to measure the height of the Great Pyramid of Cheops, based on an observation. He knew his own height, and could measure the height of his shadow. He could also measure the height of the pyramid's shadow. With these three numbers known, it was possible to calculate the fourth unknown number (the height of the pyramid.)

Science

Aristotle is considered the Father of the Scientific Method. He emphasized:

- the importance of making one's own discoveries
- collecting information
- analyzing the information
- classifying the information

Scientific Method

Find a definition of the current Scientific Method. Choose an animal or plant that you can find nearby. Observe your subject. Weigh it, measure it, poke it (if possible), smell it, test it every way you can think of. Write down everything you observe. Did you discover anything you didn't already know? What new ways could you classify the subject?

Measure

Try measuring a tall tree like this: On a sunny day, make a stake three and a half feet tall. Drive it into the ground so that it is three feet tall. Label this measurement *A*. Now measure the length of the stake's shadow. Label this measurement *B*. Measure the length of the tree's shadow. Label this measurement *C*. You can now figure the height of the tree, which we will label *X*. (A/B = X/C) Just solve for *X*.

Buoyancy

Experiment with the principle of buoyancy. You could try Archimedes' experiment by getting into the bath tub and seeing how high the water rises. Or, try dropping various materials of different weights into a jar of water. Record the different levels the water rises to. Do large items displace more water than smaller items? Do heavy items displace more water than lighter items?

Music

Pythagorus, a Greek mathematician, was walking down the street one day when he heard the sound of four hammers beating on metal. Realizing that the sounds were pleasing to the ear, he recognized the golden opportunity to determine what made them so. The littlest hammer rang out with a higher sound than the others, while the biggest hammer produced the lowest sound. Pythagorus was hearing the "pitch" of the hammers.

Pitch is the musical term used to describe the highness or lowness of sound. It is one of the five elements of music. Sing the words, "Twinkle, Twinkle, Little Star." Which word do you say when you are singing the highest sound? Which word do you say when you are singing the lowest sound? The highest sound is the highest pitch, and the lowest sound is the lowest pitch.

Try This

Using a keyboard or other instrument, have someone play two different notes. With your eyes closed, tell whether the second note is higher or lower than the first. (Thumbs up if the second note is higher, thumbs down if it is lower.) Have each member of the class or the family try this experiment.

» ***Variation:*** Play three notes in one direction. Determine if the pitches are ascending or descending. How did you do? This is an excellent starting place for learning to distinguish pitch, and for developing a "musical ear."

» When we combine different pitches, the sound can be pleasing (consonance) or harsh sounding (dissonance). What Pythagorus heard was a pleasing sound and he determined to research why these particular hammers sounded good together. What he found was that the hammer with the highest pitch was exactly one-half the size of the hammer with the lowest pitch. The other two hammers also had precise mathematical ratios with the lowest. Pythagorus came up with an explanation of which combinations of notes are consonant and which combinations are dissonant. But the amazing thing about Pythagorus was that he figured it out using mathematical ratios!

Try This

Sing together "Row, Row, Row Your Boat." Now, try singing it as a round with each new part entering when the previous part starts the phrase: ". . . gently down the stream." Listen to the sound. Can you hear the different pitches that are being sung at the same time? Is it pleasing, or harsh?

Play around with notes on the piano. Can you find pleasing consonant sounds and harsh dissonant sounds? Don't be discouraged if you can't. It takes practice!

Celebrate the miracle of Hanukkah with lots of oil! It is traditional to eat both potato cakes and fried doughnuts. (Thankfully, this feasting is not for every day!)

Cooking

Greek foods are one of my absolute favorites! There are so many recipes to choose from, but this one is one of the best.

Baklava *Serves 8*

10 sheets filo pastry (freezer section)
½ cup melted butter
1¼ cup finely chopped walnuts
¼ cup honey
½ tsp cinnamon
½ cup honey
½ tsp ground cloves
½ tsp grated orange peel
1 tsp lemon juice

Cut pastry sheets in half (20 12x8-inch sheets). Brush 7 sheets of filo with butter and layer them into a buttered 12x8 metal baking pan. Combine walnuts, honey, and cinnamon. Spread one-fourth of the mixture over filo in pan. Cover with 2 more sheets of buttered filo, then add another one-fourth of the mixture. Repeat until you have used a total of 13 sheets of filo and all of the mixture. Brush remaining 7 sheets of filo with butter, and place on top of sheets in the pan. With a sharp knife, cut pastry to form 16 diamond-shaped pieces. Top with remaining butter and bake at 350 degrees for about 50 minutes, until top is crisp. While baking, combine remaining ingredients in a small pan. Bring to a boil, then lower heat and simmer for 8 to 10 minutes. Remove baklava from oven. Top immediately with hot syrup. Cool.

Potato Latkes

4 large potatoes (peeled, grated)
1 small onion (grated)
3 eggs (beaten)
2 Tbsp flour
salt & pepper

Drop by large spoonfuls into a hot, oiled fry pan. Cook until brown on both sides. Serve warm and topped with sour cream, applesauce, or yogurt.

Student Self-Evaluation UNIT 7, PHASE 3

Dates and hours:________________________

Evaluate Your Projects

- List which of the activities listed in this Phase you did:

  ____

  ____

  ____

- Rate your enthusiasm: __________

  Explain: ______________________________________

  ____

- Rate the precision of your approach:__________

  Explain: ______________________________________

  ____

- Rate your effort towards the completion of the project: __________

  Explain: ______________________________________

  ____

Ask yourself what worked and what did not. What would you do differently in the future, and what would you repeat?

____

How specifically did these hands-on activities enhance your knowledge of Greece & the Hellenists? What made them worthwhile?

____

In the first three Phases of this Unit, what aspect of the time period has most captured your imagination? What would you like to creatively pursue to conclude your study?

____

Phase 4

In Your Own Way…

We have seen the Golden Age of Greece and its influence on the world, Alexander the Great's empire and it's hellenization of the known world, and the scientific and mathematical achievements of the Greeks. We have contrasted ancient Greek thinking with biblical truths, discovered God's great deliverance of his people from the Seleucid army, and learned about the origin of Hanukkah. Now, choose a selection of these activities, or create your own, which will best express what you have learned from this Unit.

LINGUISTICS

Journalism

- Be a reporter for the magazine, *The Modern Military*. Your assignment is to visit Sparta before the outbreak of the Peloponnesian wars. Describe the training and tenacity of the Spartan army.
- Be a war correspondent for the *Voice of the Maccabeans* and write the behind-the-scenes story of Judas Maccabaeus and his guerrilla army.

Prose

- Write the annals of Aristotle's assistant, assigned to acquire all the animals for Aristotle's assessment.
- Write a first person account about translating the Old Testament into Greek. Describe some of your Jewish translation buddies in Alexandria.
- Imagine you are a sailor and describe the Pharos of Alexandria to folks at home who have never seen it.
- Pretend you are a novelist in Ephesus, dealing with writer's block. Then Paul comes, as described in Acts 19, and inspires you to write the best-selling novelette, *A Funny Thing Happened on the Way to the Temple.*

Playing with Words

Discover the connection these words have to the Unit, and then write a rhyming poem (or poems) using them: *culture, sculpture, picture; Pericles, Themistocles, Hippocrates; Parthenon, Marathon, Xenophon.*

Poetry

- Compose a poem entitled, "To the Unknown God." (Reference Acts 17.)
- Write a poem about the Festival of Lights (Hanukkah).

ART

Painting/Drawing

Paint or draw someone lounging in Greek fashion on a Greek couch, wearing Greek clothes and eating Greek grapes.

Sculpting

Using modeling clay, try sculpting a bust in the Greek style.

Cartooning

Draw a cartoon of the shortness & wonder of the Golden Age of Greece.

Graphic Design

Create a poster recruiting Greek mercenaries to fight with Xenophon. "Uncle Xeonphon wants YOU!"

Illustration

Create a picture book showing the history of Hanukkah, and how it is celebrated today.

MUSIC

Compose

Write a song using the Dorian mode. (Dorian mode is found by playing a scale on the piano, beginning at "D," and using only white keys.) This is a Greek mode, but may not be the same today as it was to ancient Greek musicians. These modes are known as the "Church Modes" and they use Greek names, but we have no way of knowing what the Greek mode called "Dorian" actually sounded like. Dorian has a wonderful, haunting sound, however, that will be evocative of Greek music and culture.

Performance Practice

With your teacher's help, select an appropriate piece of music, which expresses some element from this Unit. If possible, find a piece written for Hanukkah. Prepare and perform the piece for an audience. Communicate with your audience the reason for your selection either in the program notes or in a short speech.

DRAMA

Comedy

- Aristotle, Pericles, Pythagorus, Thales, Themistocles, and Alexander are all going to receive an award at a Greek banquet. You are the emcee for the banquet. Introduce at length each of these famous Greeks to explain why they merit this award.
- Do a humorous skit about Archimedes' discovery of buoyancy.

Tragedy

The Greeks were the ones who dramatized tragedy, using all male casts and masks. Create a tragedy, on the model of the Greek tragedies. If you have any females in the cast, dress them as boys who dress as girls!

Reality

Perform the scene from Josephus about Alexander the Great coming to Jerusalem. Use your imagination for costumes, props, horses (!), etc.

Puppetry

Using puppets, act out the scene in the Temple when the Menorah was kept miraculously lit. Use your imagination to create props, sets and costumes. Be sure to include realistic rejoicing!

Prop Needs

____

____

____

Costume Ideas

____

____

____

Role/Player

____

____

____

Set Suggestions

____

____

____

MOVEMENT

Pantomime

Create a pantomime showing little Alex begging his father, King Philip, to let him ride that big black horse (Bucephalus.) Be sure to include the look of surprise on everyone's face while he is riding!

Dance

Choreograph a dance of Eratosthenes figuring out how to measure the world.

Miniature Action

Using LEGO bricks, papier maché, clay, or other medium, build a miniature version of Tyre. Demonstrate Alexander's successful techniques for capturing this heretofore unconquered city.

CONCEPTUAL DESIGN

Game of Conquest

Create a game which will show the extent and the speed of Alexander the Great's conquests. This may be a board game, an action game, or a computer game.

CREATE YOUR OWN EXPRESSION

____

____

____

____

____

____

Student Self-Evaluation UNIT 7, PHASE 4

Dates and hours:____________________

Evaluate Your Projects

- What creative project did you choose:

- What did you expect from your project, and how does the final project compare to your initial expectations?

- What do you like about your project? What would you change?

In Conclusion

Revisit the five Key Concepts from the beginning of this Unit. Explain how your understanding of and appreciation for each has grown over the course of your study.

Record your concluding thoughts on Greece & the Hellenists:

The Rise of Rome

UNIT 8

Key Concepts

- The rise of Rome
- The leaders of Rome
- The engineering feats of Rome
- God's plan for Rome

The largest empire begins . . .

> After this I saw in the night visions, and behold, a fourth beast, dreadful and terrible, exceedingly strong. It had huge iron teeth; it was devouring, breaking in pieces, and trampling the residue with its feet. It was different from all the beasts that were before it. Daniel 7:7

Rome. The exceedingly strong city, which would swallow the kingdom of Alexander and his generals along with many far away lands, was birthed in legendary violence. The story of the beginnings of Rome tells of two brothers, Romulus and Remus, who quarreled over who should have the honor of building a city and naming it after himself. In the end, Romulus was overcome with wrath, and struck down and killed his brother. Whether this has any basis in fact or not, there was a foundation of betrayal and bloodshed, which would later be evident in Rome's history. Romulus populated his new city by inviting all of the outcasts and outlaws of the surrounding area to live in Rome. To assist him in governing the city, King Romulus decided to establish a senate (meaning "old man") with one hundred men whom he appointed.

Rome was located halfway up the "boot of Italy," on the fertile western side of the country. The city was built along the Tiber River, on seven hills which formed a natural fortress sixteen miles inland from the Mediterranean. Cicero, a famous Roman writer from the first century BC wrote, "The site of Rome is well supplied with natural springs, and healthy, in spite of unhealthy neighboring territory. For the hills channel the breezes, and provide shade for the valley."

Early Rome

The first two and a half centuries of Rome's existence were spent under the rule of seven kings, many of whom were Etruscans, the most advanced people in Italy at the time. These kings brought about great improvements in Rome, particularly the great public works projects to drain the swamps around the seven hills and build the impressive and gigantic Capitol. But the last king, Tarquinnius Superbus, was such an unbelievably cruel and wicked ruler that the people eventually banished him and his whole family. That was around the year 510 BC, and from that point, the Roman people maintained such a continuing abhorrence for kings that, several centuries later, it would contribute to the downfall of Julius Caesar.

The story of the beginnings of Rome tells of two brothers, Romulus and Remus, who quarreled.

In place of a king, the Romans established a form of government known as a republic (meaning "public things"). Rather than give one ruler too much power, they preferred a multitude of government officials who had specific duties in the governing of Rome. These men were selected solely from the Senate, and their positions included: two *consuls*, who governed the military and were in charge of overseeing Rome; eight *praetors* to act as judges in the courts; four *aediles* to take care of the public buildings, as well as the public games and grain supply; and twenty *quaestors* who handled the state finances. These positions of power, and indeed all of the Senate positions, were only to be filled by those who could trace their ancestry back to the original advisors to King Romulus. These *patricians* were all wealthy landowners, who for the most part, neglected the poverty and starvation issues facing the common people. The common people, or *plebeians*, demanded their own voice because they greatly resented the patricians controlling the government. The result was that in 494 BC, after violent political demonstrations, the plebeians set up their own assembly, and elected ten *tribunes* to be their representatives in government. Eventually, the tribunes came to have the power to call the

Senate to a meeting, to introduce laws, and to stop unjust laws passed by the Senate. The underlying struggle between patrician and plebeian would, however, continue for centuries.

This new republic was not popular with its neighbors, probably because the neighboring kings were concerned that it would give republican ideas to their own people! As they began to attack, Rome had to fight for its life. A Latin alliance of cities defeated the Romans in 496 BC, forcing them to join the alliance. But over the next one hundred years, as they ably learned how to defend themselves, the Romans doubled their territory and became the leading city in this alliance.

The next century was spent enlarging their territory, though it started off with disaster. In 390 BC a northern European tribe called the Gauls invaded and destroyed most of Rome. The devastated Romans had to both rebuild their city and then reconquer their lost lands. By the late 300s, Rome had beaten the Gauls, as well as the powerful Etruscans, and dominated all but the southern part of Italy.

This new republic was not popular with its neighbors.

You might recall from the last unit that Greek settlers in the 700s BC had set up Greek city-states in many areas throughout the Mediterranean, including the southern part of Italy. In 282 BC when one of the Greek cities asked mighty Rome for military help to protect them from a warring tribe, many others joined in the plea. However, one Greek city, Tarentum, was not pleased with the idea of Roman "barbarians" coming into their Greek area of Italy. They ended up insulting Rome and provoking a war. Since they were not personally equipped to fight against the Roman army, the people of Tarentum sought the help of a Greek king, Pyrrhus of Epirus, and his army from northern Greece. The struggle between these two armies was very costly in lives, and, though King Pyrrhus won the first few battles, he recognized that "if we win one more victory against the Romans, we shall be totally ruined." Rome pursued the war until King Pyrrhus was vanquished, and Tarentum surrendered. With this victorious conclusion, Rome became the dominant city-state in Italy with allies throughout the width and breadth of the land—allies who were increasingly Romanized in language and culture. Rome was now one of the most significant military powers in the Mediterranean.

The Punic Wars

On the coast of North Africa, about four hundred miles south across the Mediterranean from Rome, was a fabulously wealthy and powerful city-state founded by the seafaring Phoenicians somewhere between 814 BC (traditional date) and 750 BC (archaeological date). Carthage was a thriving commercial empire, which had come to dominate trade in the Mediterranean, due to its massive navy and its strategic location, ever since the destruction of Tyre and Sidon by Alexander the Great. Carthage had colonized the western

8

part of the island of Sicily in the 400s BC as part of its commercial empire, but when it took the Sicilian city of Messana in 264 BC, the Romans saw this as a potential threat to their territory and gave an immediate military response. Thus began the Punic Wars, which would conclude with Carthage annihilated, and Rome standing as the greatest power in the world.

The First Punic War lasted twenty-three years. For the first eight years, Rome had the more powerful land army but virtually no navy, while Carthage ruled the seas but could not win on land. This put them into a virtual deadlock until, one earthshaking day, a Carthaginian ship was stranded on a Roman beach. Within sixty days, Rome had built a fleet of one hundred exact replicas of this ship and set to sea. Though they lost not only this fleet but the next one to the fierceness of Mediterranean storms, they eventually were able to use their third fleet of fighting ships to categorically defeat Carthage's navy in 241 BC and to oust them from Sicily. This ended the first war, and gave Rome the boost it needed to obtain a superior navy, which is necessary if one is to have a first-class empire.

The Second Punic War began in 218 BC. Carthage bore a hatred toward Rome from its previous defeat, and continued to seek a way of defeating the proud Romans. Since they knew from experience that an attack on Rome from the Mediterranean side was doomed to failure, Carthage looked for another, more successful means of attack.

Carthage was a thriving commercial empire which had come to dominate trade in the Mediterranean.

Unfortunately for Rome, the Carthaginian army was now commanded by one of the most brilliant generals in history, who conceived a most unexpected strategy. Hannibal, who had commanded troops in Spain, as had his father before him, took an army of 35,000 men and a secret weapon—thirty-seven war elephants—along a surprisingly unexpected route. Up to this point, the Alps mountain range across the top of Italy had been a formidable barrier for keeping out unwanted armies. Hannibal crossed them, nonetheless, in the severe cold and snow of winter. Ten thousand of his men and all but one of the elephants died, but once he entered Roman territory, his army was never defeated. For a few years, the Roman policy under Quintus Fabius was to continually harass the enemy but to avoid a major confrontation since the Roman army was not in a position to guarantee a victory against Hannibal. In 216 BC that policy changed and an army of 80,000 Romans—the largest ever assembled up to that time in Roman history—met the Carthaginian army at Cannae. Hannibal's shrewd tactics brought about the worst defeat the Romans ever suffered, with 50,000 men killed and 10,000 taken prisoner. It decimated the Roman army, and left the city of Rome vulnerable. Not recognizing his advantage, Hannibal did not attack the city of Rome at that vulnerable moment, since he felt it was still impregnable.

In hindsight, we know that if Hannibal had marched on Rome, he would have likely conquered the city at that point, and history would have been greatly altered. However, as Daniel saw in his vision, Rome was destined for a much greater role on the world's stage.

Fighting for its life, Rome decided to go on the offense against Carthage in order to get Hannibal and his army out of Italy. A Roman general named Scipio took troops first to Spain to attack Carthaginian territory, then moved on to North Africa and the city of Carthage itself. The leaders of Carthage recognized the seriousness of the threat against their city-state, so recalled Hannibal from Italy. Hannibal with his army met the Roman army under Scipio in 202 BC at a place called Zama, and this time the Romans won. Not only did they demand a huge amount of money from the Carthaginians but also celebrated their victory by seizing Spanish territories from Carthage.

The third and final Punic War lasted three years (149–146 BC). The Romans discovered that Carthage, once again strong and healthy, was rearming itself for war. Determined to defeat this city once and for all, the Romans laid siege to Carthage for three years, and in the end, utterly destroyed it. All of the people of Carthage were killed, except 50,000 who were taken away to slavery. The city was set aflame, and the land itself was salted to prevent anything from ever growing there again. They devoured it, broke it in pieces, and trampled it under foot. And they gained another province, North Africa.

The Alps mountain range across the top of Italy had been a formidable barrier for keeping out unwanted armies.

Internal strife

In that same year, the Roman army smashed a Greek uprising in the city of Corinth. The Romans had been fighting battles in Macedonia and Greece for the previous fifty years, and their military presence had increasingly infiltrated the realm of Greece. Now, with the destruction of Corinth, all of Greece came under the power of Rome, with a Roman governor ruling over them. Slowly and inexorably, Rome, with its nearly invincible army, gained control of the entire Mediterranean.

The conquering of these various lands and people caused Rome to grow in power, but it also caused increasing inequality between the rich and poor at home. As the wealthy were greatly profiting from the wars, the poor were increasingly impoverished through unemployment since more and more slaves were used for traditional jobs. Many of the soldiers of Rome were normally farmers who, during all of these wars, spent so much time away from home that their farms were ruined through neglect. Those who had profited from the conquests were then able to purchase these derelict farms, along with other lands, thereby creating huge landholdings. When the displaced farmers/soldiers went to the city to look for work, they found that most jobs were filled by slaves brought from conquered lands. An increasing number of poor people were permanently unemployed and permanently upset about it.

In 133 BC Tiberius Gracchus, grandson of Scipio, the conqueror of Carthage, proposed that the very wealthy give up the lands, which had been unjustly taken, and that these lands be divided among the poor. This passed into law while Tiberius was a tribune, but it made the patricians and the Senate very angry. They provoked a riot in which Tiberius was killed. When his brother, Caius, also sought to help the poor stand against the rich, he too was murdered.

> The city was set aflame, and the land itself was salted to prevent anything from ever growing there again.

By 120 BC two political groups had emerged to deal with the tremendous tension between the rich and poor in Rome. The *optimates* believed that things should stay as they were, that the wealthy were justified in their acquisitions, and that the Senate should be firmly in control. The *populares* wanted to give the poor more land, give grain to the starving, and let the common people rise in power. Marius, one of the most powerful generals of the time, was from a plebeian family, and he came to represent the populares position. His great military success in Africa and in wars with barbarians from the Baltic Sea made him very popular with the people, who elected him as consul seven times, beginning in 107 BC. The patricians did not dare to speak a word against him due to his popularity, but they were well aware that he was defying the law and dominating Rome in an increasingly dangerous way.

Another general, an optimate from the patrician class, was also growing in power. This man, Sulla, was elected consul in 88 BC, and then sent by the patrician Senate to lead a Roman army against a dangerous opposing king, Mithridates, in Asia Minor. After Sulla left with his army, the plebeian Assembly decided that Marius should lead the army instead. When Marius sent word to Sulla that he was coming to take over, Sulla rallied his troops to his side and turned back toward Rome to defeat these "rebels." Marius and his troops were quickly defeated, and he was condemned to die.

Escaping from Rome, Marius fled the city and eventually landed as an exile in Africa. While Sulla went back to fighting King Mithridates, a new army of plebeians was raised to fight against the patricians for the rights of the common people. This army asked Marius to lead them and he accepted. Once on the march, he quickly conquered Rome and was elected consul yet again by the people.

Do you remember the foundation of bloodshed and betrayal in the beginning of Rome? As the Republic became more and more unstable, as armies were increasingly loyal to their generals rather than their government, as the masses of poor people were won by the politicians who provided them with gladiator contests and free food, and as the rich sought only more gain for themselves at the cost of the poor, bloodshed and betrayal would become a visible part of the political and relational structure of Rome. The Republican ideals of government by many would devolve into rule by one powerful leader, and this would eventually destroy the Republic.

When Marius was firmly in control as consul, he turned vengeful eyes on the patricians—those who had driven him into exile. He personally led his murderous guards throughout Rome, killing all of Sulla's supporters. Hundreds of the most noble men of Rome were slain, until no one who had supported Sulla was left. Two weeks later, after his unappeasable fury had spent itself, Marius died.

Bloodshed and betrayal would become a visible part of the political and relational structure of Rome.

When Sulla returned victorious from his war in Asia, he learned of Maurius's hateful vengeance. Not only did he learn what had happened, he learned the lesson of striking terror into the hearts of anyone who disagreed with the ruler. When he became a dictator from 82–80 BC, Sulla's focus and purpose was patrician revenge. He ordered all the followers of Marius to be executed, and when this was finished and the intimidated people of Rome thought peace would follow, he confounded them all. Not content with the destruction of his obvious enemies, Sulla brutally continued to order the seemingly random executions of thousands of people, both rich and poor, throughout Rome and Italy. After this year long reign of terror, he gathered the stunned people of Rome together for a parade of triumph, where he showed off riches and captured treasures from his military conquests in Asia Minor. Can you imagine how absolutely surreal this parade must have seemed, and how the terrified people must have clapped and cheered in order to avoid being the next victim? After accomplishing his revenge and his triumphant war display, Sulla retired from office and died.

Next on the scene comes Pompey, another mighty military commander of Roman armies. After Pompey helped the Roman leader Marcus Crassus put down a slave rebellion, led by Spartacus in 71 BC, he and Crassus were each made consul the following year. Pompey then went on to brilliantly defeat marauding pirates who had been terrorizing ships and coastal lands of the Mediterranean, and to continue the war against Mithridates in Asia Minor. After years of conquering not only Mithridates, but Syria and Palestine as well, Pompey returned in triumph to Rome. When the Senate would not approve the distribution of land, which he had promised to his troops for their military successes, Pompey decided to find a way around their power. In 60 BC, this adored idol of the masses, along with Crassus and Julius Caesar (a rising star), formed an alliance, known as the First Triumvirate, in order to battle politically against the Senate. What Pompey did not realize was that Julius Caesar was going to eclipse him in power and popularity. He would pay for this oversight with his life.

Julius Caesar

Julius Caesar was born circa 100 BC to patrician parents, but as he came to power, he allied himself with the plebeians. He was considered one of the best orators of Roman history (second only to Cicero), a military genius, and an astute politician. Caesar was elected to a number of political positions in Rome over a ten year period, from the lowest position of quaestor all the way to top-ranking consul in 59 BC. He was, at this time, part of the First Triumvirate, and used his position as consul to force the Senate to accept the Triumvirate's policies. After his one year term as consul, Caesar was sent on a military conquest of Gaul. For the next nine years, he performed his duties ingeniously, beating not only the Gauls but beginning the conquest of Britain, as well. In 49 BC the Senate, under Pompey's prompting, demanded that Caesar return to Rome without his army. Realizing that this would leave him defenseless and at the mercy of his enemies in Rome, Caesar boldly defied the Senate, entering Italy at the head of a powerful and loyal army. Pompey and the wealthy patrician senators fled Rome, and, within sixty days, Caesar stood unopposed as the sole master of the Roman Republic. When Pompey raised an army against him in Greece, Caesar took his troops to war. In 48 BC Pompey was defeated, and, fleeing to Egypt for protection and exile, was murdered by the Egyptian ruler.

When Julius Caesar followed Pompey to Egypt, he found more than he had been looking for. Being presented with the embalmed head of Pompey provided relief for Caesar, but meeting the mesmerizing Cleopatra provided an ongoing entrapment, which would set many influential Romans against him. Cleopatra, the last of the reigning Ptolemies of the Hellenistic empire, had been co-ruler of Egypt with her brother, but now was engaged in a struggle for sole control. Caesar helped Cleopatra in her quest to be queen, and, at the same time, fathered her child. Then leaving Egypt, Caesar continued his battle against the hastily raised armies of Pompey's supporters in Asia Minor, Africa, and Spain for two more years. Once he returned victoriously to Rome, Caesar pardoned his enemies and made senators of those who had traditionally been ineligible. He embarked on a number of projects, like reforming the calendar and passing laws to improve the way the government operated. He also built aqueducts, monumental buildings, and a great library. Though the people loved him, to the point of carrying his statue in a procession which honored the gods, many of the ruling senators hated him, convinced that Caesar was on the verge of making himself king. Not only did they fear his becoming king, they also saw that, once this position was obtained, Caesar would rule much of the earth with his Egyptian queen. This would end the Republic, and these republicans were ready to do anything to make sure this did not happen. So, on the Ides of March (March 15), 44 BC, they attacked him in the Senate and assassinated him at

Statue of Caesar

the feet of the statue of Pompey. How ironic that the one who was responsible for Pompey's death was now dead at his statue's feet.

Julius Caesar's will designated his great-nephew, Octavian, as his heir and adopted son. Opposing this was Caesar's lieutenant, Mark Antony, who jealously believed that he should have been the heir of Caesar. Along with the disdainful antagonism of Antony, Octavian faced the daunting prospect of fighting two of Caesar's assassins, Cassius and Brutus, along with the army they had raised to defend the Republic. Antony and Octavian put their differences momentarily behind them in order to fight Cassius and Brutus in Macedonia. When this was successfully accomplished, Octavian, Antony, and a third ruler, Lepidus, drew up a list of 2,300 people who were considered powerful enemies. These 2,300 men were executed, their land and wealth confiscated and given to Roman soldiers. Eventually, Antony left Rome to deal with problems in the East while Octavian took care of the issues at home and Lepidus dropped out of sight. Antony, while soldiering in Turkey, met Cleopatra and, losing sight of everything else, spent all his energies to court her. Octavian, on the other hand, patiently and unerringly courted the favor of the Senate and restored peaceful order to Rome and Italy.

Caesar boldly defied the Senate, entering Italy at the head of a powerful and loyal army.

As each of these men pursued their objectives, their differences became more and more obvious to the Roman people. Antony was hated by one and all in Rome because of his illegal marriage to Cleopatra, and because he had then given Roman territory to her and her children. Octavian, the rightful heir of Caesar, was seen as a respecter of the Republic and an able leader. At last, these differences erupted into war. At the Battle of Actium, in 31 BC, Octavian defeated the combined armed forces of Mark Antony and Cleopatra. After conquering Egypt and making it another Roman province, Octavian went back to Rome as the unchallenged ruler of the entire empire. In 27 BC he was given the name "Augustus," indicating an almost superhuman status. From that point, he was known as Augustus Caesar, the First Citizen, and, in effect, the first Roman emperor.

At this point in history, Rome was the center of the largest empire the world had ever known. Through the might of its well-trained and well-disciplined armies, Rome had marched against countries and city-states throughout the western part of Europe, North Africa, Egypt, Syria, Palestine, Greece, Macedonia, and Asia Minor, relentlessly devouring one after another, turning them into Roman provinces under the rule of a Roman governor.

Daniel described the fouth kingdom as one that crushes and breaks in pieces all the others (Daniel 2:40). And now, the stage had been set for the final part of Daniel's vision: a kingdom that "shall never be destroyed; and the kingdom shall not be left to other people; it shall break in pieces and consume all these kingdoms, and it shall stand forever" (Daniel 2:44).

The best is now to come.

Phase 1

Key People

Romulus & Remus
Legendary founders of Rome

Hannibal
Carthaginian general in Punic Wars

Scipio
Roman general who defeated Hannibal

Julius Caesar
Greatest of all the Caesars

Mark Antony
Julius Caesar's greatest general

Octavian
Julius Caesar's heir

Cleopatra
Last reigning Ptolemy

Listen to This

What in the World? VOL. 1

DISC FOUR:

- Early Rome (track 2)
- The Punic Wars (track 3)
- Julius Caesar & the Late Republic (track 4)
- Octavian vs. Mark Antony (track 5)

Read For Your Life

The Holy Bible

- The Main Story: Daniel 2:33–35,40–45; Luke 2:1–3

Talk Together

Opinion Column

- What did you find to be the most interesting aspect, or the most fascinating person, you encountered in your introduction to the rise of Rome?
- Imagine you were with Hannibal as he crossed the Alps with his army and elephants. What would the trip through the mountains have been like? What would be your anticipation for the effectiveness of the elephants against the Romans?
- If you were a Roman soldier traveling to Gaul with Julius Caesar, what are some terms you could use to describe life in the army?

Critical Puzzling

- » What importance do you think the Punic Wars had in the history of Rome?
- » Julius Caesar was assassinated on the Ides of March. How do you think history might have been different if this event had not occurred?
- » The Romans created amazing bridges, aqueducts and roads which still exist in many places. Why do you suppose they put so much effort into building them?
- » Jesus came and began His Church during the Roman Empire, and the Bible describes His advent in the world as being "in the fullness of time" (Galatians 4:4). What do you think the Roman Empire brought to the world that may have enhanced the spread of Christianity?

Resources for Digging Deeper

Choose a few books that look interesting, or find your own.

BIOGRAPHIES

Plutarch—Lives of Noble Romans

Edited by Edmund Fuller • Plutarch was one of the earliest biographers in history! All the plays William Shakespeare wrote about the Romans were derived from Plutarch's biographies. Difficult reading, but some might enjoy it. Plutarch compared Roman leaders with Greek leaders. **HS+**

Famous Men of Rome

Edited by Rob Shearer • A much gentler version of the following book, it gives a good introduction to the mo important men of this empire. **E+**

Lives of Famous Romans

Olivia Coolidge • Any set of biographies on the Romans is bound to be distasteful to some extent, since so many of the ruling Romans (especially of the Empire) were given over to utter immorality. My suggestion is to read these biographies in light of Daniel 2, and the perspective given in the gospels and Acts. **HS+**

Worl
Pres

Dorc ... ok takes a sym ... emy in Egypt. Cl ... loved by Caesar a ... Learn why in

... biography of the last ... conquered both ... JE+

Ha

Robert Green • ... biography, this is an excellent introduction ... thage's greatest general and Rome's greatest fear. **UE+**

ARCHITECTURE

City

David Macaulay • Mr. Macaulay helps us to see the incredible cultural dynamic of architecture. In this fascinating book, learn how a Roman city was designed and built. **UE+**

ANCIENT ROME

The Romans—Usborne Illustrated World History

Anthony Marks & Graham Tingay • Filled with short descriptions and great pictures, this is a wonderful, concise, fact-filled book about ancient Rome. **UE+**

The Romans—Life in the Empire

Charles Guittard & Annie-Claude Martin • This is a birds-eye look at the culture and everyday life of the Roman people. Helpful for understanding the times. **UE+**

Ancient Rome

Philippa Medcalf & Jan Rolph • This Cambridge Junior History book is an excellent introduction to ancient Rome for pre-high school students. **UE+**

Augustus Caesar's World

Genevieve Foster • A fascinating book for all ages which tells the story of Augustus Caesar, describing the world in which he lived. **E+**

Growing Up in Ancient Rome

Mike Corbishley • Another book in the series, this is one of the best books I know for introducing the lifestyle and culture of ancient Rome. Excellent overview for children. **E+**

The Roman Empire (Make it Work!)

Peter Chrisp & Andrew Haslam • This is a hands-on approach to learning history! Filled with ideas for Roman clothing, art, architecture, weaponry, and more, it certainly has enough ideas to keep everyone happy. **E+**

ARCHAEOLOGY

The Lost Wreck of the Isis

Robert D. Ballard • Learn about underwater archaeology while reading a fictional tale of a ship lost at sea during Roman times. Very interesting. **UE+**

Sunk! Exploring Underwater Archaeology

Runestone Press • This is a fascinating book showing how archaeologists discover new aspects of history and ancient cultures under the water. **UE+**

Piece by Piece! MOSAICS OF THE ANCIENT WORLD

Michael Avi-Yonah • A wonderful look at this art form, this book is filled with pictures and the stories mosaics have "told" to archaeologists. **E+**

PUNIC WARS

The Young Carthaginian

G. A. Henty • Henty's fictional story of Hannibal's war against Rome, told from the perspective of Hannibal's young cousin, is a fantastic way to learn about this important moment in history. Highly recommended! **UE+**

Hannibal's Elephants

Alfred Powers • A fictionalized account of the mighty Hannibal, general of Carthage. It is told from the perspective of a boy who helps care for the war elephants during the Second Punic War with Rome. It is very interesting, especially for boys. **UE+**

JULIUS CAESAR

Caesar's Gallic War

Translated & edited by Olivia Coolidge • This version of Julius Caesar's autobiographical account of the Gallic War is fabulous! Olivia Coolidge has added enough "color" that it draws the reader in to the story. I absolutely recommend it! **MS+**

Julius Caesar

William Shakespeare • One of Shakespeare's most famous plays. **MS+**

Julius Caesar (World Leaders Past and Present)

Roger Bruns & Arthur Meier Schlesinger • An excellent book in this excellent series! I preferred this book to the one about Mark Antony, and much of the same time period and material is covered. After reading Caesar's Gallic Wars, this book will fill in the gaps. **MS+**

SCIENCE

Science in Ancient Rome

Jacqueline L. Harris • This is an excellent introduction to the scientific achievements of the Romans, perfect for younger students. **UE+**

Roman Roads and Aqueducts

Don Nardo • One of the titles in the Building History series, this is a fascinating look at how Rome was able to build such long-lasting, efficient roads and aqueducts. **MS+**

Bridges: A Project Book

Anne & Scott MacGregor • If you can find the book, there is a wonderful project for building a Roman arch bridge. **E+**

Building (Make it Work!)

Andrew Haslam • Another book from this fantastic series, this one shows many different projects for the family to do, including a keystone bridge and an aqueduct. **E+**

MILITARY VIEW

Life of a Roman Soldier

Don Nardo • Rome was able to conquer because her soldiers were tireless, fearless, well-trained, well-organized and nearly invincible. Learn fascinating details about the Roman military in this excellent book. **MS+**

For more books, use these Dewey Decimal numbers in your library:

Ancient Rome: #937

Also, look for biographies on the key people listed.

What books did you like best?

The Internet also contains a wealth of information about ancient Rome.

What sites were the most helpful?

Student Self-Evaluation UNIT 8, PHASE 1

Dates and hours:____________________

Key Concepts

Rephrase the four Key Concepts of this Unit and confirm your understanding of each:

- The rise of Rome

____

- The leaders of Rome

____

- The engineering feats of Rome

____

- God's plan for Rome

____

Tools for Self-Evaulation

Evaluate your personal participation in the discussions of this Phase. Bearing in mind that a good participant in a discussion is not always the most vocal participant, ask yourself these questions: Were you an active participant? Did you ask perceptive questions? Were you willing to listen to other participants of the discussion and draw out their opinions? Record your observations and how you would like to improve your participation in the future:

____

____

Every time period is too complex to be understood in one Phase of study. Evaluate your current knowledge of the rise of Rome. What have you focused on so far? What are your weakest areas of knowledge?

____

____

Based on the evaluation of this introduction, project ahead what you would like to study more of in the following Phases:

____

Phase 2

Research & Reporting

Explore one or more of these areas to discover something significant!

Punic Wars

- Research and write a detailed description of Hannibal's surprise route from Carthage to Rome.
- Discover and report on the Punic Wars, including such questions as: What was the short term result of the Punic Wars? What was the long term result for Carthage? Rome?

Roman Republic and Empire

- Find one of the books listed, or a book of your choice, for basic information on Rome—first, the Republic and then, the Empire. Report your findings.
- Research and report on the "Rise and Fall of the Roman Republic."
- Who were the slaves in Rome? How did the Romans acquire their slaves? What work did the slaves do? Share your findings.

Calendar

Discover and report on the changes made in the calendar by Julius Caesar.

Julius Caesar

Look up Julius Caesar in your history resources. How significant was this leader in Roman history? What is the significance of the Rubicon River in his life? How was the Republic affected by his death?

Compare and Contrast

- Towards the end of the Roman Republic there was the first triumvirate, or council of three men, who led Rome. Who were the three leaders and what was the result of that triumvirate? After Julius Caesar's death there was another triumvirate. Who were the three leaders, and what resulted from their union? Compare and contrast the first Triumvirate with the second Triumvirate.
- What can you discover about this culture in regard to their treatment of other peoples? Were they similar to the Assyrians, Babylonians, Persians or Greeks? In what ways? How were they different?

Then to Now

In the library, or on the Internet, investigate the history of Rome (Italy) from the time of the Republic to the present. Report your findings.

Builders

Discover the methods used by the Romans to build roads. Draw a diagram showing the different steps involved. Arches had been used in architectural design for centuries, but the Romans found a better design and use for the arch. Discover what made the Roman arched bridges and aqueducts so strong that many remain even two thousand years later.

Provisioning

Discover and describe the climate and terrain of Rome. What kind of crops were grown? What kind of animals were raised? How were the large cities (like Rome) supplied with food, clothing and other goods? What impact did the conquests have on the people back in Rome?

Brain Stretchers

A Scriptural View

The Romans had been described in the book of Daniel hundreds of years before they emerged as world leaders. Using a study Bible, Bible handbook, Bible dictionary, commentary, etc., research the possible reasons God intended Jesus to come during this empire. What set this empire apart from earlier ones?

Naval Battles

Find out about the use of navies in warfare during this time period. Research and report on the Battle of Actium, and why it is still studied by military strategists.

Create Your Own Research Topic

____

____

____

Timeline

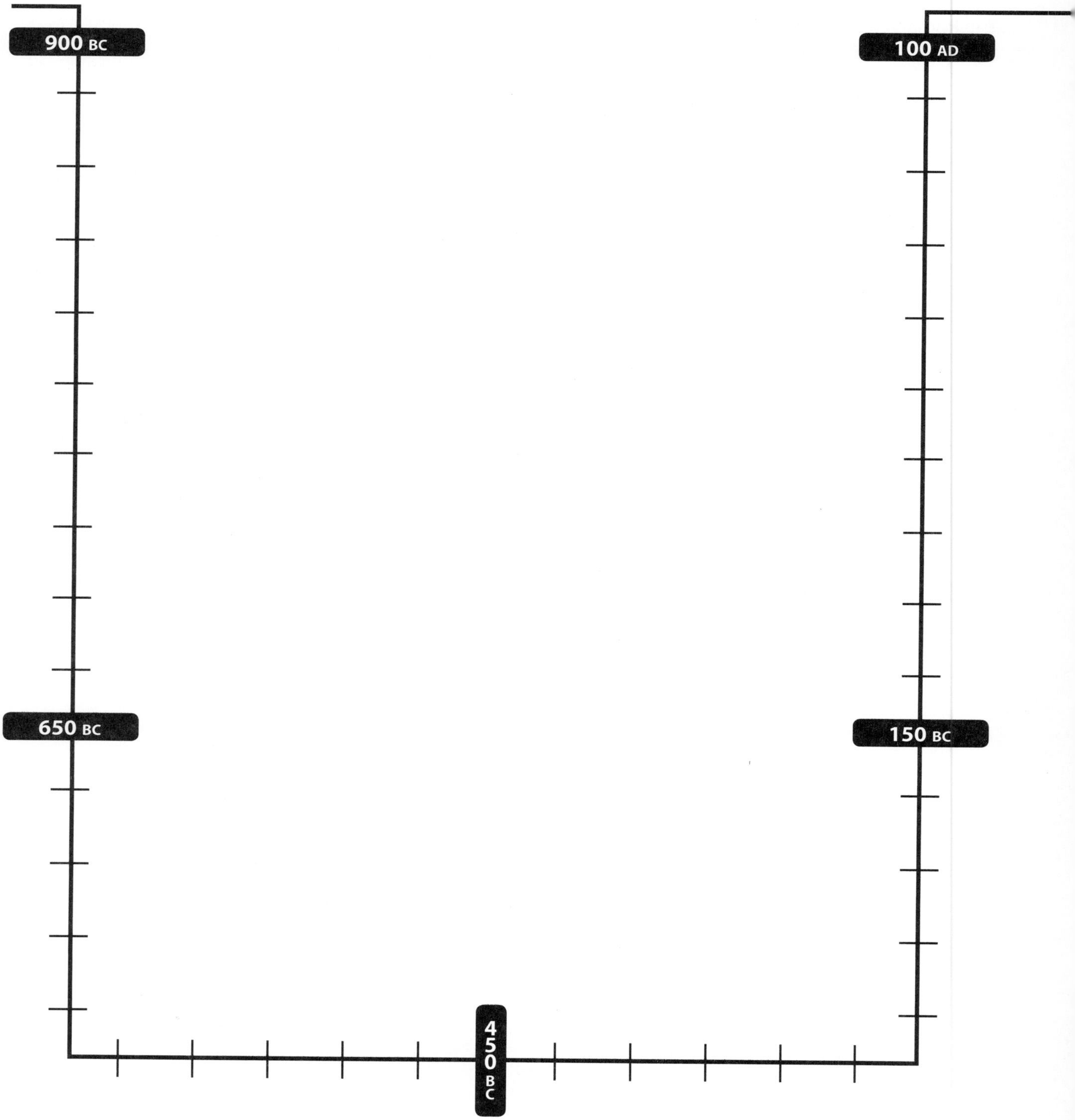

Consider this for your timeline

The Hellenistic Empire crumbled under the powerful hand of the Romans. Julius Caesar, a Roman military genius, conquered vast areas of land and people, and was suddenly assassinated. His heir, Octavian, fought Mark Antony and Cleopatra to become the sole ruler of Rome. It was this man who became known as Augustus Caesar, and through whose proclamation to tax all the people, the not-quite-born infant of Mary was brought to the City of David. How perfectly God does all things!

Key Events

The Punic Wars

Roman Republic

Roman Empire

Be sure to include the people listed in Key People in Phase 1.

Words to Watch

Remember—The easiest way to learn a subject is to master its terms:

republic	Pax Romana	triumvirate	Punic Wars
aqueduct	emperor	slave	tribune
centurion	legion	senate	patricians
empire	plebeians		

Other words you need to look up:

____

____

____

____

____

____

____

Student Self-Evaluation UNIT 8, PHASE 2

Dates and hours:________________________

Research Project

- Summarize your research question:

____

____

- List your most useful sources by author, title, and page number or URL where applicable (continue list in margin if necessary):

____

____

____

Now take a moment to evaluate the sources you just listed. Do they provide a balanced view of your research question? Should you have sought an additional opinion? Are your sources credible (if you found them on your own)? Record your observations:

____

____

Evaluate your research project in its final presentation. What are its strengths? If you had time to revisit this project, what would you change? Consider giving yourself a letter grade based on your project's merits and weaknesses.

____

____

Letter grade: ____

You have just completed an area of specific research in the rise of Rome. Now what would you like to explore in the upcoming Phases? Set some objectives for yourself:

____

Phase 3

Maps and Mapping

Physical Terrain

- » Label the land of Italy and color the "boot," which was the center of the Roman Republic and Empire.
- » Label and color the island of Britain, which Julius Caesar attempted to conquer.
- » Label and color the islands of Sicily, Corsica, and Sardinia.
- » Draw and label the Tiber river.
- » Mark and color the Alps mountain range and the Apennines mountain range.
- » Color and label the Mediterranean Sea, the Adriatic Sea, and the Tyrrhenian Sea.

Geopolitical

- » Draw the boundaries of the Roman Republic.
- » Now, using a different color marker, draw the boundaries of the Roman Empire under Emperor Hadrian.
- » Label and color the region of Illyria.
- » Label and color the countries of Gaul and Spain, which Julius Caesar conquered. What are the modern day names of these countries?
- » Label the location of Carthage and Rome. Locate the sites where Roman governors commanded. What modern day cities are close to these ancient cities?

Explore

- » ***Christian Outreach:*** What is the status of evangelical outreach today to Italy and the lands of the former Roman Empire? What opportunities and what difficulties face those who share the Gospel in these nations?
- » ***The Growth of an Empire:*** After looking at a map of the Roman Empire, consider its natural boundaries and how they were enlarged significantly by conquering other lands. What words would you use to describe this empire?

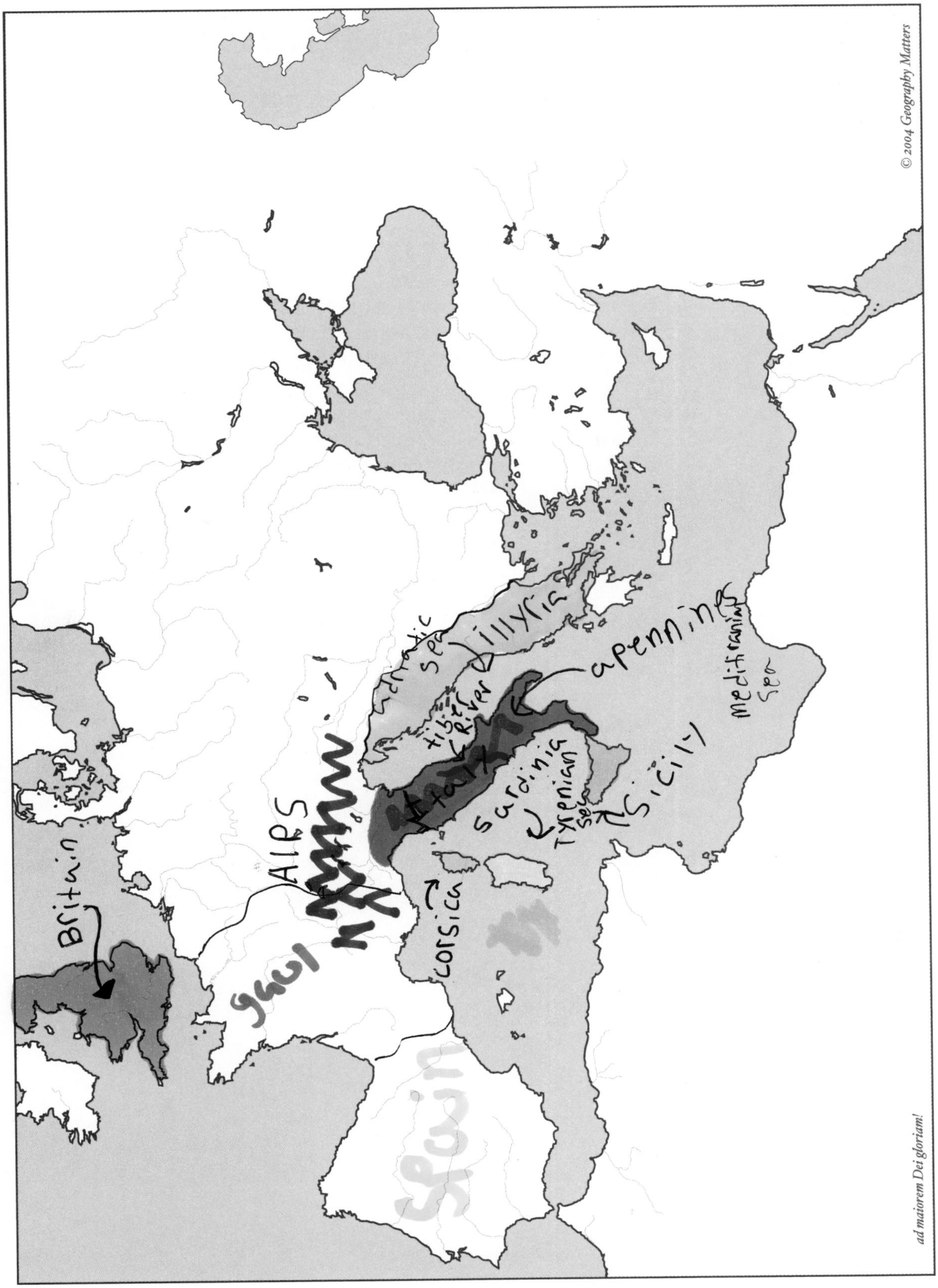

ad maiorem Dei gloriam!

CONSIDER:

From early in the Republic, the Romans showed great devotion to the concept of the family. This helps to explain their development of the individualized portrait bust. The Romans had a tradition of creating a wax, terra-cotta, or marble portrait head of the father in the family. Interestingly enough, these busts include the unique aspects of the particular person, such as wrinkles, large ears, etc., which shows an unusual respect for the individuality of the man represented.

Art Appreciation

Look for examples of Roman portrait heads.

» How would you describe these faces?

» Do they seem realistic to you?

Architecture

One of the achievements of Rome was providing clean drinking water for the inhabitants of its cities. Aqueducts (from the latin aqua for water, and ductus for channel) were constructed to carry water from the springs in the high hills down to the towns and cities. One of the most famous of the Roman aqueducts is the one in Nimes, France. It was constructed of huge stone blocks, weighing as much as six tons! This aqueduct is one hundred sixty feet tall, and consists of three tiers of arches with the top tier containing the channel for the water. Enough water traveled through this aqueduct to provide for 50,000 people. The Romans were such good engineers that this structure was able to endure high winds and flash floods. It has stood for two thousand years.

» Find a photograph of the aqueduct at Nimes. It is one of the most popular scenic attractions in France, with more than two million visitors per year. What words would you use to describe this structure?

Arts in Action

Select one or more, and let your artistic juices flow!

Imitation

Try creating or drawing a portrait bust in the style of the Romans.

Costuming

Fashion historic Roman costumes with sheets or fabric. There are many books in the library which will give you ideas and suggestions.

Mosaic

Try making an artistic mosaic. There are many ways to do this, from very simple to very complicated. One wonderful idea is to create a papier maché bowl, paint it a base color, then create a pattern inside the bowl with colored bits of paper. Complete your masterpiece by giving a coat of varnish, inside and out.

War Elephants:

Trace a picture of a war elephant. Glue on beads, rice or glitter to show their armor. They were considered to be a vital part of the military maneuvers of that time period. If available in your area, you should ride an elephant. It is a moving experience.

Diorama

Get a big cardboard box. Paint the Swiss Alps on the inside back and sides. Using miniature figures, create a diorama of Hannibal crossing the Alps with his army, horses, and elephants.

Science

Roman Arched Bridge

Make an arched bridge. We found books in the library (listed at the beginning of the unit) which gave detailed descriptions of how to do this. Be sure to learn what a keystone is, how it functions, and why it is important.

Aqueduct

Make an aqueduct. An good example is found in *Buildings (Make It Work!)*.

Music

The Romans developed many brass instruments used in military music. For example, the Roman straight trumpet (they called it a tuba) was like the herald trumpet used today at horse races. Another was the buccina, which had a wooden crossbar to allow soldiers to carry it on the march. These instruments were very simple in structure and so they had very limited range of pitches. Their purpose was not to entertain people, but for signaling: to call the soldiers to assemble, or move.

It wasn't until centuries later that further developments allowed these instruments to have more melodic ability, thereby allowing them to come inside! Now, of course, it is very common to see trumpets and tubas, etc., in orchestras and bands. But there is still a certain thrill in hearing them played outdoors at concerts and celebrations.

Listen

» Play some of John Philip Sousa's march music, such as *Stars and Stripes Forever* or the *Washington Post March.*

Try This

» Cut the bottoms off plastic pop (soda) bottles. A 2-liter bottle gives a lower sound, while a 16 oz. bottle gives a higher sound. Now, play it like a trumpet: tighten your lips, center the mouth of the bottle over both lips, blow air through a small opening between your lips very fast—fast enough so your lips will buzz. This buzzing will make sound come out of the bottle. If you tighten your lips more and blow faster, the pitch will go up. If you loosen your lips and blow slower, the pitch will go down. Try placing your fist in the bottom of the "tuba"—it will give a nice variation. Your pop bottle "tuba" will sound somewhat like those early instruments in that they weren't very pretty either!

Cooking

The Romans were extremely fond of an herb we usually use in licorice—anise. It was considered to be so delightful that kings perfumed their linen with it. (Imagine sleeping on a pillow that smelled like licorice!) This recipe is not from Roman times, but it is a delicious way to sample this favored herb.

Anise Cookies

4 eggs	2 tbsp anise seed
1 cup sugar	3 cups flour
1 tsp vanilla	4 tsp baking powder
$^1/_3$ cup milk	1 cup butter, softened

Preheat oven to 375 degrees. Beat eggs in large bowl. Add sugar, vanilla, milk, and anise. Stir well. In another bowl, mix flour and baking powder. Cut in butter. Combine both mixtures. Roll dough out onto floured board. Cut into shapes. Bake on greased baking sheet 12 minutes, or until lightly browned.

Makes about 4 dozen.

Student Self-Evaluation UNIT 8, PHASE 3

Dates and hours:____________________

Evaluate Your Projects

- List which of the activities listed in this Phase you did:

  ____

  ____

  ____

- Rate your enthusiasm: __________

  Explain: ____________________________________

  ____

- Rate the precision of your approach:__________

  Explain: ____________________________________

  ____

- Rate your effort towards the completion of the project: __________

  Explain: ____________________________________

  ____

Ask yourself what worked and what did not. What would you do differently in the future, and what would you repeat?

____

How specifically did these hands-on activities enhance your knowledge of the rise of Rome? What made them worthwhile?

____

In the first three Phases of this Unit, what aspect of the time period has most captured your imagination? What would you like to creatively pursue to conclude your study?

____

Phase 4

In Your Own Way…

We have seen the rise of Rome through the Punic Wars and onto center stage as a vast empire. In the midst of this final empire Daniel saw in the vision, Jesus, the Redeemer promised in Genesis 3, was born.

Now, choose a selection of these activities, or create your own, which will best express what you have learned from this unit.

LINGUISTICS

Journalism

- Be the newspaper reporter assigned to cover Octavian's triumphal entry into Rome after defeating Mark Antony and Cleopatra. Be sure to include the background information about Julius Caesar's will, which promoted Octavian to power.
- You are the on-the-spot reporter for the news rag, *It's What's Happening!* Your current assignment is to discover whether the two brothers, Romulus and Remus, are newsworthy. If so, write a piece on how they're contributing to what's happening.

Prose

- Write a fictional account of Rhodus, the Roman road builder. Of the 53,000 miles of road built by Rome, Rhodus has been told to build from Rome to Rhegium.
- Write a short story about a reluctant elephant on the march with Hannibal. Call it "The Meek Mammoth."

Playing with Words

Create a crossword puzzle. Choose words from this unit for the horizontal and vertical answers. Next, supply the clues which will enable your family to solve the puzzle.

Timetable

Create your own version of Timetables of History showing what is taking place in the arts, in science, in math, in family life, and in government during the rise of Rome.

ART

Illustration

Create illustrations that could be used in the short story, "The Meek Mammoth" listed above.

Graphic Design

Design a T-shirt for Octavian's troops after the Battle of Actium. Remember, they so intimidated Cleopatra, she fled from the battle!

Sculpting

Sculpt a head of clay, in the Roman style.

Cartooning

As a political cartoonist, show the attitude of the Roman women toward Cleopatra.

MUSIC

Compose

Write a marching song for Caesar's troops, entitled "We're Seeing the World One Step at a Time." Use a military-style, marching rhythm, and words which would inspire soldiers to march for hundreds of miles.

Performance Practice

With your teacher's help, select an appropriate piece of music which expresses some element from the Roman Empire, such as a military march. Prepare and perform the piece for an audience. Communicate with your audience the reason for your selection either in the program notes or in a short speech.

DRAMA

Comedy

Create a skit of Octavian (a schoolboy), receiving the news that he's now in charge of the entire Roman world!

Tragedy

Produce the assassination of Julius Caesar on the Ides of March. Include Brutus, his close friend, whose participation in the assassination caused Caesar to give up his struggle against his attackers.

Puppetry

Put on a puppet show of Hannibal's march across the Alps into Rome. You may choose to focus on the actual crossing, or, instead, on the triumphal march across Italy.

Prop Needs

___

___

Costume Ideas

___

___

Role/Player

___

___

Set Suggestions

___

___

MOVEMENT

Pantomime

Pantomime Julius Caesar crossing the Rubicon River in an arrogant manner. He does not lay down his arms, he does not dismiss his armies, and he does not enter Rome as a humble citizen.

Dance

Choreograph a piece showing the artistry and agility of horses on the march with Hannibal. Contrast them with the pondering and powerful elephants.

Action

Show through movement the actions of building a Roman road. Stylize the repetitive movements.

CONCEPTUAL DESIGN

Design-A-City

In the Roman style, design a city which includes straight, well-built roads, bridges, aqueducts, palaces, slave quarters, hippodrome, and whatever else would be appropriate in a Roman city.

CREATE YOUR OWN EXPRESSION

Student Self-Evaluation UNIT 8, PHASE 4

Dates and hours:____________________

Evaluate Your Projects

- What creative project did you choose:

- What did you expect from your project, and how does the final project compare to your initial expectations?

- What do you like about your project? What would you change?

In Conclusion

Revisit the four Key Concepts from the beginning of this Unit. Explain how your understanding of and appreciation for each has grown over the course of your study.

Record your concluding thoughts on the rise of Rome:

Jesus Christ, Immanuel

UNIT 9

Key Concepts

- The fullness of time
- The historical evidence
- Knowing Him—Philippians 3:10
- Sharing Him

An ancient Christian inscription from the early third century

The Promised One has come . . .

> For unto us a Child is born, unto us a Son is given;
> And the government shall be upon His shoulder.
> And His name will be called Wonderful, Counselor,
> Mighty God, Everlasting Father, Prince of Peace.
> Of the increase of His government and peace there will be no end.
> Upon the throne of David and over His kingdom,
> To order it and establish it with judgment and justice
> From that time forward, even forever.
> The zeal of the Lord of hosts will perform this. Isaiah 9:6–7

All of man's history from Adam and Eve to the Roman Empire had been leading up to this moment in history. The scarlet thread of redemption, which God had been mercifully weaving through the lives of people and nations, was now to become fully visible, in vibrant living color, clothed in the robes of frail humanity. The Promised One, the Messiah, Jesus of Nazareth, was to enter our world at a precise moment known to us as "the fullness of time" (Galatians 4:4).

Since Jesus would come as a baby to a specific family (the tribe of Judah, the family of David) in a specific geographic location (Palestine) at a specific time (during the fourth kingdom of Daniel's vision), it would do well for us to understand what Palestine was like for the Jews in this time period, and how they had come to have a king over them who was not of the royal lineage of David.

After the Temple was cleansed and rededicated to the Lord in 165 BC, Judas Maccabaeus continued to lead his troops against the Syrians and eventually died in battle. His brother, Jonathan, then became the leader of the Maccabean revolt from 160–143 BC. Jonathan was remarkably adept at diplomacy, which resulted in his signing a treaty with Rome against Syria. Jonathan then used his diplomatic skills with the rulers of Syria to gain the posts of High Priest over the Jews and political governor over Judea. Oddly enough, Jonathan was even made one of the Syrian nobility!

The Hasmonaean Dynasty

When Jonathan died, his brother, Simon, succeeded to the position of High Priest and political ruler over Judea (143–135 BC). Israel attained its longed-for independence when Simon, through the means of diplomacy, ended the taxation imposed on Israel by the Syrians. For this stupendous endeavor, the Jewish leaders gave Simon the name, "leader and High Priest forever, until there shall arise a faithful prophet." This was the beginning of the Hasmonaean dynasty (from the line of Mattathias), which would continue until the reign of Herod (37–4 BC). Isn't it interesting to consider that the family of Mattathias was neither in the line of Aaron the first High Priest, nor David the king whom God had promised would have a descendant on the throne forever? This means that the selection of Simon's family to rule and reign was a man-made decision, with political foundations. And, as we shall see, leaving God out of the equation resulted in a Godless rulership of His chosen people.

The scarlet thread of redemption . . . was now to become fully visible.

Israel's independence would last for only eighty years, until Pompey and his Roman army invaded Jerusalem in 63 BC. These eighty years were filled with Greek tragedy, as the increasingly Hellenized Hasmonaean rulers of Israel murdered their siblings for the throne, acquired the Hellenistic propensity for expanding their boundaries militarily, and grew as far from orthodox Judaism as the east is from the west. On the eve of civil war between Hyrcanus II and Aristobulus II, two Hasmonaean brothers who each laid claim to the throne, Pompey came from Syria to subdue this

Jewish strife. In his coming—which was justified because of Jonathan's treaty with Rome in 160 BC—he laid siege to Jerusalem for three months and, when he had gained the city, proceeded to execute twelve thousand Jews. Israel was then forcibly brought into the Roman fold, as part of the Roman Province of Syria.

Israel was then forcibly brought into the Roman fold, as part of the Roman Province of Syria.

Rise of Herod

By Rome's authority, Hyrcanus II was made governor of Judea and High Priest, though the man behind the scenes, who really controlled the throne, was a non-Jew by the name of Antipater. Before Pompey's invasion, Antipater had been the governor of a land conquered and Judaized by the Hasmonaeans. Antipater, both cunning and politically savvy, was well aware that Rome was the emerging power to be reckoned with in the Middle East. Necessity forced him to become very adept at changing loyalties in order to stay on the winning side. As you may remember from the last unit, Pompey was defeated by Julius Caesar, which did not bode well for those who had gained their power through Pompey. However, Antipater jumped sides and brought much-needed assistance to Julius Caesar in Egypt. For this, he was given the title and political position of Procurator of Judea, while Hyrcanus continued as High Priest. After Julius Caesar's assassination, Antipater and his sons quickly welcomed Cassius, one of Caesar's assassins, who had come to the area with his newly raised army. Further, Antipater took the initiative to provide to Cassius the tribute taxes belonging to Rome. When Cassius and Brutus were defeated by Mark Antony, Antipater's sons changed sides once again (Antipater having been murdered by a rival). Antipater's son, Herod, went in person to meet with Mark Antony. Convincing Antony of his family's loyalty with a generous amount of money, Herod and his brother, Phasaelus, were now made Tetrarchs of Judea.

When the Parthians from the East invaded Jerusalem in 40 BC, Phasaelus died a prisoner, and Herod, who barely escaped with his life, fled to the safety of Rome. Antony introduced Herod to Octavius, heir of Julius Caesar—a most fortuitous meeting for Herod. Through the influence of Mark Antony and Octavius, the Roman Senate voted Herod, "King of the Jews." This was most likely a political prize to motivate Herod to rid Palestine of the Parthians, who had never been defeated by Rome, but what it did, in effect, was link Herod's rule of Judea to the military might of Rome. From that point on, anyone who wanted to mess with King Herod would have to deal with the Roman Empire. It took a few years and a large Roman army to accomplish the defeat of the Parthians, but by 37 BC Herod was on his throne. Can you imagine? The ruler designated by Rome to be "King of the Jews" was not even Jewish! This was utterly abhorrent, especially to the growing nationalistic movement and to those still clinging to the Jewish faith.

There were at this time four main groups or sects within Judaism. The

Sadducees were the aristocracy of Jerusalem and the administrators of the Temple, including the high priesthood. To be a Sadducee, one had to be born a Sadducee, as membership to this aristocratic and wealthy group was restricted to those whose families already belonged. *Essenes*, the second group, were a mostly monastic group who lived in strict, isolated religious communities of the desert. They conducted their religious worship services in their desert communities, refusing to offer sacrifices in Jerusalem, since the worldly Sadducees were in charge of the Temple. The third group was the *Pharisees*, or separated ones, who held to orthodox Judaism. They considered the oral traditions of Judaism to be of the same importance, however, as the written Law, or Torah. These oral traditions had originally been delivered by influential rabbis over a period of time in an attempt to deal with the increasing complexities of living out the Law in a Greek world. But, by the time of Jesus, the strict observance of these traditions had become more important and far more legalistic than God's Law. The fourth group were the *Zealots*, the fiercely nationalistic movement to free Israel from hated Roman rule. Herod, when he had earlier ruled in Galilee, tried to brutally suppress this movement by executing a Zealot leader and many of his followers, but they continued to foment violent opposition to Rome and to seek Israel's independence. Though they seem to have headquartered in Galilee, their influence was felt throughout the land. Eventually, the Zealots's passion to overthrow Roman authority would bring about the destruction of Jerusalem in AD 70.

Jesus Christ

Now the stage is set. The place is Palestine, in the Roman Province of Syria. The date is approximately 5 BC.

> And it came to pass in those days that a decree went out from Caesar Augustus that all the world should be registered. Luke 2:1

In a tiny corner of the Roman Empire, far from the centers of political power and influential wealth, a young couple traveled sixty miles from their poor home in Nazareth of Galilee to Bethlehem in Judea. Joseph, of the house of David, had to return with his wife to their ancestral home in order to be registered. This young wife, Mary, carried her soon-to-be-born infant. Her God-given pregnant condition was both miraculous and prophetic.

From that point on, anyone who wanted to mess with King Herod would have to deal with the Roman Empire.

> Therefore the Lord Himself will give you a sign: Behold, the virgin shall conceive and bear a Son, and shall call His name Immanuel. Isaiah 7:14

Immanuel. It means, "God with us." No longer would we be alone and hopeless. God Himself would be *with* us . . . with us in our humanity because He would become human. We would be able to walk with Him in an intimacy of relationship we had not known since the Garden of Eden. The distance between the Creator and the created would change to closeness as the Creator became Immanuel, God with us.

And now, at one of the darkest and most helpless times in Israel's history, a child, who was the Son of God, grew inside this Jewish girl's womb. Beyond our ability to fully comprehend, He was conceived by the Holy Spirit, and was fully God and fully man. God the Son—the second person of the Trinity—humbled Himself to become one of us...in order to be with us.

A young couple traveled sixty miles from their poor home in Nazareth of Galilee to Bethlehem in Judea.

> Let this mind be in you which was also in Christ Jesus, who, being in the form of God, did not consider it robbery to be equal with God, but made Himself of no reputation, taking the form of a servant, and coming in the likeness of men. Philippians 2:5–7

This humbling of Himself did not end with His willingness to become a human baby. God had very precisely and specifically chosen the one who would be the mother of Immanuel. But, though Mary and Joseph were both of the royal lineage of David, they were poor. Jesus, the Son of God, entered the world He had created, not in the luxury, beauty and comfort of a royal palace fit for a king, but rather in a smelly, dirty animal stable. You see, there was no room for His human parents at the travelers' inn.

God with us, Immanuel, entered the world surrounded by all the trappings of poverty in all its hopelessness.

> For you know the grace of our Lord Jesus Christ, that though He was rich, yet for your sakes He became poor, that you through His poverty might become rich. 2 Corinthians 8:9

He did it for us. And He did it in a way that no one would expect. That is part of who God is and who we are not. He sees things from a perspective we would never perceive and He does things we can not imagine doing:

> "For My thoughts are not your thoughts, nor are your ways My ways," says the Lord. "For as the heavens are higher than the earth, so are My ways higher than your ways, and My thoughts than your thoughts." Isaiah 55:8–9

Everything about Jesus—the manner of His birth, the hiddenness of his youth (apart from one notable exception), the style of His ministry, the shame of His death, the shock of His resurrection—is so different than the way we would have written the story. His convention-breaking conversation with the loose-living Samaritan woman totally confounded His own disciples; His simple answer to the politically explosive question, "Is it lawful to pay taxes to Caesar, or not?" muzzled his opponents; His wisdom-beyond-Solomon's judgment of the woman caught in the act of adultery revealed the hearts of her accusers; His reputation of being a drunkard and a glutton destroyed any hope of seeming sufficiently religious. How could He have walked so differently than we do? How could He have so totally ignored the social and religious norms of His day? How could He love the ones no one liked, even a money-grubbing tax collector, and a friend who would betray Him? How could He resist the instant popularity of the mob by telling them they would need to eat His body and drink His blood? Beyond all this, how could He willingly offer His life as a sacrifice in order to save us? The answers all reside in who God is. We can not understand Jesus unless we recognize that He is God. God with us.

Jesus did not come to be a religious icon. He did not come to be a word in our vocabulary or a theological concept in our doctrines. He did not come to be a movie star, nor a fund-raising method, nor the origin for popular jewelry. He came for one purpose: to restore us to relationship with Himself.

The Western Wall (or Wailing Wall) is all that remains of Herod's Temple.

This is all about Jesus. History shows us our desperate need and God's divine rescue. It is not an academic subject—it is a means of pointing us to Jesus. And He, Immanuel, came to be with us. We are back where we started in Unit One: "He made us for relationship, deeper and more satisfying than anything we have ever imagined."

Are you willing? The way back to God has been made for you, and His name is Jesus.

Phase 1

Listen to This

What in the World? VOL. 1

DISC FOUR:

» In the Perfect Moment of Time (track 6)

» The Promised One (track 7)

» The Life of Jesus (track 8)

True Tales VOL. 1

DISC THREE:

» The Biblical Prophecies of Jesus Fulfilled (track 3)

Digging Deeper VOL. 1

DISC THREE:

» The First Christmas

Read For Your Life

The Holy Bible

» The Main Story: The book of Luke (or Matthew, Mark, or John)

» Other Helpful Verses: Isaiah 46:9–10; Romans 1:2–4

» Prophecies Fulfilled in Jesus's Life:

Genesis 3:15	Isaiah 7:14	Psalm 2:7
Genesis 22:18	Numbers 24:17	Genesis 49:10
Isaiah 11:1–5	Jeremiah 23:5–6	Micah 5:2
Jeremiah 31:15	Psalm 110:1 & 4	Deuteronomy 18:18
Isaiah 33:22	Isaiah 61:1–3	Psalm 69:7–9
Isaiah 40:3	Isaiah 9:1–2	Isaiah 35:5–6,
Psalm 78:2	Malachi 3:1	Zechariah 9:9
Psalm 118:22	Isaiah 60:3	Psalm 16:10
Psalm 41:9	Zechariah 11:12–13	Zechariah 13:7
Psalm 35:11	Isaiah 53	Isaiah 50:6
Psalm 22	Psalm 109:24–25	Psalm 69:4, 20–21
Psalm 38:11	Psalm 31:5	Psalm 34:20
Amos 8:9	Zechariah 12:10	

Key People

Jesus
Messiah, Redeemer, Lord

John the Baptist
"Prepare the way of the Lord"

Peter
The impetuous disciple

John
The beloved disciple

Mary and Joseph
The parents of Jesus

Caiaphas
The High Priest

Herod the Great
Idumean ruler who kills the infants

Herod Antipas
Idumean ruler who murdered John the Baptist

Talk Together

Opinion Column

- What did you find to be the most interesting aspect you encountered in this introduction to Jesus Christ?
- Imagine you are one of the shepherds who had heard the angelic announcement. Consider your surprise, your amazement and your awe at actually seeing the Christ child. How would you describe your experience?
- Read Matthew 11:28–30. What does Jesus tell us to do, and how do we obey Him? How do you think this will change your life?

Critical Puzzling

- Why do you think God sent Jesus to be born of peasants rather than kings?
- Read the book of Mark. It clearly reveals the miraculous power of Jesus to heal the sick, calm the storm, cast out demons, feed the multitude, die a sacrificial death, and rise from the dead unto eternal life. What do you think someone who believes in a "closed system"—one who does not believe in God and does not believe in the supernatural—would say about these miracles?
- There is a significant difference between a person who says, "I don't know, but let's do some research to find out" and the person who says, "I already know it isn't true"? Why will the second person not believe any historic evidence for the truth of Christianity? What do you think will help them believe?
- The amazing thing about studying Jesus is that He is ALIVE! When we studied Moses, King Nebuchadnezzar, Xerxes, Alexander the Great, and Julius Caesar, we studied about important men who had accomplished much during their lifetimes. But they are all dead. When we study Jesus, He is with us, revealing Himself, changing us, making us into His image. Take some time, either alone or with your family, to talk to Jesus about what you are studying. Ask Him your questions, bring Him your thoughts, allow Him to show you that He is faithful and trustworthy; that He is the same, yesterday, today and forever.

Personal Application

- Ask the Lord to draw you into a closer walk with Him every day, to reveal His infinite love in your life. Keep an ongoing journal to show how this prayer is answered.

Resources for Digging Deeper

Choose a few books that look interesting, or find your own.

APOLOGETICS

Evidence that Demands a Verdict

Josh McDowell • This is not a book to sit down and read, it is a book to study. It will teach you the historical evidences for the Christian faith. (A term often used for this is "apologetics.") Filled with historical, archaeological, medical, and legal references, this book will give you a very firm foundation for the defense of biblical Christianity. **MS+**

Mere Christianity

C. S. Lewis • One of the classics of Christian apologetics, this considers the issue of whether Jesus was a liar, a lunatic, or Lord, as well as many other concepts. **HS**

HISTORICAL FICTION

Titus: A Comrade of the Cross

Florence Morse Kingsley • A classic, this book helps make the events of the Gospel come to life. **MS+**

The Bronze Bow

Elizabeth George Speare • Written for children, this is an absorbing tale about a young Jewish boy who struggles with his hatred for the conquering Romans. A very good insight into the mood of the times. **E+**

The Runaway

Patricia St. John • A very good story about a Phoenician boy whose sister is demon-possessed. The Scriptures come to life as you see the boy encounter many different people who have met Jesus. Our family couldn't put it down! RA

Ben Hur

Lew Wallace • This classic is written from the perspective of a prince of Judah who is thrown into Roman slavery. When he regains his freedom, he joins the guerrilla fighters who want a political Messiah. Having watched the movie and also read the book, I would highly recommend the book as it contains far more understanding of the culture, the times, the thoughts of the people. **MS+**

Ben Hur

Edited by William Kottmeyer • If reading the original is beyond your students, you may want to consider getting a younger version. **E+**

Vinegar Boy

Alberta Hawse • This is the story of the boy assigned to bring vinegar to those who were crucified. It is a story of the bitterness of defeat being turned into the joy of victory **UE+**

The Robe

Lloyd C. Douglas • This is an excellent look at Roman ways and their conflict with Christianity. **MS+**

BIOGRAPHIES

Pontius Pilate

Paul L Maier • Historical fiction, the events of this book are based entirely on historic documentation. It is a fascinating look at this historic person. (There is one scene I would avoid, when Salome dances for King Herod.) **MS+**

The Jesus Story Retold from the Bible

Mary Batchelor • Though I prefer to have the actual story directly from Scripture, this is an excellent adaptation of the life of Jesus for younger students. **RA E+**

For more books, use these Dewey Decimal numbers in your library:

Bible: #220

Ancient Palestine: #933

New Testament: #225

Gospels & Acts: #226

Jesus Christ: #232

Also, look for biographies on the key people listed.

What books did you like best?

____

____

____

____

The Internet also contains a wealth of information about Jesus Christ.

What sites were the most helpful?

____

____

____

____

Student Self-Evaluation UNIT 9, PHASE 1

Dates and hours:________________________

Key Concepts

Rephrase the four Key Concepts of this Unit and confirm your understanding of each:

- The fullness of time

____

- The historical evidence

____

- Knowing Him—Philippians 3:10

____

- Sharing Him

____

Tools for Self-Evaulation

Evaluate your personal participation in the discussions of this Phase. Bearing in mind that a good participant in a discussion is not always the most vocal participant, ask yourself these questions: Were you an active participant? Did you ask perceptive questions? Were you willing to listen to other participants of the discussion and draw out their opinions? Record your observations and how you would like to improve your participation in the future:

____

____

Every time period is too complex to be understood in one Phase of study. Evaluate your current knowledge of the time of Jesus Christ, Immanuel. What have you focused on so far? What are your weakest areas of knowledge?

____

____

Based on the evaluation of this introduction, project ahead what you would like to study more of in the following Phases:

____

Phase 2

Research & Reporting

Explore one or more of these areas to discover something significant!

Fulfilled Prophecies

Using either a Bible handbook, study Bible, commentary, or *Evidence that Demands a Verdict*, make a chart showing the Old Testament prophecies of the Messiah, the date they were written, and the fulfillment of these prophecies in Jesus.

The Time of Jesus

- Read the Gospels in the New Testament. Report on these questions:
  - To whom did Jesus come?
  - What was His message?
  - How did the people respond?
  - How did the Resurrection impact the rulers of Jerusalem; of Rome?
  - How did it impact the disciples?
- In reference books, research what was happening in the Roman Empire during the time of Jesus's life. Find the poem, *One Solitary Life*, and show how it is historically accurate.

Apologetics

- *Apologetics* is basically the intellectual defense of Christianity. Research and report on one area of apologetics, such as, fulfilled prophecy, evidence for the resurrection, the uniqueness and reliability of the Bible, etc.
- Research and write about the claims of Jesus Christ. Who did He say He was? What did He claim to be able to do? What evidence exists to validate His claims? (Consider: I highly recommend investing in a copy of *Evidence that Demands a Verdict* or something similar. It will open up a whole world in understanding the reasonableness of our faith.)

Miracles

Make a chart showing the supernatural—outside of natural law—acts of Jesus. What did He do? What were the results of his miracles, both in the lives of those receiving the miracles and in the attitude of those watching Jesus do the miracles? In what ways do you see the same attitudes in people today?

Brain Stretchers

Prophecy

Research the mathematical probabilities that one man could fulfill all the prophecies of the Messiah.

Apologetics

C. S. Lewis in Mere Christianity wrote: *"I am trying here to prevent anyone saying the really foolish thing that people often say about Him: 'I'm ready to accept Jesus as a great moral teacher, but I don't accept His claim to be God.' That is the one thing we must not say. A man who was merely a man and said the sort of things Jesus said would not be a great moral teacher. He would either be a lunatic—on a level with the man who says he is a poached egg—or else he would be the Devil of Hell. You must make your choice. Either this man was, and is, the Son of God: or else a madman or something worse."*

Research and report on the current arguments against Jesus being God's Son and Redeemer. How would C. S. Lewis's words effectively counter these arguments?

Fullness of Time

Research and write on the flow of history from Creation up to the time of Jesus. Show how Daniel's vision has been fulfilled through the four great empires. Galatians 4:4–5 indicates that God chose the perfect moment for the Messiah. In hindsight, how can we demonstrate that this was the case?

Create Your Own Research Topic

____

____

____

Timeline

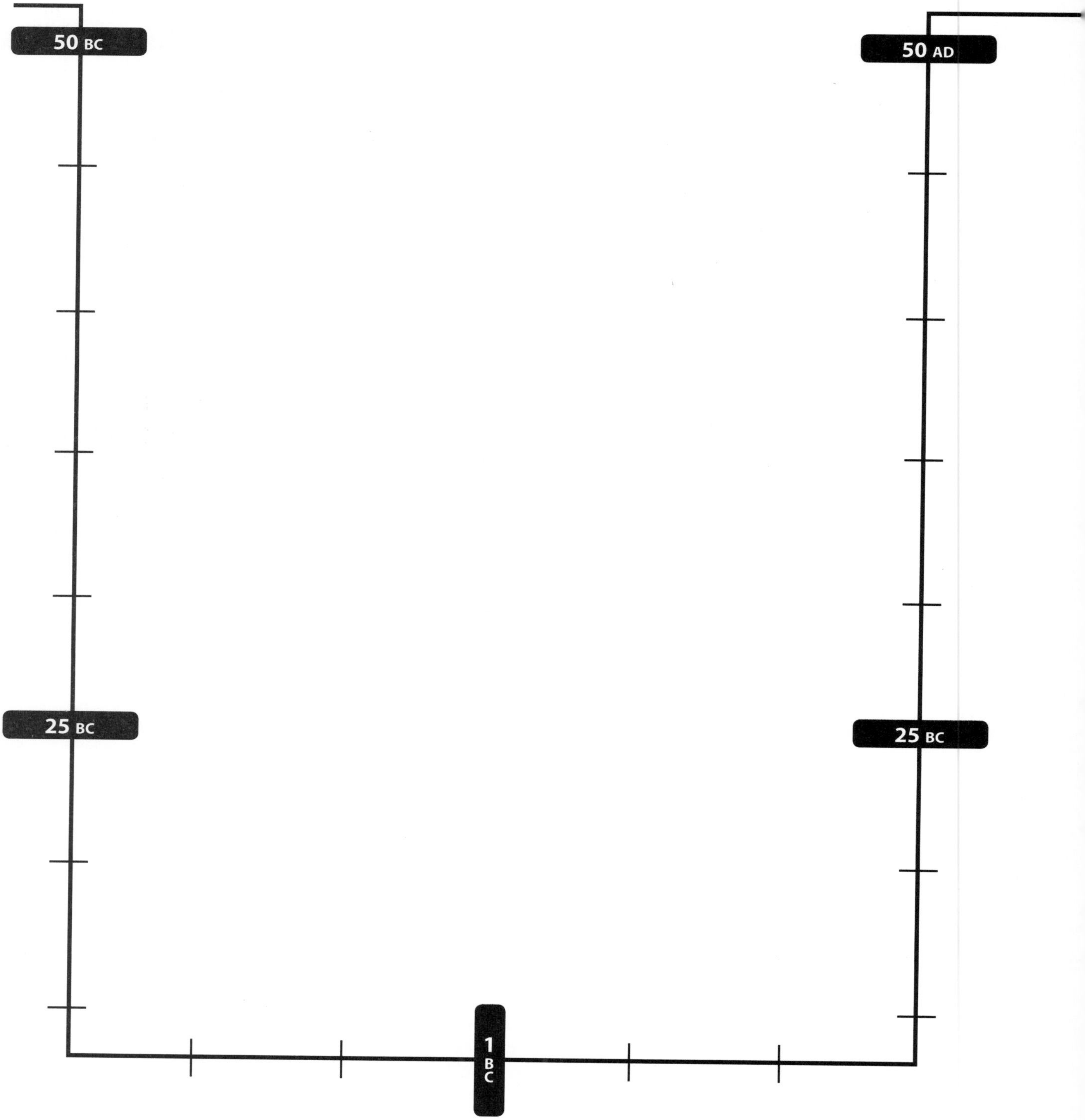

Consider this for your timeline

Galatians 4:4–5 tells us that in the fullness of time, "God sent forth His Son, born of a woman, born under the law, to redeem those who were under the law, that we might receive the adoption as sons." As you create your timeline for this Unit, think about the amazing timing of God, that He chose the perfect moment to send His Son into the world. It's not an accident that Jesus was born in Bethlehem, in the earliest years of the Roman Empire. It was exactly right. And, in the same way, His second coming will be at the exact moment in time to fulfill all of God's purposes and plans. This is not just about history, this is about eternity!

Key Events

- Birth of Jesus Christ
- Death & Resurrection of Jesus Christ

Be sure to include the people listed in Key People in Phase 1.

Words to Watch

Remember—The easiest way to learn a subject is to master its terms:

natural	supernatural	miracle	hoax
history	validate	Lord	myth
Messiah	Emmanuel	Christ	disciple
apostle	resurrection	ascension	commission
crucify	tomb	swoon	theory

Other words you need to look up:

Student Self-Evaluation UNIT 9, PHASE 2

Dates and hours:____________________

Research Project

- Summarize your research question:

____

____

- List your most useful sources by author, title, and page number or URL where applicable (continue list in margin if necessary):

____

____

____

Now take a moment to evaluate the sources you just listed. Do they provide a balanced view of your research question? Should you have sought an additional opinion? Are your sources credible (if you found them on your own)? Record your observations:

____

____

Evaluate your research project in its final presentation. What are its strengths? If you had time to revisit this project, what would you change? Consider giving yourself a letter grade based on your project's merits and weaknesses.

____

____

Letter grade: ____

You have just completed an area of specific research in the time of Jesus Christ, Immanuel. Now what would you like to explore in the upcoming Phases? Set some objectives for yourself:

____

The Hands-On Week

Phase 3

Maps and Mapping

Physical Terrain

- » Label and color the Dead Sea, the Sea of Galilee, and the Mediterranean Sea.
- » Label and color the Jordan River.
- » Locate and indicate the mountain ranges, deserts, and green areas.

Geopolitical

- » Draw the boundaries of Israel in the time of Jesus. Where are the boundaries of Israel today?
- » Label the cities of Bethlehem, Nazareth, Jerusalem, and the cities of the Decapolis.
- » Locate and label the area known as Samaria. What is the modern name of this area today.

Explore

- » ***Geography of the Promised One:*** Though Israel was a backwater, out-of-the-way country of the Roman Empire, God chose to send His Son to that geographic location. Looking at a map, consider and discuss God's unfailing wisdom and perfect knowledge in bringing the promised Redeemer for all the families of the earth to that nation.

ad maiorem Dei gloriam!
© 2004 Geography Matters

CONSIDER:

Jan van Eyck was a fourteenth century Flemish painter with an amazing grasp of Biblical truth. He perfected the technique of painting with oil paints, which can be seen when studying his master-piece, *The Adoration of the Lamb*. His painting, *The Annunciation*, is a stunning example of Biblical symbolism, which antici-pates the restoration of Sola Scriptura in the Reformation by nearly a hundred years.

Art Appreciation

The Annunciation by Jan van Eyck

» Do you think this reflects what the Bible describes?

» How does it differ from your own impression of this historic event?

» How would you describe the *Annunciation*?

» How many symbols can you find in this painting?

The *Pieta*—A Sculpture by Michelangelo

» Do you think this reflects what the Bible describes?

» How does it differ from your own impression of this historic event?

» How would you describe the *Pieta*? Why do you think it is considered to be one of the best sculptures ever created?

- Michelangelo was in his early twenties when he created this life-size sculpture of Mary holding the crucified Jesus in her arms. He created this in less than two years from a single slab of marble—one of the most magnificent sculptures ever created!

Architecture

Though Solomon's Temple was destroyed in 588 BC, the repatriated Jews returned to Jerusalem, under the patronage of Cyrus, to rebuild it. In 20 BC King Herod began an ambitious undertaking to Hellenize the look of the Temple. It took eighteen months and 1,000 specially trained priests (only priests could walk in the sacred area) to complete the main work, though craftsmen continued on sections until AD 64.

The Temple platform was thirty-five acres in size, and the massive enclosure walls were up to fifteen feet thick! The western section of the wall is known today as the Wailing Wall.

» Look for an artist's rendition of The Second Temple (built by Zerubbabel, refashioned by Herod the Great, destroyed in AD 70).
  - In what way does this reflect the Greek style of architecture?
  - How would you describe this structure?

» Find a photo of the Wailing Wall in Jerusalem.
  - How would you describe the Wailing Wall?
  - What do people do at this sacred site?

Arts in Action

Select one or more, and let your artistic juices flow!

Animal Crafting

Sew a Passover lamb out of fleecy acrylic. Check in the library for the how-to information. Remember, the Passover lamb had to be without spot or blemish.

Crèche Making

Build a crèche for a Nativity scene using twigs, wood, moss, bark, etc. This would be a great present to give your mother! To complete the crèche, try to find a craft book to show how to make bread dough figurines which can be painted. Or, it may be possible to buy greenware, clean it, paint it, and have it fired in a kiln. Ask a local ceramics or crafts expert how to do it.

Imitation

Try your hand at creating a Biblical scene in the style of van Eyck

Diorama

Create a miniature Resurrection day scene with bread dough, clay, or papier maché. Form it, paint it, add figures. The most important element is the empty tomb!

Science

Leaven

» Jesus said, "A little leaven leavens the whole lump." Leaven is another term for yeast. Learn the meaning of Jesus's words by making a loaf of bread from scratch. How much yeast do you use in comparison to flour? What happens if the water is too hot? What if the water is too cold? What is the application to our lives?

Diffusion

» 2 Corinthians 2:14 says ". . . and through us diffuses the fragrance of His knowledge in every place." Experiment with diffusion. Borrow a bottle of perfume from your mother. Set the closed bottle on a table. Does it smell? Now, hold your breath and spray the perfume in the air. Quickly step out of the room, and then return, breathing deeply. Can you smell the perfume? Try setting a bowl of potpourri in the kitchen. Can you smell it throughout the house? Now try heating the potpourri. Can you smell it throughout the house? Why? What can we learn about our life in Christ from this experiment?

Music

"By faith we understand that the worlds were framed by the Word of God." Hebrews 11:3

Have you ever noticed the remarkable structure evident in the universe? Rain falls, the moisture waters the earth, the water evaporates, the evaporation forms clouds, and the clouds produce rain. Everything that God created has structure and form, even if it is invisible to us.

In music, there is also a structure, a form. Form is the fifth element of music, and it is what holds all of the rest together. Without form there would not be familiar songs. There would only be random high notes and short notes and loud notes and low notes and fast notes and slow notes without any order. Does this sound somewhat like an evolutionary worldview—meaningless, chance and chaos? Actually, there are 20th century composers whose music reflects this worldview.

To reflect the Biblical worldview, our music will have some form, some structure, some purpose. Handel's Messiah is a wonderful piece of musical literature about Jesus the Messiah. It incorporates many Old Testament prophecies in a rich setting of voices.

The Messiah is an oratorio, which means that it has a special form: a long text, usually religious—rapid dialogue between characters performed in a church or theater—scenery, costumes, and action emphasis on chorus, with solos—emphasis on solos, with chorus accompanied by orchestra—very long sections.

The form of the oratorio is what distinguishes it from operas, symphonies, or choir concerts.

CONSIDER:

"For by Him all things were created that are in heaven and that are on earth, visible and invisible . . . All things were created through Him and for Him. And He is before all things, and in Him all things are held together." Colossians 1:16–17

And Paul wrote in I Corinthians 14:40 that "all things should be done decently and in order."

Listen

» Listen to these different pieces of music:

- Handel's *Messiah*
- an opera such as Mozart's *The Marriage of Figaro*
- a symphony such as Beethoven's Fifth Symphony.

» Notice the differences in form, or structure, between these types of music. Name the differences you hear.

Try This

» After the above listening exercise, play "drop the needle" (which is an old-fashioned name since the advent of CDs!). One person will be the maestro and will secretly choose a recording and select portions for the others to listen to. Play the recording at some randomly chosen spot and see who can identify the form of music being played.

- ***Variation:*** Select any three different kinds of music for the maestro to choose from, such as country, jazz, and gospel. Can anyone in your family or class identify the form of music being played?

Cooking

The fish was chosen to be one of the earliest Christian symbols. Taste & see!

Stuffed Baked Whitefish

3 cups bread cubes
¼ cup melted butter
¾ cup chopped cucumber
¼ cup chopped onion
3 tbsp water
½ tsp salt
⅛ tsp freshly ground pepper
3 pounds whitefish, cleaned and boned

Combine the first seven ingredients and toss to mix well. Place stuffing lightly in fish cavity. Place in a greased baking pan; brush with oil. Bake at 375 degrees for 30 min. or until fish flakes easily. Baste occasionally with oil. Serves 6.

Student Self-Evaluation UNIT 9, PHASE 3

Dates and hours:____________________

Evaluate Your Projects

- List which of the activities listed in this Phase you did:

____

____

____

- Rate your enthusiasm: __________

  Explain: ____________________________________

  ____

- Rate the precision of your approach:__________

  Explain: ____________________________________

  ____

- Rate your effort towards the completion of the project: __________

  Explain: ____________________________________

  ____

Ask yourself what worked and what did not. What would you do differently in the future, and what would you repeat?

____

How specifically did these hands-on activities enhance your knowledge of the time of Jesus Christ, Immanuel? What made them worthwhile?

____

In the first three Phases of this Unit, what aspect of the time period has most captured your imagination? What would you like to creatively pursue to conclude your study?

____

Phase 4

In Your Own Way…

We have seen the fulfillment of the promise made by God, that He would send a Redeemer to save His people from their sins at the perfect moment in time. We have observed the life, death, and resurrection of Jesus Christ, Immanuel. We have considered the historical evidences, and how we might share Him with others. Now, choose a selection of these activities, or create your own, which will best express what you have learned from this unit.

LINGUISTICS

Journalism

- The magazine, *Religion Today*, has asked you to do an eyewitness report on the miraculous healings that are being reported throughout Judea and Galilee. Join the throng following Jesus and write what you see, including interviews with those who have been healed.
- Be a newspaper reporter for *The Temple Times* investigating the incredible story of the empty tomb! You should include the background information that leads to this event.

Prose

Write a short story of the birth of Jesus from the perspective of the donkey who carried His mother to Bethlehem.

Poetry

Mary, as she watched the unfolding of the events in Jesus's life, "pondered these things in her heart." Write a poem, from her perspective, on her son, Jesus the Messiah.

ART

Painting/Drawing

Paint or draw the scene from the Gospels where the little boy gives Jesus his loaves and fishes.

Graphic Design

Design a timeline for young children showing Jesus Christ as the Centerpiece of all of human history. You will be able to add to this as you study further in history.

Sculpting

Sculpt a "pieta" (like Michelangelo's Pieta) in the material that seems best to you. It can be anything from realistic to abstract, as long as there is reverence shown.

Cartooning

Create a political cartoon showing how Satan's plan for killing Jesus backfired in an unexpected way!

MUSIC

Compose

Compose a song about Immanuel, God with us.

Worship

Choose your favorite hymns, worship choruses, and/or songs about the resurrection of Jesus, and then prepare to share a time of worship, scripture, and praise to our God for what He has done through our Lord Jesus Christ.

Performance Practice

With your teacher's help, select an appropriate piece of music which expresses some element from this unit, such as the wonder of His birth, the sorrow of His death, or the joy of His resurrection. Prepare and perform the piece for an audience. Communicate with your audience the reason for your selection either in the program notes or in a short speech.

DRAMA

Heavenly

Act out the angels listening to Augustus Caesar's proclamation to register all the people in the Empire. Caesar is trying to make up his mind how and when he wants this done. The angels know the prophecies, so they are very excited when he finally makes a decision. They all get in line to volunteer for messenger duty to the shepherds! Use your imagination to create props, sets and costumes.

Comedy

Do a humorous skit about the sower who went out to sow his seed. Be sure to include birds, hot sun, shallow roots, weeds, and fruitful plants.

Role Playing

Role play a conversation using apologetics to explain to a non-believing friend the historical foundation of Christianity.

Prop Needs

____

____

Costume Ideas

____

____

Role/Player

____

____

Set Suggestions

____

____

MOVEMENT

Pantomime

Choose some scenes from the miracles of Jesus to pantomime. Find some appropriate recorded music (or have another student or someone in your family perform) while these miracles are acted out.

Dance

Choreograph a dance of Lazarus being raised from the dead. If there is more than one involved, you could each dance a different character.

Action

Create a stylized movement showing the betrayal, trial and crucifixion of Jesus. If this ends at the death of Jesus, be sure to have someone read the scriptures or tell the story of His resurrection—on which our living faith depends.

CONCEPTUAL DESIGN

Multimedia

Plan, and if possible, create a multimedia presentation for nonbelievers, showing who Jesus is and what He has done. As you create this, use only the most compelling music, video, artwork, photos, etc., so as to best represent both His humility in dying for us and the majesty of His resurrection.

CREATE YOUR OWN EXPRESSION

Student Self-Evaluation UNIT 9, PHASE 4

Dates and hours:____________________

Evaluate Your Projects

- What creative project did you choose:

____

- What did you expect from your project, and how does the final project compare to your initial expectations?

____

____

- What do you like about your project? What would you change?

____

____

In Conclusion

Revisit the four Key Concepts from the beginning of this Unit. Explain how your understanding of and appreciation for each has grown over the course of your study.

____

____

____

____

____

____

Record your concluding thoughts on the time of Jesus Christ, Immanuel:

____

____

____

About the Author

Diana Waring has been fascinated by history since she was old enough to discover that World War II had ended ten years prior to her birth in Germany. As a child, she always wanted to understand the chronological march of kings, the connection between momentous events—especially wars—and the international tapestry of fascinating people throughout the ages. The first glimmers of understanding came in a rapid-fire African history course at college, but the full explosion of light dawned when she began teaching world history side by side with the Bible to her three children. It was at that point, with the research required to answer their innumerable questions, that all the pieces began to fall in place. The contagious excitement of discovery led to her speaking and writing about history.

While writing this book, Mrs. Waring lived in a small town in the Black Hills of South Dakota with her husband and dog. She now resides in a small town in Washington state, when she is not visiting her adult children or traveling around the world to educate teachers and parents on the wonders of learning.